CISTERCIAN STUDIES SERIES:
NUMBER ONE HUNDRED NINETY-NINE

The Search for God:

Conferences, Letters, and Homilies

Bernardo Olivera OCSO

CISTERCIAN STUDIES SERIES:
NUMBER ONE HUNDRED NINETY-NINE

The Search for God:
Conferences, Letters, and Homilies

Bernardo Olivera ocso

CISTERCIAN PUBLICATIONS
Kalamazoo, Michigan
2002

Available from

Cistercian Publications
Editorial Offices and Customer Service
Institute of Cistercian Studies
Western Michigan University
Kalamazoo, MI 49008

British and European Customer Service
97 Loughborough Road
Thringstone, Coalville, Leic. LE67 8LZQ

http://www.spencerabbey.org/cistpub/

The work of Cistercian Publications
is made possible in part by support from Western Michigan University
to The Institute of Cistercian Studies

Library of Congress Cataloguing available upon request.
ISBN 0-87907-699-2 (pb)

TABLE OF CONTENTS

INTRODUCTION

MORE THAN TEN YEARS HAVE PASSED since the election of the current Abbot General of the Cistercians of the Strict Observance. Chapter conferences, circular letters, homilies, and other writings have accumulated. Because they were sometimes spoken or written in response to very specific circumstances they are not all of equal value, and it is very likely that much will be carried away by the purifying wind that occasionally sweeps through history. Some reflections, however, will be of more lasting value, since they apply to realities of today and of all time. Though the topics addressed cover a whole range of questions, they have as a common denominator the subject of monastic renewal.

Renewal implies 'newness', not just any sort of newness, but rather a newness as distinct from both the outmoded and the new-fangled. We grasp readily enough that 'new' means the opposite of old. Old, however, is not necessarily synonymous with old in age or ancient in time. Likewise, there is a strong contrast between the newness of renewal and the novelty of fashion which is intrinsically ephemeral. Were fashion to endure, it would go out of fashion, all of which shows the foolishness of such unstable transitoriness.

Some will miss the circular letters and conferences on the martyrdom of the Brothers of Atlas in Algeria. These, however, have already been published elsewhere.[1] The same applies to a series of conferences given to members of the Spanish region on the subject of heterosexual friendship which has been published as a separate small book.[2] Both of these publications fall within the framework of monastic renewal, at least this was the intention.

These times of ours are full of challenges and surprises. They evoke interest and invite reflection. May the Risen One, the Lord of history, grant that this collection awakens the mind, enkindles the affections, and motivates the heart of those who read it.

Rome, 15 August 1999
Bernardo Olivera OCSO

---

1. *Martirio y Consagración: los mártires de Argelia* (Madrid: Ediciones Claretianas, 1999). In English, *How Far to Follow? The Martyrs of Atlas* (Petersham, MA: St. Bede's Publications, 1997).

2. *Consagrados y Consagradas Amigos: amistades entre géneros diferentes* (Madrid: Ediciones Claretianas, 1999).

TABLE OF ABBREVIATIONS

ad Abbat	*Sermo ad Abbates*
Anal. Cist	*Analecta Sacri Ordinis Cisterciensis; Analecta Cisterciensia*
Asspt	*Sermo in assumptione BVM*
C = Cst	Constitutions
Conv	*Sermo de conversione ad clericos*
Dil	*Liber de diligendo Deo*
Div	*Sermo de diversis*
Ep	*Epistola*
Oasspt	*Sermo dominica infra octavam assumptionis*
OC	Cistercian Order
OCSO	Cistercian Order of the Strict Observance
Palm S	*Sermo in ramis palmarum*
Pasc	*Sermo in octava paschae*
Prae	*Liber de praechepto et dispensatione*
Pur	Guerric of Igny, *Sermo in purificatione BVM*
RB	Rule of Saint Benedict
SC = Serm. Cant	*Sermo super Cantica canticorum*
Sent	*Sententia*
TCL	Theology of our Cistercian Life
VC	Apostolic Exhortation on Consecrated Life

Conferences at the ocso General Chapters

SELF-INTRODUCTION AND PROGRAM

Conference at the General Chapters,
September 1990

SOME OF YOU HAVE UNDERSTANDABLY WONDERED who our new Abbot General is: what does he want and what will he do? So I will try to present myself to you as briefly and as simply as possible. I know you will listen to me as a brother and receive me as one.

My forbears came from Spain and arrived in South America during the sixteenth and seventeenth centuries. I was born in the city of Buenos Aires on June 17, 1943, baptized a few days later and given the name of Luis José. I am the third of six children: five brothers and a younger sister. My father died two years ago at the age of seventy-four but my mother is still doing well, having just turned seventy.

I went through grammar and secondary school at Saint Elizabeth's College, run by the Salesians. The year after graduating from there, I entered the School of Agriculture and Veterinary Science at the

University of Buenos Aires. Toward the end of 1961, I seriously thought of studying philosophy and literature, and training to be a diplomat: all of this, of course, without giving up my career as a veterinarian. You can see that I know first hand that the young can do anything, especially when they are in love!

In 1962, I began to work in order to be more economically independent. I would study during the day and work at night, from midnight to 6 am. The values that governed my life at that time were basically: good friends of both sexes, money, daydreams and plans, and a deep respect for truth, goodness, and religion. Yet, all of this was shot through with the feeling of an inner void.

Then came June 28, 1962, the day of my first conversion, which happened as follows. I was going by bus to my veterinary classes. The weather was cold and I was cold. It was early morning, and day was dawning. There were others in the bus, and they were just anybody. Everything was just as normal. Suddenly I sensed a presence in front of me. I recognized it immediately. It was the Lord. Then some words came into my heart: 'Come and follow me'. He had to repeat them three times, because the first two times I hesitated. Why did I hesitate? There were other plans and another love. However, the third time my whole being melted and I wept as I never had before, with deep grief and a tender sweetness. From that moment on, I began to understand that my whole life had to be simply this: listening to the beating of the heart of God.

On September 8, 1962, I made my first visit to the trappist monastery at Azul and entered there as a lay brother on October 28 of the same year. The Lord knows what happened during those first years . . . Thanks to the Decree of Unification, I made profession as a monk on May 1, 1966. Very soon afterwards, I was sent to Spencer for two years. That is where I began my studies in Sacred Scripture, Theology, and cistercian spirituality while working in the infirmary and in the jelly factory.

I made solemn profession at Azul on March 19, 1969, and was ordained priest on July 25, 1971. During all this time, I continued studying as well as serving the community as librarian, infirmarian, submaster of novices, and cellarer. In 1973, I studied at the School of Theology of the Catholic University of Argentina and was able to cooperate with the Lord in founding a movement of contemplative marian spirituality that has continued through the years and is still growing.

The suffering and joy caused by all of this was like a second conversion for me. May God reward with his grace the faith of my superior and of my brothers.

From 1974 to 1984, I worked as novice director and teacher of theology and spirituality. This was interrupted in 1978, when I went to Rome to study at the Gregorian University in their Institute of Spirituality, returning to Azul the following year. In June of 1983, I was named Superior Vicar and elected as abbot in February 1984.

So we come to September 8, 1990, and the beginning of my third conversion. In the context of the reading of the House Reports during this General Chapter, you could easily ask about my main weak point and strong point. I think I could answer as follows:

- principal weak point: besides being too thin, there is the tendency to become impatient, although this seldom turns into anger, thanks be to God.

- principal strong point: the ability to bear witness to the constant, active presence of the Risen Christ and his Mother at the heart of the Church; and also a very good sense of humor.

Perhaps I should add something more: my singing is terrible, my knowledge of Latin is superficial, and Canon Law is definitely not my strong point.

You probably want to know what I plan to do, God willing, in the next few months. First, I plan to return to Azul to help the community in its preparation for an abbatial election. I will return to Rome at the end of October in order to meet with Dom Ambrose and the new Permanent Councillors. I will immediately take an intensive course in French and then visit Cîteaux, La Trappe, and a few other monasteries. Perhaps then I will write a letter of presentation to all the communities of the Order.

Let me conclude with a synthesis of the basic direction my service as Abbot General will take, as I see it at present:

1. A constant return to Jesus and to his Gospel of love for the Father and all the brothers, in the hands of Mary.

2. Formation in the cenobitic school of Saint Benedict, with the contemplative and mystical qualities characteristic of Cîteaux.

3. Openness to new expressions of the cistercian charism, with its inculturation and firm establishment in the local churches.

4. Particular attention to the unity of the Order, formed, as it is, by both monks and nuns, by two General Chapters working together in the search for and discovery of the good which is common to each one of us within this communion.

5. Participation and careful listening at the meetings of the Regional Conferences to help communication among them.

6. A discreet and timely presence wherever there may be special needs, partly to solve problems, but especially in order to carry the Cross together, since the Cross is always the way of salvation.

7. Special love for the younger members, the older members, and the sick members of our communities.

It only remains for me to ask you to pray earnestly for this poor man who, by the will of the Lord as clearly expressed by all of you, is here today as your Abbot General.

THE ORDER TODAY

Conference at the General Chapters,
September 1993

THREE YEARS HAVE NOW PASSED since the last election of an Abbot General. During this time, I have had the opportunity to visit one hundred forty-three of the one hundred sixty-four houses that compose the Order. In the majority of these houses, I have been able to stay four days. This gave me the opportunity to speak with all the brothers and sisters, and to enter in some way into the rhythm of their daily lives. Now seems to be the right moment to share with you my ideas and impressions relative to the Order.

I am aware of the fact that in his circular letter of January 6, 1990, Dom Ambrose presented an overall view of the situation of our monasteries. His general impression was positive. In fact, the situation had not changed very much since his previous evaluation in 1980.

I shall now attempt to give you my own vision. The result will probably not differ too much, but perhaps the angle does differ, just as do the eyes of this observer.

STATISTICS

Statistics have their limits, but they can serve us well, provided we have the knowledge to put them at the service of life.

From the last statistics of the Order it is possible to draw five simple conclusions, that affect our present, and which may perhaps affect it even more in the future.

- First, it is obvious that the communities are smaller today and will be still smaller in the future than they were in the past. The cause is obvious. The number of persons is decreasing while the number of communities is increasing.

- Second, in the last three years the nuns have shown greater daring and have been more prolific in making foundations than have the monks. The number of foundations and their locations speak eloquently for themselves.

- Third, the role of the nuns will be increasingly active and important in the life of the Order. The reasons that support this affirmation are two: What has been said above about foundations, and a loss in personnel considerably less than that of the monks.

- Fourth, the Order is shifting slowly but firmly toward the South (Africa and Latin America) and toward Eastern Asia. This movement parallels the greater movement of the shift of Catholic Christianity during these last years.

- Fifth, we can say that the Order as a whole is participating in the paschal mystery of the Lord Jesus. The *kenosis* of some communities, above all in the Western First World, is accompanied by the rise of other communities, especially in Third World, and in non-Christian countries.

These simple data that stem from statistics, when discerned with the eyes of faith, can also be considered as words of the Lord, who is speaking to us in history through the medium of our own lives.

Evaluation

Recently I have been asking myself: is it possible after only three years of service as Abbot General, to discern our present situation and to make a general evaluation concerning our spiritual health? Is it possible for me to evaluate the ensemble of one hundred sixty-four communities scattered over five continents, differentiated by cultures, histories, age, and number of members? Counting on your kindness, I dare to say: yes, it is possible.

In reality, the problem is simplified when clear and effective criteria of discernment are available. Thank God, we have them—to wit: a sense of identity and a desire for growth.

If we judge the Order in the light of the criterion of identity, the verdict is highly positive: we do not have an identity crisis. It is relatively easy to proclaim our own name and place in the Church. We have no doubts concerning what is proper to us; it is permanently ours and it permits us to differentiate ourselves thanks to our mutual relations. We recognize and present ourselves as Christians and monks in the Cistercian-Benedictine tradition. The new Constitutions are a clear reflection and sign of our own name.

The fact that we do not suffer from an identity crisis, after twenty-five years of *aggiornamento* is no small accomplishment. It speaks of a gift of the Lord and of a grace of correspondence to His grace.

However, it is evidently not all. From word to act, there can be a long way to go. A second criterion of discernment imposes itself: the effective desire for growth.

By visiting the houses of the Order and speaking with so many brothers and sisters, I have been able to perceive an eagerness, a longing, and a desire for full life in the Lord. Once again, this is a gift of divine grace. The Lord is inviting us and enabling us to respond to his call.

In conclusion, we know who we are, and we want to be what we are in ever-greater depth and fullness. This is our present reality and I do not hesitate to judge it positively.

REALISM

The preceding affirmation could sound too optimistic and perhaps, for certain people, even unrealistic. It is therefore necessary to clarify and complete the panorama.

Being a realist is not opposed to being an optimist. Realism refers to a true or correct perception of what exists. Optimism is an existential disposition—or a choice—that allows one to face reality and to be in control of it rather than to be controlled by it.

The positive affirmation of our present reality is realistic. It is also realistic to note the shadows that dim the light that we ought to reflect. Called to be the salt of the earth, we run the danger of becoming earth without salt.

Our capital sins, under which are to be found many others, can be reduced to three: activism, individualism, and inconstancy. This is not the time to discern the nature, causes, species, and remedies for each of them. It suffices to say that these vices are very bad and deadly for they eat away our life from its very marrow. Activism militates against the contemplative dimension; individualism deals a mortal blow to our cenobitic charism; inconstancy makes our *conversatio morum* inoperative.

Within this context, in order to complete the inventory of our present reality we must also mention: the lack of vocations, progressive aging, and personnel shortage in some communities due to deaths and departures. All of this represents a real challenge and requires on our part creative imagination and absolute trust in Providence. One region has already had the courage and good sense to face this situation and has thus opened a way that could help others in the not too distant future.

As for the rest, in the document which I and the Permanent Council sent you last year for the first centenary of the ocso, you will find listed other realities, positive in nature, as well as some challenges. There is no need to review them at this time.

Nevertheless, we still must mention that which is most precious and real in the Order. Each of us, particularly the elderly, has been called by the Father to be recreated in the image of his Son through the action of the Spirit! Each of us desires to live in a radical way, with the help of grace, the good news of Jesus Christ. Each of us, pilgrims to the absolute, companions in joy and sorrow, witnesses of the monastic Church and to the kingdom to come!

RENEWAL

I wish to add a last word. It is obvious that with the approval of the Constitutions in 1990 we concluded one stage in the life of the Order—a stage begun twenty-five years earlier and characterized by the *accomodata renovatio* proclaimed and programmed by Vatican Council II.

This stage fulfilled its task: to give priority to the Gospel, return to our patrimony, adapt to modern times, and renew structures and institutions.

It is permissible that some should ask: 'and now what?' The answer to this question is evident to me.

Brothers and Sisters, the Lord is inviting us to a new stage in the renewal of our Order. The *accomodata renovatio* of yesterday must continue in the spiritual *inculturata renovatio* for today and tomorrow. Indeed, the *magisterium* of the Church teaches us that:

- 'Renewal and adaptation cannot be realized once and for all without being continually lived through fervor and the medium of Chapters and superiors' (ES, III, 19).

- 'The best adaptations to the needs of our times can produce their effects only when animated by a spiritual renewal' (PC, 2. e).

- 'The manner of life, of prayer and of work must be duly adjusted . . . to the exigencies of the culture and of the social and economic circumstances in so far as it is required by the character of each institute' (PC, 3.).

The texts just cited tell us the how and why of renewal, but it is still possible to explain better the reasons that motivate this new state.

- In the first place, our clear and definite identity together with a profound desire for growth in the same.

- The deep conviction that Cîteaux, known in its day as 'the new monastery' was born in order to make new life possible, as new creatures, in the new creation, living anew the new commandment. Our Fathers and we ourselves are all disciples of him who says: 'See, I make all things new!'

- Finally, the fact that we are an international Order that aspires to be an intercultural and supracultural Order.

I stop here because all of this will be the theme of a next conference if the Lord continues to want it. So be it.

INCULTURATED SPIRITUAL RENEWAL

Conference at the General Chapters,
September 1993

I N THE CONCLUSION OF MY INAUGURAL CONFERENCE I
began to present to you what I discern as the Lord's will for
us today and in the near future: the gift and the conquest of
a spiritual and inculturated renewal.

Now I present to you the context, the guiding ideas, the instruments, and the agents of the spiritual and inculturated renewal.

CONTEXT

Our previous stage of 'accommodated' renewal was carried out in the context of a conciliar and post-conciliar Church. Most of us shared and experienced the conciliar and consequent post-conciliar stages in some form or another. There is no need to characterize it.

Suffice it to say that the Church wanted to listen and dialogue with the modern world and catch up with the times.

The present ecclesial moment is not easy to define. But beyond all opinions and stands, there are three realities that are emerging with ever increasing clarity: the Church is at last and in fact 'catholic', that is, universal; the Church understands herself as a mystery of communion in the image of the Trinity; and the Church is committed to a global project of new evangelization.

The world has suffered incredible changes relative to the world in which we lived thirty years ago. In these last three decades, we have experienced a profound and accelerated social, political, economic, and cultural transformation. It suffices to mention the facts that are known to everyone:

- the end of the cold war and of the arms race by the disappearance of one of the hegemonic blocks.

- costly rise of nationalities because of the collapse of the USSR.

- predominance of the capitalist system due to the failure of the socialist alternative.

- passage from the industrial revolution to the technological revolution.

- globalization of the world economy and the appearance of regional economic blocks.

- emergence of post-modernity within Western cultural modernity.

The Order, for its part, has also undergone notable changes in these last years. The same conciliar renewal has been the cause of the vast majority of them. A simple comparison of the new Constitutions with the preceding ones speaks for itself.

As for the rest, since the beginning of Vatican II, fourteen foundations of monks and twenty-three of nuns have been made. Only eight of these are in Europe, the Order's place of origin. For this reason, the geographic theme of the universality of the Order is opening to the anthropological reality of interculturality. From a culturally monocentric Order, we have become a culturally pluricentric Order.

Many other points could be indicated, but what has been said suffices to show that the ecclesial and worldwide context of the current renewal differs not a little from the preceding context. The Order itself, by preserving its profound identity is also finding itself in a new period of its centuries old history. To a new context and reality, there is a corresponding new step or stage of renewal.

Lines of Inspiration for the Future

I shall now attempt to characterize in a few lines the new and current stage of spiritual and inculturated renewal.

The principal and fundamental—in the sense of being first and basic—inspirational leads, can be reduced to three. I present them in these terms:

- the following of Jesus with Mary in accordance with the radicalness of the Gospel, leaving behind everything that is not Christ in order that we might live united and poor with the poor Christ!

- ongoing cenobitic formation according to the Benedictine rule and tradition—ready to give one's life for the other by not seeking one's own interest but that of others!

- oriented toward the Mystery and under the guidance of the cistercian mystics: only the spouse of the Word, become one spirit with Him by conformity of wills, can know and taste the intimate life of the triune God and his plan of salvation.

Basing ourselves on these lifelines, or even better, plunging our roots into them, we must also accentuate these others:

- the meaning of the Order, understood as communion among persons, thanks to which each monk and nun shares in the living patrimony of Cîteaux and in the institution that expresses and favors it.

- communion with the life and mission of the Church: the ecclesial character of our life must be translated into a communion of love and obedience to the Pope and bishops, and the ecclesiology of communion invites us to be and to labor in mutual relation with other states and forms of christian life.

- a deep and fruitful solidarity with the men and women of today. Everything that is truly human must echo in our hearts!

As a consequence of the foregoing, or as a more detailed explanation of some latent aspect in these last three lifelines, we must exert every effort to attain:

- the inculturation of our patrimony and an openness to intercultural dialogue.

- discernment of the signs of the times and contemporary challenges.

- interreligious and ecumenical dialogue according to the orientations of the ecclesiastical magisterium.

Obviously, each of these nine lifelines will ultimately have to be reconsidered and elaborated, by precisely determining its extent and its implementation in concrete projects at different levels. Nevertheless, what has already been stated suffices for the present.

INSTRUMENTS

I shall now consider the instruments. Obviously, there is no need to demonstrate that without tools we can do nothing; without them, we cannot exercise the art of spiritual and inculturated renewal. In addition, tools provide instruction: it is a question of working, yes, but with meaning, that is, with a purpose and with an end in view.

What instruments do we count on? First, and above all, we count on the Gospel of our Master and Lord Jesus Christ.

The ultimate norm of the consecrated life is the following of Christ, as set forth in the Gospel. Only by taking the Gospel as our guide can we follow in his footsteps until we meet him face to face in his kingdom.

Of course, we have to look at the whole Gospel. Nevertheless, it is possible to emphasize some texts. Which? Those that have always been a source of inspiration and renewal of the consecrated life, that is, those radical, paradoxical and demanding texts that break with the ordinary and usual ways of behavior, those texts that reveal the inexhaustible in the evangelical life.

If there is a text that takes us to the roots of Jesus' teaching, that text is the beatitudes. The matthean beatitudes give us the picture of the true disciple, a picture of the Master himself, whose footprints we must follow and whose sentiments we must possess. For man this is impossible, but for God nothing is impossible!

We also have the *Rule* of Saint Benedict. The Benedictine Rule is a most apt tool for summarizing the evangelical demands in a monastic key. We speak of the Holy Rule not because its author may be considered a saint, even though he is, nor because it is considered as the fruit of an inspiration from heaven, although the Spirit of God is present in it, but because in all its pages we find the Holy Scriptures and the teachings of the holy Fathers.

True, the *Rule* is presented as an elementary rule, as a handbook for beginners. For that very reason, if we do not put this elementary medium of the Gospel into practice we will not be able to live as cenobitic monks.

The *Rule* of Saint Benedict has a heart. Chapter 72, on the good zeal that monks and nuns should practice, beats with the most ardent love of the patriarch of cenobitism.

The works of our Fathers constitute the tool that is most properly ours. They teach us to live monastically, accompany us in the liturgical celebrations, captivate us with lively formulas, and transmit spirit and life to us.

The cistercian spirituality of the twelfth and thirteenth centuries is outstanding for the coherence of its doctrine and the unity of its theory and praxis. For our Fathers, the monastery is a school of charity, a place where there is teaching and learning, a place where the monk trains, a place where he seeks and finds God by living in unity with his brothers.

In the cistercian school one is taught and one learns, in theory and in practice: who is a human being, in what the efforts and exercises of the ascetic life consist, the centrality of Jesus Christ, venerated, celebrated and imitated, the mystery of love which by departing from itself and embracing others leads to mystical union with God.

This whole doctrine of life reaches its summit in the commentaries on the *Canticle of Canticles*. Why does the soul seek the Word, our

Fathers ask themselves. Unhesitatingly, they answer: in order to rejoice and be transformed into him. Mystical love is the desirable goal of the search for God.

We also have the renewed tool of our Constitutions. They are the concrete and contemporary expression of our special following of Christ according to the Gospel and the *Rule* of Saint Benedict. They are the stable expression of our patrimony and express the awareness that all the members of the Order have of themselves.

I do not hesitate to consider the Constitutions as a 'book of life'. Indeed, they proceed from life and lead to greater life. They offer a harmony of means and ends, of observances and values for living the Christian life in its radicalism, the Christian life centered on the search for God and the encounter with him.

Speaking of tools, we can also say something about the documents of the conciliar and post-conciliar magisterium. They are the voices of God for the Church today. Every effort of renewal must be carried out within the heart of the Church, and for that very reason cannot be alien to her teaching.

We have no lack of instruments. Neither do we lack the will to grasp and use them, or so I believe. If on judgment day we give them back incarnated in our own lives, we shall receive a recompense surpassing anything that can be conceived or merited.

AGENTS

The agents of this new stage of renewal are each and all of the monks and nuns of the Order. Each one with his grace and his struggle, each one trying to return to that first love which led him to consecrate his life to the Lord for the glory of the Father and the salvation of all. All of us, without exception are invited to collaborate actively. We renew ourselves all together, or no one is renewed!

Local superiors—monks and nuns—have a special responsibility. It falls to those who hold the place of Christ among their brothers and sisters to encourage one and all to run the road of their vocation in depth and without reserve. To that end, the superiors themselves— monks and nuns—must be the first in the march to the Father.

The Fathers Immediate, for their part, are called to watch over the progress of their daughter houses, and at this particular time it is not solely a question of watching over but of supporting and helping—better still, of giving life that there may be life.

Without the help and organic collaboration of the Assemblies of Superiors, we cannot go very far. Above all, it is for the General Chapters, as the supreme authority of the Order, to promote renewal. Our mutual pastoral solicitude for the common good of each community now has a name: spiritual and inculturated renewal.

The regional conferences for their part have the task of fostering fraternal cooperation and inter-culturality in all that refers to renewal. I invite you to draw up projects indicating the basic responsibilities, means of action, and short and long term goals, which will make concrete the lines that have been indicated.

Without this joint action, the service of the Abbot General as the promoter of the spiritual renewal of the communities becomes a utopia lacking all reality.

To conclude, it only remains that we should ask the Holy Spirit, the providential agent of our new life to instill light and fire in our hearts as he did in the Virgin Mary at the beginning of the new creation.

Brothers and Sisters, the grace and the effort of a spiritual and inculturated renewal is our contribution to the Church-Communion dedicated to the service of a new evangelization and to the contemporary world that searches in the darkness for him who guides and draws it with his providence and his love.

VARIOUS PERSPECTIVES
ON THE ORDER

Conference at the General Chapters,
October 1996

I N MY TALKS DURING THE MIXED GENERAL MEETING OF
1993, I presented a program of *Inculturated Spiritual Renewal.*
While explaining the features and guiding principles that
inspire this renewal, I spoke of a 'sense of the Order'. During
the present General Chapter I wish to explain in more detail what
this is.

In the first place, I should say that I use the word, 'sense', to designate
a double reality, namely: belonging and participating in a conscious,
affectionate and effective way. In a word, it is a matter of feeling
and knowing that you are an active member of the Order.

I am not going to treat this theme systematically. My purpose is
more modest. In my talks, I will first offer some reflections for the
sake of knowing the Order better. Then, from a more practical
point of view, I will present three basic principles for an 'ordered'

functioning of the Order, if you will excuse this redundancy. Finally, I will let myself dream and invite you to do the same, so as to project our hearts toward the future, as toward a utopia.

THE ORDER FROM DIFFERENT POINTS OF VIEW

Without going into the different uses of the word, 'Order', I wish to speak about applying this word to our concrete reality. Let us try to look at it from different viewpoints so as to understand better what we see, without forgetting that those who most love the Order are the ones who know it best.

The Historical Perspective

From an historical point of view, we can say that the Cistercian Order, with its form of government based on co-responsibility, has existed since 1119, when Pope Calixtus II approved the *Charter of Charity*. In his Bull of confirmation, the Pope points out that our document sprang 'from the consent and common deliberation of the abbots and brothers of your monasteries'. A few years later, around 1123, the *Charter of Charity* was confirmed by twenty abbots, that is, all there were at that time. This act was also the confirmation of the existence in the Church of a new monastic institution, the Cistercian Order.

The Cultural Perspective

It is said that monasticism is a transcultural phenomenon because no one culture has a monopoly on it and monks often withdraw into solitude on the margin of their own culture. To a great extent, this is true. Nevertheless, it is also true that monasticism is a cultural phenomenon, since it exists in a particular culture and inaugurates a subculture within that broader cultural context.

In the same way that we speak about a 'christian culture', we can also refer to a 'monastic culture', although it is better to use the plural, 'monastic cultures', rather than the singular, as is shown by the different forms or styles of monastic life down through the centuries. Benedictine life and the benedictine tradition is a monastic culture, or subculture. So is the cistercian tradition and the Cistercian Order taken as a whole. The success and expansion of Cîteaux in the twelfth century can be explained by its knowing how to incarnate the culture of its time and place. Above all, it knew how to embody that culture's deepest spiritual aspirations.

This is valid for us today. The Order is, in a broad sense, a 'monastic subculture' in the midst of various cultures. That is, it is inculturated in different cultures without prejudice to its unity, or common-union. By this very fact, it is 'transcultural'. The meeting between the Gospel and the world's cultures produces evangelization and inculturation: evangelization of cultures and inculturation of the Gospel. Inculturation of the Order is part of the larger event of inculturation of the Gospel and evangelization of cultures.

All this is simply a rough sketch of what could very well serve as a theme for a future Mixed General Meeting. This, at least, is clear: the Order in its totality cannot separate itself from cultural realities and their changing dynamics; the Order is not identified with any particular culture but has to be open to the values of all cultures, since they are new mediating realities which can enrich and communicate the wealth of cistercian culture.

The Theological and Spiritual Perspective

From a theological and spiritual viewpoint, we can say that our Order is formed by communities united by the bond of charity.

This is how they help each other in their difficulties, or when they need to understand or live in practice their common patrimony. That is, the Order is a communion of communities and persons, thanks to which each community, and every monk and nun, has a part in the living patrimony of Cîteaux and in the organization that expresses this patrimony and promotes it.

It is also possible to understand the Order as a *Schola caritatis,* that is, as a School of charity for 'schools of charity'. This means that the purpose of the Order is charity and all its structures and institutions are meant to be means and expressions of the same charity.

The Ecclesiological Perspective

Since the Order is an ecclesial event, it is possible to apply analogously to it what is said about the Church. Therefore, we can say that the Order is for us: the Body of Christ and the Temple of the Spirit; a sacrament of communion; charism and an institution; and the historical incarnation of the mystery of salvation in Christ through the Spirit.

Just as the Church is not simply an institution but a mystery, so it is with the Order. Both the Church and the Order are charismatic realities and institutional ones. However, it is not a question of two separable or distinct realities, but of two essential dimensions of a single mystery. The Church is the Body of Christ made dynamic by the Spirit, and so is the Order!

Since the Church is the fruit of the two missions, of Christ and of the Spirit—and we can say the same for the Order—it will be helpful, in order to understand ourselves more deeply, to place ourselves explicitly in a charismatic and Spirit-centered perspective.

The Charismatic and Spirit-centered Perspective

If we look at our origins from the perspective of the Holy Spirit, we will say that the Order has, as its basis or foundation, a charism, that is, an experience of the Father though a gift of the Spirit for building up and serving the Body of Christ. Even more, I dare to say that the Order is itself a charism of the Spirit in the Church and for the Church. Thanks to our Order, the Church relives a particular dimension of the life that Jesus led on this earth. That is why the Order is such a vital charism. Through it the Church—and we as her members—can continue to live Jesus' own way of life.

The founding charism, or charism of the Founders, is meant to be constantly lived, kept, deepened and developed in harmony with the Body of Christ and in a process of continual growth.

The signs that distinguish the Order as a charismatic reality are the following:

- a truly new contribution to the spiritual life of the Church.

- a special effectiveness that may even become an occasion of conflict.

- constant verification of our faithfulness to the Lord and our docility to the Spirit.

- prudent attention to the signs of the times and to different circumstances.

- the desire to be inserted in the Church.

- consciousness of our own subordination to the Hierarchy.

- daring in taking initiatives, constancy in our self-gift, humility in trials and contradictions.

- interior suffering and the cross, without which there is no true charism or originality.

Our founding charism—and the Order taken as a charism that is vital to the Church—is a complex entity. So is every living and many-sided reality. Using a schematic outline, we can distinguish the following elements or stages:

1. Charismatic inspiration and empowering of the founding group.

2. Charismatic verification and enrichment of the founding group's charism by those who join them.

3. Progressive institutionalization of the charism:

    a. Institutionalization of inner life: organizational guidelines and structures.

    b. Institutionalization of outside relationships: ecclesiastical recognition and approval of a specific statute.

We should bear in mind that our first institutionalization was part of the founding charism. The following steps of institutionalization were meant to flow from the charism itself, to let it to be lived and expressed in space and time. Of course, all this process does not take place without successes and failures, as the redactional history of our Constitutions so clearly shows.

Still speaking from this Spirit-centered viewpoint but with greater precision, we should say that the Order is a collective, shared charism implying a specific mode of being, a specific mission and spirituality, a life style and a specific structure at the service of communion and mission within the Church.

Collective charisms or gifts of the Holy Spirit are dynamic impulses in continual development at the service of the Body of Christ, which is always growing. They are confided to human groups in order to be lived, interpreted, made fruitful and witnessed to at the service of communion within the Church, in the different contexts offered by the various cultures. Participation in a collective charism helps the formation of the group's members, produces greater cohesion among them, creates a stronger sense of identity, gives a sense of belonging to a spiritual family, and is a source of creative energy for a quick response to the signs of the times.

Through the action and gifts of the Spirit, persons who belong to different states of life can share a collective charism. In our case, for example, these persons could be consecrated clerics, consecrated laypersons, or oblates. That is why it can also be thought of as a charism; that is 'open' to new forms of presence and historical modalities.

The Canonical Perspective

Let us take a very quick look at our reality as an Order from a canonical point of view. First of all, the new Code of Canon Law never speaks of Orders, but rather of monastic Congregations. Thus from the viewpoint of the Code, an Order—as a decentralized canonical entity—is a monastic Congregation. This is our case. The Code of 1917 defined a monastic Congregation as: several autonomous *(sui iuris)* monasteries under a single superior. (*CIC* 1917, c. 488.2; Cf. *CIC* 1983, cc. 613 and 620)

However, something more has to be stated. The Order of Cistercians of the Strict Observance is a monastic Congregation *sui generis*, that is, it is constituted by two branches with two autonomous General Chapters, a single patrimony and a single Abbot General as a bond of unity *(unitatis vinculum)*. Moreover, the two branches of the Order are bound together by a system of filiations and an interdependence based on mutual consent in case of any change touching the integrity of the common patrimony.

There is still more. The Order exists thanks to charity and its practice as expressed in the Constitutions. It is precisely the bond of charity that gathers, that 'congregates', in unity the communities of the Order scattered throughout the world.

Our Belonging to the Order and Our History of Following Jesus

In the light of all that has just been said we can ask ourselves, 'What does participation in the life of the Order mean in real life?' Whatever might be our reply to that question, it would have to take into account the following elements:

- shared participation in a single spiritual patrimony.

- reception of a tradition and its communication to other generations.

- active fellowship in the Order's organization and with its highest authority.

- mutual collaboration while respecting complementary differences.

- respectful submission to the different levels of authority.

- belonging as an active member to a local community.

In conclusion, let us say that our Order finds its identity through the story of its own history. This history is one of following Jesus Christ. Since this following of Jesus continues today, our history is an open one and projected toward the future.

THREE UTOPIAS: INTEGRATION, COMMUNION, ASSOCIATION

Conference at the General Chapters,
October 1996

THERE IS NO SADDER WORLD THAN THE ONE that has no dreamers. Daydreaming is not part of my temperament, but sometimes I let myself be carried aware by a creative imagination. It is not bad to build castles in Spain, provided that your intention is not to live in them permanently.

Now there may be some among you who prefer crude reality to dreams. But you may be open to utopias, if they are well understood. So let us speak of utopias, or dreams. Each of you can choose according to your own taste and preference.

Etymologically, the word, 'utopia' comes from one of two different roots: *ouk-topos:* no place; and *eu-topos*: place of happiness. In the first derivation, it is a question of something unreal, in the second, of something pleasant. I am in favor of this second interpretation.

We can say that a utopia consists in a criticism of what exists and a proclamation or preparation of what could exist to make everyone happy. This, however, requires some clarification.

- It is not a question of a 'reasonable' project or proclamation, but of an impulsive, intuitive, and 'symbolic' one.

- The project or proclamation springs from deep longings rooted in the desire for happiness and fulfillment.

- The utopia, therefore, is not in the area of opposition between what is true, that is, what exists, and what is false, or utopian; nor between what is real, by existing, and what is unreal, or utopian. Rather it is an opposition between what is known, because it exists, and what is unknown, or utopian; and between what is the same as everything else, because it exists, and what is different, or utopian.

In this sense, we can now say that a utopia consists in a symbolic project that anticipates a future that is better than the present and therefore desired. That is why a utopia is an agent of change and a motor of history. Its principle functions are to protest against the present situation, to prepare for a future that is intuited and desired, to anticipate the future now, with passion.

What, then, are my passionate desires that make a dreamt-of future present, in relation to the Order? What do I dream about when I let my creative imagination go, in the perspective of the ninth centenary of the founding of Cîteaux and the beginning of the next millennium?

INTEGRATION WITHIN THE OCSO

If the Order's renewal contains anything like a utopia, it will be in the line of imagining how to strengthen the bonds that unite us.

The personal integration in each of our hearts has to express itself also on the level of the Order, with its services and institutions.

Between Genders: Monks and Nuns

We read in our Constitutions: *Monks and nuns of the Strict Observance constitute a single Order. They participate in handing on the same patrimony. They collaborate and give mutual help in many ways, having due regard to their healthy differences and the complementarity of their gifts.* (C.72.1) This text of the Constitutions anticipated by a few years the following text from the Post-synodal Exhortation on Consecrated Life:

> *The Church fully shows her manifold spiritual riches when she overcomes every type of discrimination and welcomes as an authentic blessing the gifts bestowed by God to both men and women, judging them in their equal dignity. . . . It is urgent, therefore, to take concrete steps, beginning by letting women participate in different sectors and on all levels, even in those processes in which decisions are reached, especially in those matters which more directly concern women.* (John Paul II, *Vita Consecrata*).

In this context we could wonder if there is not room in our Order for an evolution in our life, which would be made official at the opportune moment and would take into account: the Abbesses of founding houses along with the Fathers Immediate, Mothers Immediate (for nuns and for monks), Abbess Visitators (for nuns and for monks), interdependent Permanent Councils, an Abbot or Abbess General, nuns preaching retreats, and so forth.

Between Communities: Filiations, Visitations, and Regions

Opening the Constitutions again, we read the following:

The communities of the Order spread all over the world are gathered into unity by a bond of charity. Through the union that results from this association, they can help one another in coming to a more complete understanding and practice of their common patrimony and they can offer mutual encouragement and support in difficulties. This communion assumes juridical form in the government of the Order according to the Charter of Charity as interpreted by the norms of these Constitutions. The abbots and abbesses meeting in two Chapters are active in their common solicitude for all the communities of the Order in matters both human and divine. This pastoral care has been exercised traditionally through the institutions of filiation, visitation, and the General Chapter (C.4.1–2).

In the light of this text, we have to admit that the 'common solicitude', at least as regards Filiations and Visitations, is seriously limited by the following facts:

- The Abbot General, not the Fathers Immediate, has the right of Visitation over the sixty-six monasteries of nuns.

- There are almost ninety potential delegated Visitators but this number is cut in half when you take into account the criteria I use to name them, namely:

  –the Father Immediate at least every six years.

  –if possible, two Visitations made by the same Visitator, to favor continuity.

  –not to overburden the Fathers Immediate who have many daughter houses.

  –the opinion of the local Abbess.

  –attention to the travel expenses of the Visitator.

- Only fifty-five abbots—out of the ninety-nine male superiors and sixty-six female superiors (a total of one hundred sixty-five superiors)—are Fathers Immediate.

- Thirteen Fathers Immediate, all but two of them Europeans, have five or more daughter houses; that is, they exercise their fatherhood over seventy-four daughter houses.

In the light of these facts—and of others that I omit here for the sake of brevity—we could dream of:

- redistributing the filiations.

- crossed filiations, that is, of monks from nuns and vice versa.

- greater delegation of Visitations for the monasteries of nuns.

- delegating Visitations to former abbots and superiors *ad nutum*.

- Regular Visitations that are crossed, that is, made by monks to houses of nuns and vice versa.

- intercultural Regular Visitations, that is, from the northern hemisphere to the south and from the south to the north, from east to west and vice versa.

- the pastoral role of the Regions.

The process of greater integration could continue in the area of relations between Regions in the same country and between different countries. The Presidents of Regions could be invited to other Regional Meetings. There could be joint meetings of two or three Regions. All that helps culture exchange in the Order will have to be recognized and promoted.

As you listen to me you will surely be thinking the Abbot General is a dreamer! Yes, and more besides. I believe in the utopia of our

Order as united and well integrated on all levels, launched toward a greater sense of communion in our charism.

CISTERCIAN COMMUNION

Spiritual renewal has to produce a greater integration of the Order, and this integration has to be open to a broader communion, which begins, in the first place, in the context of the Cistercian Family.

The Cistercian Family

There are presently five groups that make up what we can call, 'the big Cistercian Family'. For today, however, I will simply underline the relationship existing between two of these groups: the Cistercian Order (OC) and the Cistercian Order of the Strict Observance (OCSO). They are presently made up of one hundred thirty-five and one hundred fifty-four communities, respectively. These communities are composed of 2,451 persons in the OC and of 4,483 persons in the OCSO.

Let us look briefly at our history. The Strict Observance came to Rome in 1892 by ways that were not always the straightest. In Rome that year, the union took place thanks to which we exist today as the OCSO. It is correct to say, as I just did, that the union took place. However, a division also took place, a break with an important part of what was, until then, the Cistercian Order. From that moment on, the 'Cistercian Order' became the Cistercian Family composed of two Orders. That is how Pope Leo XIII put it ten years later in an Apostolic Letter that is both important and forgotten. He wrote:

> *The Abbot General and the other abbots and monks of the Reform,*
> *that is, of the Strict Observance, despite the union which constitutes*

*them as an autonomous Order—as we have just recalled—are and
remain true members of the Cistercian Family in the same way as
the Abbot General and the other abbots and monks of the Common
Observance are. We therefore establish and declare by the aforemen-
tioned authority and power, that they possess all the same privileges,
favors, indulgences, faculties, prerogatives and indults that could have
been granted in whatever way to this Cistercian Family, and which
the Abbot General and the other abbots and monks of the Common
Observance possess and use, without any difference whatsoever*—Leo
XIII, *Non mediocri,* July 30, 1902.

A Little History

Shortly before the Apostolic Letter just quoted, there was a serious attempt at union which came to nothing. It would seem that
the most prudent means to this end were not used, nor was the
method truly transparent and the motivations of some of the persons involved were very shortsighted. To be convinced of this it
is sufficient to read the *dossier* for 1896 on the project of Union,
which we have in our archives, and the historical studies already
made on the subject.

It is worth noticing the conference of the Abbot General at the
General Chapter of 1952, commemorating the Sixtieth Anniversary
of the Chapter of Union that gave birth to the Order. The Chapter
Fathers unanimously approved the following conclusion: *The union
cannot be achieved unless the Common Observance decides to return to the
purely contemplative ideal of the Founders (Minutes, Session 5).*

In fact, the union was not achieved. Worse still, two years later the
'Spain *Affaire*' occurred. This was a project of the Abbot of Cardeña
working behind the scenes with the Abbot General of the Common
Observance to reestablish the Congregation of Castille and reunite
in it all the Spanish communities. Such a scheme worsened the
situation and created new obstacles (cf. General Chapter of 1954,

Minutes, Session 2). Because of this incident, Dom Gabriel Sortais wrote to Dom Kleiner in the following manner:

> *While sharing with you the deep regret I have felt about all this, I would like to tell you simply and sincerely the course of action which I have thought it my duty to take, and which I have also asked the Reverend Father Capitulants meeting in Cîteaux in September to take: while observing toward your Order the signs of respect which charity demands, we will no longer enter your monasteries. I would be grateful . . . if you would kindly show the same reserve concerning our monasteries*—Letter of Oct. 1, 1954.

The relations between the two Observances began to change somewhat in 1987 with the preparation for the Congress on Saint Bernard of 1990. During the General Chapter of 1990, Dom Ambrose reported:

> *A month ago, I had an interview with Dom Polycarp. He told me that, in the context of the 1998 Centenary, we should have a dialogue between the two Orders as a preparation for union.* (Session 27.2)

All the foregoing explains why, in the Circular Letter of 1992—on the occasion of the first centenary of the OCSO—I wrote as follows:

> *This centenary of the Chapter of Union should make all of us more aware of preparing the ways that will let us achieve someday, with our brothers and sisters of the Common Observance, what was the final purpose of the Chapter Fathers of 1892, namely, to achieve the full unity of the whole large Cistercian family.*

This is not the time to describe in detail what has happened and the contacts that have been made during the last four years. The most significant fact is certainly this one: on September 1, 1995, our Procurator General, Dom Armand, represented me at the General Chapter of the Cistercian Order and, speaking in my name, asked forgiveness for the past history of rejections. He also suggested a *Carta Fraternitatis,* to be signed by all who share in the cistercian patrimony, and he invited their Chapter to establish different forms of *spiritual associations* between neighboring monasteries of one or the other observance.

Perhaps I am dreaming, even though I am wide-awake. In any case I am attracted by the utopia of celebrating the ninth centenary of the founding of Cîteaux by having a General Cistercian *Congreso* in which a *Carta Fraternitatis (Sororitatis) et Pluralitatis* is drawn up and signed by the entire Cistercian Family. This *Congreso* would also study the possibility of a *Carta Communionis* between monasteries of different Congregations or Orders, as well as different types of intercongregational associations. Can we dream of a new formula of cistercian communion so that we can begin to bring the Cistercian Family together again?

Charismatic Associations

In various places where the Order exists today we see how lay persons or groups who want somehow to share our charism have sprung up. Various groups already exist. They have varying degrees of organization and are associated with different monasteries.

Such events are relatively new for our Order. They correspond to the rising position of laypersons in the life of the Church. In many countries, lay movements have modified the vision and perception of the Church herself. The new Code of Canon Law 'canonized' the desire of the laity to share in the life and spirituality of religious institutes. According to can.303, all institutes can establish some type of association with laypersons.

The Exhortation after the Synod on consecrated life is aware of this phenomenon, discerns it and offers some stimulating words of encouragement:

> *In the case of monastic and contemplative Institutes, their relations with laypersons are principally characterized by spiritual bonding. . . . Due to new situations, not a few Institutes have come to the conviction*

that their charism can be shared with laypersons. Thus, the latter are invited to participate more intensely in the spirituality and mission of the Institute. Based on the historical experiences of the different 'secular Orders or third Orders', it can be said that a new chapter has begun in the history of the relations between consecrated persons and the laity. It is a chapter rich in hope. These new paths of communion and collaboration deserve to be encouraged for a diversity of reasons. . . . Therefore, whatever activity or ministry consecrated persons carry out, they should remember that their duty is to be, above all, expert guides in the spiritual life—John Paul II, *Vita consecrata*, 54–55; cf.31.

How are we to interpret these events? What is the Lord trying to tell us through this sign of the times, which for us seems certainly to be also a sign from God? These questions are not without significance for the service of the Abbot General. The Constitutions say specifically of him that he *is the watchful guardian of the Order's patrimony, ensuring its growth* (C.82.1). Moreover, if the Abbot General cannot ignore these questions, much less can the General Chapters ignore them.

I have treated this theme elsewhere and now is not the time to repeat what I have already stated. So let these few ideas, colored with a little utopia, suffice.

Lessons from History

I have already pointed out that the cistercian charism is a collective one. We can now add that it is a charism open to different configurations. The establishment of Laybrothers, Oblates, Familiars, and Military Orders are examples of this. However, is it possible to conceive of the cistercian charism as a grace shared with seculars in the world so as to create the possibility of a secular form of the cistercian charism?

In the first place, let us say that our charism, like every charism, is a gift from the Spirit in order to build up the Church as the Body of Christ. No one possesses the cistercian charism as private property. Our charism belongs, at its root, to the Church. The Spirit can share it with whomever He wishes and in the form and measure that He wishes. As Cistercians, we have given a monastic and historical form to this particular gift of the Spirit. This monastic form is an integral part of the original charism of the Founders. Nevertheless, as we have seen above, that did not prevent the charism from being shared with Laybrothers, Oblates, Familiars, and Knights of the Military Orders.

So now the question is: Can the fact that, in our day, seculars feel drawn to and identified with the cistercian charism be understood as a sign that the Spirit wants to share it also with them, so that our charism might receive an additional secular form in our historical moment today?

Our Charism Shared with Seculars

The monastic nature of our Order (C.2) does not mean that many elements of its spirituality (C.3) cannot be shared with laypersons in the world. In fact, the *Rule* of Saint Benedict has been lived for centuries by oblates living outside the monastery. Moreover, various monasteries of the Cistercian Order, belonging to different Congregations, have lay oblates who live in the world.

Separation from the world (C.29), though it is a special feature of our monastic life, should not make us forget that, as members of the Church, our life has an authentic secular dimension that is rooted in the mystery of the Incarnate Word. Of course, all members of the Church share in its secular dimension, but we do so in a different way. The secular nature of the lay faithful is different from, and complementary to, the secular dimension of monks and nuns. (Cf. John Paul II, *Christifideles laici,* 15)

Our monastic zeal for the spread of God's Kingdom and the salvation of all (C.31) also includes restoring all the temporal order of creation (cf. *Christifideles laici*, 15). Our secret apostolic fruitfulness (C.3.4) finds a deep resonance and complementary in the vocation of the lay faithful who are called by God to contribute from within, like yeast, to the world's sanctification through the exercise of their own responsibilities (cf. *Christifideles laici*, 15).

Our mission of evangelization by our contemplative presence (C.68.1) is not exclusive, nor does it exclude others. On the contrary, it admits the complementarity of the contemplative presence of laypersons immersed in the heart of the world. The mission belonging to our charism is not limited to our form of living it and revealing it. The inclusion of laypeople within our charism and mission will make the significance and usefulness of these spiritual realities more evident to all. In practice, the mystery of the Church as Communion implies an exchange of gifts at the service of the new evangelization.

Therefore, to respond to the original question above, it seems to me that the fact that some laypersons today feel attracted to and identified with the cistercian charism can indeed be understood as a sign that the Spirit wishes to share it with them, too, so that our charism can receive an additional secular form at the present moment of our history.

I have already mentioned the existence of Oblates residing in our communities. This phenomenon has recently been discerned and structured by the General Chapters. The fruit of this discernment process is the *Statute on Oblates*.

It could be asked if the time will come, or if it may have already arrived, to draw up a 'Statute of Confraternity' in order to regularize the association of present and future lay groups that share or will share our charism. If this is done, then we will no longer speak of a utopian dream. The Cistercian Family will enter the third millennium with a new look and a new service in the Church of God. Otherwise, let us keep on dreaming, without drowsing or going to sleep.

If the new stage of the Order's inculturated spiritual renewal becomes a reality, we can wait in confidence for the arrival of our ninth centenary and the third millennium. This renewal should awaken in each one of us a living, active 'sense of the Order'. A renewed heart is not closed in on itself. On the contrary, it broadens its boundaries. The local community as a *School of Charity* will pave the way for an Order that is also a *School of Charity*. Moreover, this school of charity will include all the Cistercian Family. It will even give birth to other schools of charity formed by laypersons and Christian families. Are these dreams? Life is a dream and dreams are life.

THE ORDER TODAY AND TOMORROW

Conference at the General Chapters,
October 1999

NINE YEARS HAVE NOW PASSED SINCE MY ELECTION as Abbot General. If God, the General Chapters and I myself remain willing, by the next Mixed General Meeting I will have exceeded the average length of the Abbot General's stay in office; in fact, the last eight Abbots General remained in office for an average of eleven years and eight months. During this time, I have had occasion to make sixty-nine international voyages and four hundred three visits to communities, without counting the communities in Italy. Those of you who were present at the time will recall that at the 1993 General Chapters, I presented my vision of the Order, as I perceived it then.

My evaluation at that time was positive and continues to be so today. It was precisely because the situation was positive that, discerning the Lord's will, I took the liberty of inviting each and every one to go a step further along the path of renewal. I would like now to return to those same topics. What was said in 1993 retains its value, at least according to my own view and judgement. What I will say today, as we cross the threshold of the third millennium, will serve to fill out the picture and look at some aspects in greater depth.

STATISTICS AND INTERPRETATIONS

It is an easily proven fact that the population of **monks** has been gradually decreasing for some years now. The number of monks reached its high point in 1958 with 4400 persons and from that date began slowly to decrease. In the year of my election as Abbot General in 1990 there were 2797 monks; today there are 2512, that is to say, two hundred eighty-five fewer.

The **nuns'** situation is different. They reached their peak in 1961 with a total of 2010 persons. From that date on, the total began to drop off gradually, slightly rising and falling in turns. In 1990 there were 1876; today there are 1863, that is to say, thirteen fewer nuns. This more stable monastic population among the women enables us to foresee an increasingly active role on the part of the nuns in the life of the Order.

It would seem that the drop in numbers, especially among the monks, will still continue for some years. One reason in support of this claim is the high average age of some communities of monks; this means that there was a notable influx of vocations at a given moment in the past, i.e. at the end of the 1940s and the beginning of the 1950s.

The **regions** with the highest average age at present are Canada, the Isles, and Holland. The regions with the lowest average age, on the other hand, are Africa, ASPAC, and REMILA. This holds for both monks and nuns. This means, moreover, that the latter three regions have a higher number of young people in formation. It is easy enough to guess what these figures mean for the future of the Order that continues slowly to shift toward the south and the east.

AN INCREASE IN FOUNDATIONS

The increase in the number of foundations in the Order these last years reflects the above statements. Since 1980, the **monks** have made eleven foundations (Brazil, Japan, Mexico, Venezuela, Dominican Republic, Taiwan, Spain (two), Indonesia, Lebanon, Ecuador) and two pre-foundations (Algeria and Nigeria).

The **nuns**, for their part, have made sixteen foundations (Chile, Japan, Nigeria, Angola, Venezuela, Indonesia, USA, Korea, Spain, Zaire, Ecuador, China, Philippines, India, Madagascar and Norway). In the last twenty years, then, the Order has made twenty-seven foundations and two pre-foundations with the following geographic distribution: four in Europe, one in North America, eight in Central and South America, six in Africa, and ten in Asia.

Along with the above, we must also include the incorporation of Kurisumala in India, the foundation **projects** of Sept-Fons, Klaarland, and Hinojo, and the **annex** houses of Huerta (Monte Síon) and Laval (Meymac). For the sake of being exact, we must also mention the closure of Orangeville, a foundation of Oka in Canada, and the existence of various monastic projects in China.

It is easy enough to realize the influence these new foundations have in the renewal of participants at the General Chapters. It is not only a matter of new members, but also of new experiences, new points of view, and new life.

In this context, I would like to share with you a few ideas that have been finding their way into my heart over the last few years.

The first of these ideas is in reference to the **criteria of discernment** for making a new foundation. The *Constitutions* mention community growth, the desire of participating in a monastic manner in fulfilling the mission of evangelization as the contemplative presence of the Church, and other *signs of Providence*. Special attention is to be given, in all of this, to the Second Vatican Council's invitation *to establish monastic life in the new Churches.* Lastly, the General Chapter urged that possibilities for foundations be carefully examined, *not only prudently but also boldly and generously* (C.68). The *Statute on Foundations* groups all of these considerations together by referring to *various signs of divine providence* and then adds a few practical aspects: the community's capacity for making a foundation (personnel and economics), the possibility of vocations, local conditions, the counsel of third parties. Be that as it may, it is nonetheless a matter of *discerning* God's will (1 and 3).

Our legislation, then, offers us two kinds of criteria for discerning a foundation. These criteria can be presented as follows:

- the natural criteria of **human prudence**: number of persons, personal capacities, economic means, possibility of vocations, local conditions, and seeking the counsel of experienced people; and

- the theological criteria of **divine prudence**: to help a local church express its contemplative dimension, witness to the Gospel through one's prayerful way of life, offering a place in which to live and grow monastically.

Obviously, these two series of criteria are not exclusive one from the other; rather they must mutually complement each another. One might ask, however, which takes precedence? We can perhaps find the answer in the *Constitutions* themselves when they speak of *confidence and generosity*. Without a strong dose of generosity and bold confidence, I think it is impossible to discern the *signs of God* hidden in the signs of the times.

Now then, what are the main **motives** for making a foundation? The motives coincide with the criteria of discernment, and the main motives are to be found in the theological criteria of divine prudence. While it is true that many concrete problems in foundations come from not having sufficiently taken into account the criteria of human prudence, nonetheless, a foundation that is not based on the criteria of divine prudence will lack the 'meaning' needed to sustain the motivation of the founders, foundresses, and communities that undertake to found.

The second idea is with reference to the **teachings** we can glean from new foundations. History and experience show that foundations teach us some important lessons that can be presented in a synthetic way as follows.

- **A sense of what is essential**: the basic values and observances are experienced without adornment, in all simplicity, with the possibility of adaptation as indicated in the Constitutions.

- **Radicalness**: it is necessary to leave everything behind in order to follow the Lord, in a foreign country or with people coming from other countries.

- **The value of poverty**: not only material, but also intellectual and liturgical poverty, or poverty in terms of formation . . . freely embraced, even if dictated by necessity.

- **Trust in Providence**: since insecurity—economical, political, and vocational—is part of daily life.

- **A sense of the Church**: an intimate bond is formed with the local church that a foundation both serves and makes manifest.

- **Revaluation of the Tradition**: in order to be firmly rooted, sound doctrine and experience approved by the centuries.

- **New ways of adaptation**: many things are found to be relative—food, clothing, certain behaviors, and structures.

- **Inculturation**: it is less a matter of implanting than of germinating, fostering dialogue, and discerning values and counter-values.

- **Vitalization of the motherhouse**: thanks to its own fruitfulness, for the sake of opening new horizons and of being challenged by what is different.

- **Cenobitism**: is often fostered by the demands of a small community, which requires no little virtue.

- **Catholicity**: a communion is created between geographically distant churches.

- **Rejuvenation of the founders**: given the fact that a new *habitat* often favors a new rebirth.

- **Ways of founding**: experience teaches what is best and the *Statute on Foundations* provides orientation.

- **A sense of the Order**: one learns to act locally and to reflect universally.

The capital importance of foundations for the Order of the present and of the future cannot leave us indifferent. For this reason, we can **raise the question** if it would not be better to reserve the approval of foundations exclusively to the General Chapters (cf. St. 84.1.C.a). Or, on the other hand, what does it mean concretely, on the part of the superiors who approve a foundation, to *encompass the new offshoot with fraternal care* (C. 69; Statute on Foundations 9)? We must all feel responsible for the consolidation of new communities, but this does not mean placing an artificial control on the expansion of the Order. It is not easy to strike a balance between consolidation and expansion. I am of the opinion that a certain amount of 'ferment' can help us avoid immobility disguised as prudence.

A SHIFT OF CENTERS

The founding activities of recent years, as I have indicated, likewise allow us to speak of a certain shift in the Order. To put it more concretely, at the Order's birth in 1892, eighty percent of the communities were in Europe and twenty percent outside of Europe, the percentage between monks and nuns being about the same (seventy-nine percent and twenty-one percent). Current data offers the following figures:

- communities of **monks in Europe**: fifty-one, with 1326 persons (average age of sixty-three) of whom 145 are novices and simply professed.

- communities of **monks outside of Europe**: forty-nine, with 1186 persons (average age of fifty-seven) of whom one hundred ninety-nine are novices and simply professed.

- communities of **nuns in Europe**: thirty-seven, with 1121 persons (average age of sixty-two) of whom eight-seven are novices and simply professed.

- communities of **nuns outside Europe**: thirty, with 742 persons (average age of fifty-five) of whom one hundred forty-two are novices and simply professed.

Once again—taking into account the higher number of persons in initial formation, the lower average age and the higher number of foundations outside of Europe—it hardly seems presumptuous to affirm that, if the present situation continues to obtain, in less than ten years the ocso will be a predominantly non-European Order.

This situation will very likely entail several consequences. One of these will be a new balance between fidelity to the tradition and creativity based on the tradition; perhaps rather than speak of 'creative fidelity', we will for a time speak of 'faithful creativity'. It is also likely to bring about a re-discovery of roots, recognizing the fact that these are what hold up the tree, not the leaves, flowers and fruit. Moreover, the original charism, by being lived out and interpreted in other cultural milieu, will bring to light facets and possibilities little known until now.

Throughout this process, younger communities have to show prudence by being open to the time-proven experience of older communities. In addition, the glory of older communities will consist in the fact that sons and daughters become in their turn teachers.

A Few Challenges

In 1992, on the occasion of the first centenary of the ocso, I wrote a circular letter in collaboration with the Permanent Council. In this letter, we looked at our past, present, and future. The present was characterized by positive signs and challenges to address. Rereading what was said there, I find that it fully retains its value. A few of these realities were taken up again in one of my conferences at the last General Chapter in 1996 in the form of three 'utopias': integration within the Order, cistercian communion, the association of lay-people in the same charism. Lastly, in the circular letter of 1998 I articulated the challenge of anthropology.

As we come to the end of this second millennium, the Lord of history invites us to respond in a creative way to what the following facts require of us.

- The need to **re-structure** the work, economies, and buildings of some communities that in past years were very flourishing but that now have a very high average age and no vocations. Eventually decisions will have to be made, and we know that necessity is not a good counselor. It is preferable to make choices and decisions before they are forced on us by necessity. It would a lack of responsibility within the context of salvation history to allow monastic communities to die in a world so urgently in need of re-evangelization.

- The situation of structural poverty and **economic crisis** affecting certain monasteries of the 'Third World' and the need for on-going help from the Order. Such situations will likewise entail the need to seek, find, and establish an economic and work structure adequately adapted to the local reality. When the help required is beyond the capacity of the motherhouses, there will be need to obtain means of assistance coming from the rest of the Order. Thus, solidarity will be the new name for poverty.

- Discernment of the values and counter-values of local cultures, of generational cultures, of the cultures proper to each gender (men and women), and of the culture predominating world-wide. Only in this way will it be possible to bring about in a prudent way the needed **inculturation** of our patrimony which reduces the distance between different generations, masculine and feminine culture, strong and weak cultures. The phenomena caused by a monopoly on cultural globalization that does not respect differences and the cultural nationalisms that close themselves off from anything that is not their own merit special attention.

- Openness to **'liturgical rites'** for the celebration of the Eucharist and the *Opus Dei* other than the Latin rite. The foundation in Lebanon and the incorporation of the monastery of Kurisumala in India have introduced the Maronite and Syro-Malankar rites into the Order. There is much to be gained from all of this, not only with regard to symbols and ceremonies, but also in the areas of theology and spirituality. A future updating of the cistercian ritual will not be able to overlook this reality.

- Dialogue with the **Cistercian Family** in order to mutually draw nearer and better understand each other, all of which could lead to new and effective forms of communion. The celebration of the Ninth Centenary of the foundation of Cîteaux signaled the beginning of a new phase. It seems best for now to put the emphasis on dialogue with the Presidents of the various Cistercian Congregations. Moreover, we need to rediscover the symbolic importance of the community and Abbot of Cîteaux and their role as a mediator within the Family. Perhaps it is now the vocation of the Abbot of the 'New Monastery' to be the *unitatis familiae vinculum* bringing us together once again, we who are still far off.

- Sharing **formation** resources with those monasteries most in need in this respect and that, at the same time, have the most young people in formation. An important task for the Regional Secretaries and the Central Secretary for Formation will be to continue putting the wisdom of the old world at the service of the new, without forgetting that genuine newness renders the wise wiser still. On the other hand, we are all aware that intellectual impoverishment is a terrible epidemic. Several Brothers who were specialists in various branches of knowledge and who served the Order well for many years have died recently. What can we do to fill this void? Our future is built on the present by means of a careful formation, which holds true for the monks as well as for the nuns of the Order.

- A special invitation to the Order on the part of churches immersed in the **islamic** world following the witness of the martyrs of Atlas. These minority churches, lost in the Muslim ocean, especially in the Maghreb, need to show that christian action is ordered to contemplation, that evangelization is not proselytism, and that the God of the Kingdom is more important than the Kingdom of God (at least according to the meaning we usually give to this Kingdom!). When the time comes to discern a foundation in these circumstances, will the likely absence of native or local vocations be a decisive criterion? I believe that here there is no little need for *generosity and bold confidence* in order to discern the *signs of God* hidden in the signs of times and places.

• Association with **lay groups** in view of sharing the wealth of the cistercian patrimony has continued to grow during the last years. It is easy to account for this in the context of a globalized world and in a Church that is fundamentally a communion. Perhaps it would yet be premature to draw up a 'Statute of Confraternity'. Nonetheless, it seems that the time has come to offer some 'pastoral orientations' that would help communities committed to or about to commit themselves to this kind of association. Such orientations would have to establish criteria to determine whether a community is sufficiently mature to open itself to this kind of charismatic communion, criteria with regard to formation, criteria for safeguarding our respective identities, and criteria for the links to be established among those involved.

• **Extreme situations** that call for prayer, sacrifice, understanding, and help on the part of everyone. I am referring especially to:

-Our Lady of the **Rosary** (China): under political surveillance that renders easy contact with the exterior impossible. The same applies to the groups of young people gathered around former monks of Consolation and Liesse who in turn maintain relations with other monasteries of the Order.

-**Marija-Zvijezda** (Banja-Luka, Bosnia): the community survived the war of 1993–1996. There remain only five solemnly professed monks with no possibility of vocations.

-Our Lady of **Bela Vista** and **Nassoma y'Ombembwa** (Angola): without stable monasteries and in the middle of the state of war between the government and the UNITA forces.

-Our Lady of **Mokoto** and Our Lady of **Clarté-Dieu** (Democratic Republic of the Congo): the monks' community is dispersed to various monasteries of the Order, while the nuns' community is physically divided between Africa and France.

SPIRITUALITY OF COMMUNION

I would like now to say a word about a reality as ancient as the human being yet which appears today in a new form, by this I mean the spirituality of communion. It is not exactly a challenge, but rather a state of mind or 'mood'. Acquiring this attitude, however, may in fact prove to be very challenging. In the Apostolic Exhortation *Vita Consecrata*, the Holy Father, entrusting the consecrated life with the task of promoting the spirituality of communion, says: *The Church entrusts to communities of consecrated life the particular task of spreading the spirituality of communion* (51). This invitation is entirely consistent with our cenobitic life and the mystery of *koinonia* that is at its very root.

To be *true experts of communion and to practice the spirituality of communion as 'witnesses and architects' of the plan for unity that is the crowning point of human history in God's design* is beyond our ordinary strength; it is at one and the same time a task and a gift (*Vita consecrata* 46).

Ecclesial communion has to develop into a spirituality of communion, that is to say, *a way of thinking, speaking, and acting that enables the Church to grow in depth and extension*. In this way, the charisms of consecrated life help the Church to grow ever deeper its own being, as a sacrament of intimate union with God and of the unity of the whole human race (*Ibid.* 46).

The spirituality of communion must be lived out in four dimensions: within one's own community, in the Order, in the local and universal ecclesial community, and in the midst of the world, above all in those places where this world is most torn and divided.

Within the context of the Order there are particular groups characterized by a wealth of internal solidarity: autonomous communities, filiations, and regions. Their existence is simultaneously a factor of solidarity and of division: division *ad extra* with respect to others in order to create a solidarity *ad intra* with respect to ourselves. Finding a healthy balance between these two realities will always be a delicate task.

Clearly, this spirituality of communion, expressed in a dialogue of charity and communion in the charism, must be a new incentive for our charismatic association with lay people and for seeking out forms of union within our torn Cistercian Family.

That our Order in general and our General Chapter in particular, brings together people from so many different cultures and countries, is a sign and an instrument of the trinitarian communion reflected in humanity. It is likewise a privileged place for living the spirituality of communion beyond the merely local level.

RENEWAL ON THE THRESHOLD
OF THE NEW MILLENNIUM

Conference at the General Chapters,
October 1999

W E Cistercians have a long history to tell of and we like to think that a history to build lies before us. We are invited to be faithful to our past and to be creators of our future. Without creative fidelity, our tomorrow will amount to a mere yesterday. On the other hand, without sanctity and boldness, there will be neither fidelity nor creativity (cf. *Vita Consecrata* 37).

Six years ago, at the 1993 General Chapter, I shared my convictions about the necessity of *inculturated spiritual renewal.* On that occasion, I presented the causes, the context, the guiding ideas, the instruments, and the actors in a new stage of renewal. In short, it was a pressing invitation to center our lives on *the person of Jesus, following together in his footsteps, entering into the Mystery of the Father.* The program was and is, therefore, christocentric, evangelical, cenobitic, and mystical. Today I return to this same topic, highlighting other aspects.

UNAVOIDABLE URGENCY

In their recent years of renewal, all forms of consecrated life have gone through *a difficult and trying period . . . The difficulties however must not lead to discouragement. Rather, we need to commit ourselves with fresh enthusiasm, for the Church needs the spiritual and apostolic contribution of a renewed and revitalized consecrated life . . .* As a consequence of the above, it is the Holy Father's wish *that reflection will continue and lead to a deeper understanding of the great gift of the consecrated life . . . and that consecrated men and women, in full harmony with the Church and her Magisterium, will discover in this Exhortation further encouragement to face in a spiritual and apostolic manner the new challenges of our time* (*Vita Consecrata*, 13).

Concerning the above, I in no way mean to call into doubt the many assets our monastic life has received from post-conciliar renewal, whether on the institutional level or in daily life. At the same time, I cannot overlook the price that has been paid. I mean by this a certain impoverishment in some aspects of our 'monastic culture.' Indeed, some values, as for example fraternal correction and fasting, have all but disappeared. In like manner, we are feeling a certain lack in the areas of law (the penal code), ritual (the weekly *mandatum*), symbol (vestments, posture), and custom (prayer when beginning work). It remains true that, with too much of this, one can lose sight of the essential, yet it is also true that we lacked creativity at the time of the changes, for it is easier to eliminate than to substitute. The impoverishment of our monastic culture could be the cause of a weakening of fraternal unity and of the structures of coherent living. The mediation of monastic culture is essential in the area of formation; without it, it proves almost impossible to give 'monastic form' to our own existence as monks and nuns.

To be sincere, we must also confess another serious limitation in our renewal effort. I am referring to **misunderstandings** that need to be cleared up, such as between poverty and economy, personalism and individualism, generosity and activism, liberty and independence, unity and uniformity, pluralism and individualism, charity and tolerance, fidelity and habit, authenticity and spontaneity, incarnation and conformity to the ways of the world, dialogue and debate, asceticism and gymnastics, fasting and dieting, prayer and emptiness, inculturation and folklore, charism and hobby, autonomy and self-sufficiency, transformation and change, perseverance and survival, and so on.

These confusions are no doubt different from those Saint Bernard evoked with a certain mischievousness in his *Apologia* for Abbot William: *they count frugality avarice, and sobriety austerity, while silence is reputed gloom. Conversely, slackness is called discretion, extravagance liberality, chattering becomes affability, guffawing cheerfulness, soft clothing and rich caparisons are the requirements of simple decency, luxurious bedding is a matter of hygiene, and lavishing things on one another goes by the name of charity (Apology* 17). Though the confusion be different, it remains true that a disorder in language sustains a disorder in the mind.

There is yet another reason urging us to welcome renewal as an ongoing process. The young monks and nuns were not instrumental in the renewal of yesterday, but they are called to be so in the renewal of today. They also have a contribution to offer since the creative and renewing Spirit is present in their lives. It would be an idle display of pride to consider renewal as something already complete, leaving no room for further innovation.

In present day literature on religious life there is no lack of an ever more urgent reflection on the 're-foundation' of religious institutes. Though the term may be ambiguous, it fully retains its value when referring to being faithful to the Lord as he speaks through each new historical situation. For some institutes the challenge is considerable, admitting only two alternatives—life or death. The situation of institutes of monastic life is perhaps not so urgent. Nonetheless, if we do not re-evangelize our concrete structures and ways of living out the charism that sustains us, we will fall into ecclesial anonymity. We will be 'bad news' for the man and woman of today and end up in the wastebasket of history.

A THREEFOLD MEANING

It now seems important to me to clarify briefly the meaning of the programmatic phrase 'inculturated spiritual renewal'. We will take up each of the three words separately in inverse order. We will see very quickly that they form an inseparable unity.

Renewal

Renewal obviously refers to 'newness', not just any sort of newness, but rather that which is contrary to both the 'outmoded' and 'the very latest'. The apostle Paul tells us this: since Christ has risen from the dead, *we walk in newness of life* (Rm 6:4). The *Exordium parvum* defends the newness of early Cîteaux, using an expression from Paul: *stripping off the old self, they rejoiced to clothe themselves with the new* (XV,2; Cf. Ep 4: 22–24; Col 3: 9–10). Consequently, the newness of renewal is quite different from mere 'innovation' or the latest fashion, which is intrinsically ephemeral. Were fashion to endure, it would go out of fashion, all of which shows the foolishness of such unstable transitoriness.

Our new life implies above all else a return to the person of Jesus and to the good news of his Gospel. Moreover, as Cistercians, our 'newness' requires a return to our origins since the founding charism of Cîteaux remains a life-giving source without which there is no possibility for originality.

Let it also be said that originality has the advantage of continually remaining in the present time, just as the essential of what is truly traditional always remains current. The present-day situation of an institute can be judged on the basis of its ability to incarnate values and make them manifest in a way appropriate to the reality of its time. It is important, therefore, to know how to avoid the modernization of inessentials and the kind of being-up-to-date that lacks history. This return to our origins requires a capacity for mobility, mobility like that of a circle that turns on an unmoving center, mobility as opposed to settling in or being unavailable. Returning to the origins is a re-creation, not so much of the outer events, but rather to what inspired them from within.

The history of institutes of consecrated life shows us that any effort toward renewal is a cause of conflict. Clearly, it is less a matter of useless antagonisms occasioned by loud protagonists than of conflict arising from faithfulness to Jesus and his Gospel. Whether a conflict is genuine is discerned by the fruit it bears in terms of the regenerativity of persons, communities, and structures—regeneration that, starting with the personal, attains to the organizational, by way of the communal.

Spiritual

The word 'spiritual', in the context of renewal, refers above all to the activity of the Holy Spirit. Indeed, it is thanks to him that we can *live by the Spirit and be guided by the Spirit*, that we can *be renewed in the spirit of our minds and clothe ourselves with the new self* (Ga 5: 25; Ep 4:23–24). Consequently, spiritual is opposed above all to 'carnal' and not to bodily or temporal. Moreover, it refers to 'metanoia' or inner conversion of heart.

The interiority I allude to at present implies at one and the same time: the human person as conscious, free, responsible, and social; living in order to love and be loved; and the divinizing life that is present in sanctifying 'grace' and expresses itself in faith, hope, and love. This spiritual interiority must never lose sight of the fact that the human being is a corporal being, that is to say, an embodied spirit.

Living in the Spirit is both a gift and a task involving both receptivity and effort. Moreover, if it is to continue over time, the initial grace must be brought to completion through the gift of perseverance.

Inculturated

Culture is something distinctively human. Human beings alone 'cultivate' their relationship with God (religion, worship), with other humans (language, social, and political life) and with creation (economics, work, technology, art). Since each people has its own culture, we can speak of 'cultures' in the plural. Each of us is at one and the same time the child and the parent of the culture we live in. Thanks to our own culture, we live in a human way. Because of our culture, we live in a limited way. Though every person exists in a specific culture, there is more to us than just culture: there is something in us that transcends culture (cf. Pontifical Council for Culture, *Towards a Pastoral Approach to Culture*, 1999).

It is also possible to speak of 'sub-cultures' in reference to groups differentiated by reason of gender (masculine and feminine culture), generation (culture of the elderly, youth culture), vocation (monastic culture, military culture), place (urban culture, rural culture), and so on.

Inculturation of our cistercian charism is an aspect of the inculturation of the Gospel, and inculturation of the Gospel is a consequence and a prolongation of the mystery of the Incarnation. The inculturation of our charism is the process of its incarnation in a specific culture and the consequent enrichment of both. It is a natural process that cannot be induced artificially, though it can be given orientation.

Our charism goes beyond all cultures and yet is in and from cultures. This is to say that our cistercian charism is transcultural, in reference to what is specific to human beings and Christians, but that it exists only within specific cultural forms.

Any process of renewal implies an inculturation that occasions new forms. Early Cîteaux uprooted itself from feudal cultural forms in order to inculturate itself in the cultural forms coming to light at that time. The whole of cistercian history can be interpreted as a succession of inculturations.

Today's inculturation has to take into account the pluricultural reality of the Order; it is therefore not possible to produce formulas or orientations that apply to all new places and situations. Certain monastic cultural forms can be up-to-date in one context and out-of-date in others. We are all aware that it is not easy to live out unanimity within pluriformity, but difficult does not mean impossible.

The purpose of inculturation in any process of renewal is: to express the charism more fully for the enhancement of cultures; to render our cistercian life more viable, credible, and universal; to communicate monastic life to local churches in a deeper way; and to allow for the creation of other forms or models of cistercian life.

Inculturation is a process that begins and never ends, for cultures change and interact. Likewise, the degree of 'enculturation' (the internalization of one's own culture) among the members of a given culture is also changeable.

The renewal and inculturation of a charism such as ours is a process that knows no end. Each generation, based on the preceding one, is called to bring about progress in the way this charism is lived out and interpreted. In this way, the charism is deepened and more fully expressed, along with the Body of Christ as incarnate in history.

REALISTIC UTOPIANISM

There will never be true renewal without an unconditional openness to the One who says: *See, I make all things new*. Among other things, this means that we have to learn to envision or conceive of our life, whether in its totality or in the elements it is made up of, with new categories or frameworks of thought. Without at least a minimum of freedom in thought and action, we will never be able to create what is not yet from what already is.

I have already explained elsewhere the meaning of the term 'utopian'. Pope Paul VI, in his Apostolic Letter, *Octogesimo adveniens*, speaks of utopias in the following way: *this form of criticism of established society often stimulates the imagination both to find previously unknown possibilities latent in the present and also to provide orientation toward a better future. It thus supports the dynamics of society by giving confidence to the inventive powers of the human mind and heart. Lastly, if it remains completely open, it can also re-discover the Christian calling* (37).

Consequently, I do not consider utopian to be synonymous with impossible. The utopian is not something impossible to carry out, but rather something that is premature. However, in the realm of human realities, what is truly possible? What is 'utopian' (in quotation marks so as to mean unreal)? Moreover, what is in fact a real possibility? Many things once considered to be impossible (or 'utopian'), as for example the abolition of slavery or the elimination of world hunger, were or still are considered to be so simply because they were not really or are not really wanted. The same can be applied to the Order. Mixed regional meetings, and the abbesses' right to vote in the election of the Abbot General or his Council were considered to be 'utopias' in the sense of unrealistic or as things that simply could not be brought about, and yet . . .

Within the order of divine grace, of new life in Christ, where is the dividing line between the possible and the impossible? Even the apostles considered monogamous and indissoluble marriage impossible (Mt 19:3–12)! Nevertheless, the Mother of Jesus knew very well that *with God nothing is impossible* (Lk 1:37; 18:27). There is nothing more utopian than the Gospel; one has only to reflect a little on the Sermon on the Mount or on the Our Father—for new wine, new wine skins! (Mt 9:17). This was the understanding of the early Christian community of Jerusalem (Ac 2:42–47; 4:32–35; 5:12–16) and of the founders of the 'New Monastery'.

It is impossible for a utopian world to supplant an extant world without a certain freedom of mind and action with regard to the latter. This attitude implies overcoming a passive acceptance of the world as it is, and at the same time avoiding a general condemnation of what is currently in place. Radical non-conformity is just as imprudent as systematic and uncritical conformity. It is not always easy to find one's right place on the continuum between passivity and refusal, intimacy and distance, fusion and divorce.

Living tradition is the very source of consistent progress, and an open future is the necessary condition for safeguarding the tradition as it moves on. Traditionalism, on the other hand, clings to the material aspects of the tradition, whereas progressivism advocates novelty without continuity, roots, or coherence.

Tradition and progress must learn to go hand in hand and not become 'isms' (traditionalism, progressivism . . .). The very worst is when such 'isms' become ideology, that is, a coherent, articulate, and operative system of thought that offers proofs and motivations for solving everything. Ideology, by simplifying reality, very often supplants it and modifies persons according to pre-established patterns. Ideology can become a mental straightjacket that warps, bridles, and hardens, in order to justify the unjustifiable.

For progressivist theology, evil lies in the past and good in the future, and vice-versa for traditionalist ideology. Cistercian history abounds in examples of tensions between traditionalists and progressivists. Nor has the ideologist demon been absent, though perhaps in a more subtle way, turning spirituality into ideology.

The current stage of renewal is urging us to give free scope to the creativity of our utopian thought and practice. Here perhaps lies the path most apt to provide answers for some of the challenges we have to face. Concretely, I am thinking of the question of the Cistercian Family and of the need to re-proportion economic and work structures to fit the needs of the local reality. A bit of utopianism will perhaps be needed likewise to find renewed meaning and new ways of incarnating certain monastic values such as silence, separation from the world, evangelical poverty, and fasting.

MEANINGFUL PRESENCE

Lastly, I would like to speak of another reality that, to a certain extent, encompasses all that has been said thus far. I am referring to the attractive evangelical witness we have to give simply by our presence. Our monastic life must be *a sign of the heavenly kingdom in the changing conditions of our time* (*Perfectae Caritatis*, 1 and 2): our very identity demands 'meaningfulness'.

Our identity and the vitality of this identity show themselves in the form of meaningful presence, presence being the visible manifestation of our identity. Our monastic charism has drawing power precisely because of its particular form of presence. Sociologically speaking, we exist because we are present and seen.

Our presence encompasses many different realities, bringing together all the fundamental aspects of our life. The most influential aspects of our presence are:

- for each one of us, **monks and nuns** of the Order: the dedication of our lives, our perseverance, our risk for the sake of the absolute, our radical daily options, our joyfulness, or, to the contrary, our mediocrity, discouragement, greed, selfishness.

- for each of our **communities**: the kind of relationships among its members, how welcoming it is, its sharing and communion, its insertion into the local area, its prayerful witness.

- the kind of **work activity** and participation in a given **economy**: agriculture, various types of factories, stores that sell one's own and others' products, employees serving the monastery.

- **buildings and properties**: where they are sited, the type of construction, the amount of land.

- other **visible signs** that indicate other realities: clericalism, medievalism, mystery, welcome, separation.

Our various forms of presence, then, manifest our identity and our charism to a greater or lesser degree. We must also take into account in this context that the secularized culture of certain areas of the globe is little inclined to recognize signs of transcendent values. Nevertheless, we might ask ourselves if our presence is:

- **production-oriented**: we are there because of what we do or make (cheese, beer, chocolate . . .).

- **patronizing**: we are there because others depend on us or are at our service (those who benefit from our presence, those we employ, various monopolies . . .).

- **provocative**: our simple life raises questions, makes people wonder (what are they seeking? They are like everyone else, and yet there is something more . . .).

- **contradictory**: the signs are unintelligible or self-
  contradictory (poor but at the same time wealthy, dressed up
  or disguised in an outmoded way . . .).

- **prophetic**: the Lord uses our presence to speak to believers
  and unbelievers alike (the Kingdom of Heaven is already in
  your midst . . .).

- **mystical**: the offering of one's life and the primacy of
  personal and communal dialogue with God are clearly visible
  to all (the mystery is revealed to the simple and pure of
  heart . . .).

Surely our presence will communicate more than one message and
will have more than one meaning. I consider it urgent—in the era
of social communication—to evaluate the visibility of our charism
and identity, since our witness depends on them. This will imply at
least:

- distinguishing whatever might obscure or confuse the witness
  of our life.

- shortening or lengthening distances to avoid confusion or
  estrangement.

- being attentive to the signs of the times and knowing how to
  inscribe new signs into the times.

- learning the difficult art of public and social communication.

Our monasteries are present in forty-four different countries. The
cultural, religious, political, social, and economic circumstances are
extremely varied. Nonetheless, there are common demands and
necessities. Contemporary reality invites us to see how our presence
and witness measure up against:

- the **poor and poverty** in all its forms.

- the **young people** who want to play an active role today and certainly will tomorrow.

- the thirst for **spirituality** on the part of the men and women of today.

- the desire for **communion** in a world torn by so many divisions.

I do not think I am mistaken in affirming that the quality of our meaningful presence and witness depends, in the final analysis, on a single reality: the deep living out of an integral spirituality abounding in divine and human values. Only thus will we be able *to make visible the marvels wrought by God in the frail humanity of those who are called* (*Vita consecrata* 20).

Our simple presence must make our monastic charism and the distinguishing characteristics proper to it visible. This presence must inspire, within our immediate environment, the desire to share in the life that shines forth in us. There is no better vocational program than the witness of a meaningful presence.

While it is true that every presence has something about it that remains unclear or inexpressible, it is also true that some signs can only be read by means of faith and openness to mystery. Nonetheless, today it is imperative that we ask ourselves if indeed our light *shines before others, so that they may see our good works and give glory to our Father in heaven* (Mt 5:16).

A BASIC REQUIREMENT

Because renewal requires effort and is likely to occasion conflict, the only ones who persevere in it are those who have a good sense of humor. Indeed, if you take life with a sense of humor, God will free you from what is tragic. If you are able to distinguish between mountains and molehills, you will avoid many worries. More concretely, if you reflect before you set to work, and if you laugh while you are reflecting, you will avoid doing many foolish things.

A sense of humor—an expression of cistercian joy—in the context of renewal keeps one from making absolute the relative and allows one to make relative the absolute in relation to the one and only Absolute. This gift of God, which renders human beings so attractive, is:

- something more serious than just funny, better understood by the humble than by the joker or the wit.

- a vaccine or an antidote against the venom of pride or megalomania.

- the ability to see the seriousness of what is foolish and the foolishness of what is serious.

- a source of relaxation and refreshment when we are tense and hot.

- the simplicity of the child with the experience of the elder.

A great mediaeval reformer and advocate of renewal, Bernard of Clairvaux, reminds us of a truth that we must not forget: *charity is laughter, for it is joyful* (Various Sermons, 93; Letter 87:12). Scripture, for its part, teaches us to call on God saying: *Lord let your face shine on (smile at) your servant* (Ps 31:17; 119:35). And likewise recommends that we *look to him and be radiant; so your faces shall never be ashamed* (Ps 34:6).

The unavoidable and urgent task of taking a step forward in renewal leads us to call on the intercession of that Mother who received into good soil the seed of God's humor and brought forth fruit a hundred-fold:

To you, our Mother, who desire the spiritual and apostolic renewal of your sons and daughters in a response of love and complete dedication to Christ, we address our confident prayer. You who did the will of the Father, ever ready in obedience, courageous in poverty and receptive in fruitful virginity, obtain from your divine Son that all who have received the gift of following him in the consecrated life may be enabled to bear witness to that gift by their transfigured lives, as they joyfully make their way with all their brothers and sisters toward our heavenly homeland and the light which will never grow dim. We ask you this, that in everyone and in everything glory, adoration and love may be given to the Most High Lord of all things, who is Father, Son and Holy Spirit (Vita Consecrata, 112).

Circular Letters to the Members of the Order

SEVEN WORDS

Circular Letter to the Members of the Order, January 26, 1991

Dear Brothers and Sisters:

During my closing talk at the last General Chapter, I promised to write an introductory letter to all the communities of the Order. I do so today, on the Feast of our Holy Founders, hoping that they will inspire my words.

I think that the best way to introduce myself will be to speak from the bottom of my heart and to show you what is in it. Having read what is in my heart and meditated in the presence of the Lord, I set myself to write without further preamble.

JESUS

Jesus, the Christ, is in the deepest recess of my heart. He dwells in me through faith and through his mysterious presence as the Risen

One. He is always present and acting. I can witness to the truth of his word: *I am with you always unto the end of the world.*

I confess him as truly God and truly human—only-begotten of the Father, born of the Virgin Mary by the work of the Holy Spirit.

Christ Jesus came to save sinners; he became human in order to make us human. He lowered himself in order to raise us up; he died in order that we might rise. He reached out to me and embraced me; he sought and found me. He called and invited me: *come and follow me.* He did the same for each one of you, sisters and brothers. There is nothing, absolutely nothing that we should prefer to Christ. Every day is an opportunity to return to our first love.

Exalted, risen, vivified, and vivifying, he made himself Bread and Wine. Consuming him, we are consumed. His Easter passing over is not a passing thing; he will remain present unto the end of the world.

MARY

I know—and I can proclaim it—that where the Risen One is, there also is his Mother, assumed into the glory of heaven. She is the Full of Grace who maternally graces us with the power of the Spirit.

She, Mary of Saint Joseph, the first believer and first disciple, has always been for me an attractive model of christian life and of the following of Christ.

Jesus offered her to us on Calvary as one of his last gifts, shortly before giving forth his Spirit. Jesus' Peace, his Love, his Word, his Bread, his Mother, and his Spirit are our christian inheritance.

Mary is never alone; the Saints always accompany her—all of them, Marian and Christian. The Saints, along with their Queen, manifest to us the face of God and offer a sign of his Kingdom.

To receive her is to offer oneself. To welcome her is to confide oneself. To embrace her is to abandon oneself into her hands. Whoever will consecrate himself and let himself be consecrated will possess her presence and a vital communion with her, and will be under her effective influence. Moreover, he will hear her say: *Do what he tells you.*

GOSPEL

I discovered the Good News of Jesus before reading it in the Book: Christ, who died and was risen for our salvation—who died, yes, but most of all was risen!

I rediscovered it in the monastery. The whole life and the whole message of Jesus may be summed up in this: filiation and brotherhood. Indeed, the prayer that the Lord taught us does not say *my Father* but *our Father.* We are all brothers and we have one common Father; and precisely because this Father is common to all of us, we are all brothers.

Whoever lives this filiation and this brotherhood will never say: *my will be done,* but rather: *thy will be done.* Moreover, living in this way, he will find his joy in the beatitudes of the Gospel.

CHURCH

I am, we are, members of one sole body—that of Christ. I know and feel that truth. We are Temples of the Spirit, Spouses of Christ, Sacrament of salvation, People and Family of God. We are a community of faith, hope, and love gathered in the communion of the Father, the Son, and the Holy Spirit. In this communion, we experience ourselves as—and become—the Family of God.

Mary, Mother of the Church, awakens our filial heart and tightens the bonds of brotherhood. The Spirit is the heart and soul of this family life.

I belong—we belong—to a large community that has no limit either in space or in time; a community without borders except, unfortunately, those of the heart of the person who rejects the Lord. Because I know that the unity of sons is realized upwards, I accept an authority and I go forth to meet it listening and assenting.

Rule

Now I must confess a sin that, I hope, you do not have to confess. During my first fifteen years of monastic life, I paid little attention to Benedict and his *Rule*. Fortunately, however, I came to the day of discovery and encounter. Then I learned how to read the Gospel with the eyes of a monk.

The *Rule*, embodiment of the life of Benedict, teaches me how to live daily as a cenobitic monk. It has shown me the path of humility and obedience; above all, however, it has shown me the path of the good zeal, or of the ardent love, that leads to the Father and to eternal life.

The *Rule*, echoing the Master who did not come to do his will, invites me always to seek not what is useful for me but for the others. The *ascesis* that Benedict teaches me is the passage from what is 'my own' to what is common—passing over of the 'I' to others so that the 'We' may be generated and may grow.

Cîteaux

I found Cîteaux and Saint Bernard before finding Saint Benedict. Cîteaux gave me eyes to read the *Rule* 'mystically' and, in that way, discover that it is entirely oriented toward the 'mystery': Christ, hidden in us and in our midst.

The cistercian fathers, without forgetting the objective reality of the mystery, give the primacy to the gratuitous experience of that mystery, and to the necessary letting go and the inseparable ascetical effort. That experience transforms us interiorly and makes us one with God.

God is a hidden God. He is sought and found in the ardent obscurity of loving faith. Moreover, when God manifests himself to us, he hides us in him in order to transform us into him. Therefore, as he divinizes us, he humanizes us.

HUMAN PERSON

Discovering myself as a person—someone in relation—I discovered humanity, and loving the human person, I loved myself. It then became evident to me that by loving my neighbor—created in the image and likeness of God—I also loved God, since love comes from God and returns to God.

Every human being, man and woman, is the object of the infinite wisdom and bounty of God, whence his supreme dignity. The human being is the only personal being of the whole creation; the only one that is conscious and free for loving in truth. We have fallen and we have disfigured ourselves, truly, but we have been redeemed and restored by the blood of the Son of God.

Every human being, without any type of discrimination, is worthy of love, but more so are those whom Jesus prefers: the poor, the weak, and those who suffer.

Every human being, any one of you, brothers and sisters, merits my respect and my love, just as I merit the same from you. Pardon me for my lack of love; once more, I enter the journey of conversion.

Sisters, brothers, my intention was to introduce myself. I think that these seven words express well what I am, what I desire to be and want to live: Jesus, Mary, Gospel, Church, *Rule*, Cîteaux, and Human Person.

It is easy to realize that these words are a program for living. Indeed, they are the basic realities of what I like to call 'The Gospel of the School of Charity'. However, I leave this here; it will be the theme, with God's help, of the next letter.

THE SCHOOL OF CHARITY

Circular Letter to the Members of the Order,
January 26, 1992

Beloved Brothers and Sisters:

I trust that the reception of this letter finds you well: helping one another in all your necessities, weeping with those who weep and rejoicing with those who rejoice, in prayer, and in contemplation of the deep mystery of God and his plan of salvation.

At the conclusion of my letter of introduction last year, I alluded to the 'Gospel of the School of Charity'. However, it was not the time to develop this theme. Today it is.

I wish to present for you, in some way, the Good News of the *Schola Caritatis* of Cîteaux. I beg you to receive my words with hearts open and well disposed, as I, in my turn, will endeavor to receive any comments. Only in this way will the fruits be abundant.

New Evangelization

The decade of the 1980's and the beginnings of the present decade, have been marked by a series of events that have changed the historical destiny of humanity. Moreover, it is precisely during these years that John Paul II, our pope, proclaimed a new evangelization. From the first announcement made in Latin America, the pope passed to Europe and then to the whole world, announcing the need for a new evangelization for the universal Church. It is the first evangelical plan on a global scale.

The proclamation of John Paul raises numerous questions. What? Why? Whom? How? And so many others. This is not the time or the place to respond to these questions.

For my present intentions, it is enough to be clear on the following. The new evangelization proposes to set in motion a Church that is evangelized and evangelizing; a Church given over to a new evangelization in its fervor, its methods, and its expression; and an evangelization capable of instilling in the whole world the civilization of love, as we approach the third millennium of Christianity.

We know that the Church exists to evangelize and that in this evangelizing action lies its most profound identity. We are also aware that in this same Church, given to action and contemplation, the visible is ordered to the invisible, and apostolic activity is ordered to contemplative activity. That is why the Church evangelizes with words and deeds, but most of all by witness and prayer.

Monastic Evangelization

The entire Church, we included, is missionary; evangelization is the fundamental duty and privilege of all the People of God. We, monks and nuns, evangelize by 'being' rather than by 'doing' (various works) or 'giving' (various goods)—unless by 'give' is understood 'hidden gift of oneself'.

Brothers, Sisters, our own consecrated life is a privileged and efficacious medium of evangelization. Our consecration situates us in the heart of the Church athirst for holiness and the Absolute, given over to the radicalism of the Beatitudes and in total availability to the Lord. Without all of this, there is no evangelical Church!

I believe, without the slightest doubt, that the life hidden with Christ in God possesses the mysterious apostolic fecundity of the prayer and gift of Christ himself to the Father.

I believe that living and sowing transcendence in the cultural ethos of the peoples—that is, in the nucleus of cultural values and in the final meaning of life—we are evangelizing cultures and enabling people to develop deep and true relationships with God, among themselves and with creation.

I believe that through our cenobitic life and organized work—in which each finds his fulfillment in the good of all—we witness to a new way of social solidarity that makes real the message of evangelical fraternity.

I believe, unwaveringly, that our conversion and adhesion to God with all our hearts redounds to the good of all the Church and is an efficacious cry of hope for all men and women.

EVANGELIZERS EVANGELIZED

Let us be realistic! If we wish to have a practical part at the heart of the New Evangelization, we must, first, allow ourselves to be re-evangelized. It is imperative to receive anew the Good News of Jesus: Repent, the Kingdom of God is near, believe! Return to the first Love!

If we wish, and certainly we do wish, to be performers—and not just bored spectators—in the mystery of an evangelization we must be:

- new in fervor: for union with Christ and his Spirit, fountain of most fervent love.

- new in methods: for the participation of all the members of People of God, each according to his vocation and mission, without allowing the diversity to fragmentize the union of action and communion.

- new in expression: utilizing symbols and words understandable to different cultures.

If we wish to be performers, then, in this evangelical plan, we must be each day disciples of the discipline taught us by the Master, Jesus Christ, in his cistercian 'School of Charity'.

THE MESSAGE OF THE SCHOOL OF CHARITY

I can think of various ways of presenting the teaching of our *Schola Caritatis*.

I could do it by analyzing and expounding on the *Mirror of Charity*, masterful work of our brother Aelred of Rieveaulx, true manual or compendium of that art of arts, the art of love.

It would also be possible to comment on the program offered us by the new Constitutions, above all the second part regarding the House of God, underlining what refers to the observances and formation.

But I am going to follow a more daring road. I am going to proclaim my own gospel: that which I have received, taught and enacted, with more or less fruitfulness according to my own cooperation with the action of the Holy Spirit. I will be brief, I want to shout it out, and he who shouts cannot indulge in long discourses. There will be passion in what I say, but reason will not be lacking.

CHRISTIAN AND CATHOLIC FOUNDATION

God the Father loved us first. He gave over to death and resurrected his own Son for our salvation. For us, also, Christ offered his Body and Blood, his Spirit and his Mother. Blessed with such precious gifts, we are sons of the Son and brothers of the Brother. All together, in communion, believing, hoping, and loving, we are his People, we are his Church, first-fruits and seed of the Kingdom— for the glory of God the Father and the liberation of the world.

CENOBITIC LIFE

By the design and predilection of the Father we have been called, each by name, to a consecrated life, under a rule and an abbot, in a stable community of brothers/sisters who love each other and seek God in sincerity of heart under the guidance of the Gospel.

- Blessed are they who live in unanimity and are of one soul, they already share and will rejoice without measure in the Trinity of the only God!

- Woe to those who isolate themselves in the individualism of their own 'I', aborting their ability to relate, these suicides and murderers of community have received their due!

We have made ourselves strangers to worldly ways and to things that are foreign to God's designs. We have distanced ourselves from the world of the men and women of today, not to reject but in order to place nothing before the love of Christ, to commune with all in him, and to recognize him and welcome him in each one. Solitary, yes, but in unlimited solidarity!

ASCETICAL LIFE

Those of us who wish to grow in humanity and Christianity know that nothing is gained without effort and practice, without discipline and *ascesis*. God shares with us the work of our own transformation. God works, true, and we do the sweating (well we know it).

Because we are flesh, because we are spirit, our *ascesis* is corporeal and spiritual. We have received an arsenal of weapons with which to emerge victorious from the battle. Clothed in:

- vigils—watchful in overflowing hope.

- fasting—moderate desert of the stomach.

- work—the toil of creativity.

- poverty—alienation, communion, and solidarity.

- chastity—sexual integration and relationship, without sex.

Thus clothed, therefore, we can subjugate the rudeness of the flesh and strengthen its weakness. We will then follow in the footsteps of Christ, rejoice in the anticipation of the final resurrection and render an inestimable service to all humankind.

- Blessed those monks and nuns who possess nothing, and monasteries that do not become rich or who share their goods generously, all these will have a share with the poor in the Heavenly Banquet!

- Woe to those monks and nuns who cherish personal goods and monasteries that trust in their goods and properties, their fasts will be turned to bitter retching for all eternity, their vigils will become anxiety-ridden insomnia, and the work of their hands will avail them nothing!

Effort, the work of God, leads to depth. The means are: the obedience that hears and assents, the reserve that allows silence to give birth to words and words to resound in silence, and the humility that raises as it plunges us into the abyss.

We arrive at the deepest center when self-denial transforms self-will into common will. Self-denial liberates love from the cruel tyranny of selfishness, allowing us to love freely through a complete gift of self.

- Bless those who can pray with total sincerity: Thy Will be done; these blessed will receive, like Mary, the Son of God in their hearts!

- Woe to the selfish who, turned in upon themselves, suffocate in their own self-love, the cries of their own self-condemnation choking them!

To deny self-will, much freedom and strength of will is needed. He who loves himself and denies himself, loves. Denial of oneself is an affirmation of oneself in the love of God.

All of this effort and ascetical practice is accompanied by an increased knowledge of oneself. Therefore, humility is a recognition of what one is. The humble soul is well rooted in the humus of his true humanity. Humility is a root, in truth.

After all of this, what then? To confess with a heart full of compunction the impotence of self-effort and transform this penitential humor into another humor: good humor! This jovial humor humidifies, heals, expands, and refreshes the tense and overheated who take themselves too seriously.

LIFE OF PRAYER

Without an ascetical life, there is no prayer life; and without a life of prayer, there is no contemplative life. In the same way, without a faith vivified by love, there is no contemplation. Nor is there prayer, for us cenobites, without the bond of peace in mutual charity.

If we want Christ and obedience to his Word to occupy the first place, nothing must come before the *Opus Dei*. If we wish to progress in the 'School of Charity', let us be solicitous and persevering disciples in the Work of God that is a School of Prayer.

Lectio divina is 'the reading of God' with the eyes of a son, the ears of a spouse, the heart of the Church. In addition, as a School of Contemplation, it prepares, deepens, and prolongs the work of God. *Lectio* without *oratio* is not *divina*.

- Blessed are those who live attentive to the Word, I am and will be for them an eternal response!

- Woe to those who do not wish to hear me and fill their ears with silliness and false learning, I will respond to their too-late questioning with silence!

At privileged moments of the day, as the grace of God allows, the praying heart should be turned toward, recollected, silenced, centered, and rested in God. In this intense, yet relaxed, interior attentiveness, we are divested of the old man and vested in the New.

At every moment, the constant mindfulness of God should actualize his presence in the cenacle of the spirit, thus allowing us to travel together—he and us—the paths of this life.

However, the source and summit of it all is in the Eucharist: sacrifice, banquet, memorial, and presence. We eat him in order to be eaten by him. From the many seeds that we are, he changes us into the one bread, his Body. When we drink his Blood, we receive love incorruptible.

PINNACLES

There is now a great silence in heaven. The heart, pure and purified, contemplates. Charity is aflame in the union of spirits and communion of wills. The presence of the Resurrected, with or without form, conforms us. It conforms because it reforms and transforms us. Now it is, that the feelings, affections, and mind of Christ are ours habitually. Now it is, that fraternity with the other and filiation with the Father have become indissoluble. Now it is, that in all truth we can say: we are worthless servants! Now only love, truth, and peace remain and irradiate.

I stop, the voice has left me.

Brothers and Sisters, if my letter is to have effect it is necessary that it harmonize with the call and vocational response of each of you and become a daily *conversatio*. However, this is not all, this *conversatio* needs continual motivation. How? I suggest three means.

Before all else, let us apply ourselves with joy and solicitude to the reading and rumination of our cistercian fathers. Then, let us commune with and participate in, with full responsibility and commitment, the life of our own monastic community. Finally, allow ourselves to be evangelized by the poor and simple, Christians and non-Christians, near and far.

The 'School of Charity' has a word to say in the world project of a new evangelization orientated toward a civilization of love: this word is our own life.

THE FIRST CENTENARY OF THE OCSO

Circular Letter to the Members of the Order, 1992

We celebrate the first century of the life of the OCSO. We celebrate an historical fact, aware that any perusal of history implies some kind of interpretation. Even more, we can speak of interpretations.

The birth of our Order lends itself to more than one interpretation. However, we do not propose to endorse one, or more than one, of these. Our aim is to celebrate.

To celebrate is not merely to recall times gone by, nor simply to commemorate the past. It is to remember with gratitude and praise of the Lord, and it is also a sorrowful recollection of past mistakes.

Historical remembrance is the foundation of identity; it permits us to know who we are and who we are meant to be. Historical forgetfulness goes hand in hand with loss of identity.

A Look at the Past

A long history of tension

The rapid expansion of the Order of Cîteaux in the twelfth century is something unique in the history of religious institutions. Among many other factors its success was due to the structure that our first Fathers gave the Order in the *Carta Caritatis*. The period of expansion and the golden age were followed by centuries of tension, at times decadence, that was due to the general situation of the Church and society as well as to various internal causes. The Congregations that began to appear in the fifteenth century were, as a whole, local or regional efforts at reform and at revitalization at a time when the whole body of the Order did not have the energy necessary to carry out such a task.

From the beginning of the seventeenth century on, we witness the division of the Order into Observances that, though based on respectable motives, led to what was called the 'War of Observances' that was not always edifying on either side. Following the Revolution, wars, and other political circumstances, this division between Observances was further complicated by divisions within the Strict Observance itself. Because the historical circumstances just mentioned had long made it impossible to hold General Chapters, the juridical situation itself was not altogether clear, particularly as regards the Abbot General. Though Pius VII had conferred on the Abbot President of the Congregation of Saint Bernard in Italy the rights and privileges of the Abbot General of the Order of Cîteaux, his rights were more formal than real, and outside Italy they were limited to confirming elections.

The events of the nineteenth century are very complex and historians as well as jurists often give them opposing interpretations. Needless to say, we do not intend to cast any new light on this matter. We even want to avoid as far as possible taking a stand for one or the other interpretation.

The General Chapter of 1892

The interpretation given to the events of 1892 obviously depends much on that given to those of the preceding decades or centuries. For most of us in the OCSO, the Chapter of 1892 was a turning point after which the Cistercian Order remained divided in two branches, which had grown from the same trunk, drank of the same sap, and shared the same tradition and history, and enjoyed the same rights. Our brothers of the Common Observance, for their part, consider that 1892 was a sad date on which an important part of the Order (the majority, in fact) left the Cistercian Order to create a new Order, autonomous and distinct. Although it is very unlikely that we could some day arrive at one common juridical and historical interpretation of the facts, we should all the same remain attentive to these different sensitivities in our fraternal relationships.

Although the Chapter of 1892 sanctioned a certain division, it was rooted in an ever growing desire for union. The immediate goal was the union of the various Congregations that had grown out of La Trappe and various attempts in that direction had been made during the preceding decades; but at least the more insightful of the promoters of that union saw it as a step toward 'the reunion of the whole cistercian family', Common and Strict Observances, as Dom Sebastian Wyart himself wrote in a letter just a few months before the 1892 General Chapter (Cf. *Anal. Cist.,* 1978, p. 335).

Perhaps the most important decision of that Chapter, in terms of its consequences, was the decision to create an autonomous Order, with its own Abbot General, rather than a Congregation under the authority of the Abbot General of the Common Observance. That decision is easily understandable in the contemporary context, and one might be led to think that, especially after the General Chapters of 1869, at which the abbots of the Strict Observance were not convoked, and of 1880 and 1891 at which an Abbot General was elected without the participation of the Strict Observance, the division was already effective both psychologically and in fact. One may wonder however whether the Capitulants of 1892 were fully aware of the radical division that their vote either created or sanctioned. In the years that followed, however, a project for the union of the two Cistercian Orders was developed along the lines of a desire for full unity. That project, certainly premature and not always put forward with the necessary tact, met with little sympathy on the part of the Common Observance, which felt wounded by the 'division' of 1892, nor even did it receive a positive answer from the majority of monasteries of the Strict Observance.

A Century of History

The Cistercian Order of the Strict Observance has been in existence for a century. That century is a chapter in the history of Cîteaux of which we can be proud, for it was a century of grace. As we begin the second century of the OCSO and prepare for the ninth centenary of the whole Order, it is only fitting to take an overall look at both the bright spots and shady areas of these hundred years.

As did the *Carta Caritatis* in the first years of the Order's growth in the twelfth century, the Constitutions written by the OCSO in the very first years of its existence gave it a solid juridical identity and contributed greatly to its development and its expansion. The purchase of the property of Cîteaux in 1898, which allowed for the Abbot General to be officially the Abbot of Cîteaux up to a recent date, was also an important historical fact.

The years from 1892 to World War II were years of consolidation and constant growth, though at a moderate pace. Those years were characterized by a spirituality in which the observances played an important role. Formation in general and intellectual formation in particular were often deficient, except in a few monasteries— Scourmont, for example—that were the exception.

From the time of World War II on, the Order experienced a rather extraordinary numerical growth, especially in America and, from 1950 on, a whole series of foundations were made, first in Africa, then in Latin America, and also in various other parts of the world. From being almost entirely European and, for the most part, French-speaking, the Order grew into a truly international one in which the various mentalities confronted each other at times, but above all enriched each other.

Because of this development, along with the general evolution of society and of the Church, the centrality of 'observances' and uniformity as the foundation of the Order's unity were brought into question. Already in the fifties we see the General Chapters revising the observances in order to allow a greater respect for geographical and cultural diversity.

In the same period, continuing along the lines of the basic aspiration toward union that had brought the OCSO into existence—but obviously at a quite different level—the 'Unification' of our communities was brought about, allowing all their members to be 'monks' with the same rights and obligations, while maintaining some pluralism within each community, but without the division into distinct 'categories'. The preparation for this 'Unification' began several years before the Council at a time when people were much less sensitive to dialogue, and Dom Gabriel, who started the whole project, was unable to bring it to completion before his sudden death. There are wounds that still need to be healed and modifications may still be necessary but the basic process of union, which allowed everyone to make monastic profession, is irreversible.

The years that followed the Council were difficult ones during which our Order, along with many other Orders or Congregations, lost several of its members, although it was the male branch of the Order that was most affected by this crisis, the female branch less so. Later on the influx of vocations slowed down in both branches, especially in Europe and America. This did not, however, diminish faith in the cistercian vocation and the desire to bring it to other places, mostly in response to calls from the Young Churches. Vocations were particularly numerous during the fifties and sixties. When we add a few incorporations—mostly in the female branch— we realize that the Order acquired thirty-six new monasteries of nuns and thirty-six of monks since the year 1942.

The preparation of the Constitutions, which lasted from 1967 to 1987, was for the Order a period of reflection and dialogue, on the community level as well as on the regional or inter-regional level. The role of the regions, along with that of the Central Commission, has taken on more and more importance as befits an Order that is gradually becoming more international and intercultural. Due to the frequent consultations made throughout the Order over a period of twenty years, the Order's new Constitutions truly express the collective understanding that the monks and nuns have of their vocation and their charism at the present time.

Coinciding with this effort of reflection, all the Regions of the Order, and the Order as a whole, during the same years, made great efforts at improving the formation of the monks and nuns at every level. These efforts produced a new *Ratio* on formation, approved at the last General Chapter, and led to a more vivid awareness of the contemplative dimension of our life and of the primordial importance of some monastic 'observances', *lectio divina* in particular.

For centuries, the nuns of our Order were under the General Chapter that was entirely composed of abbots. In the fifties, the abbesses began to hold meetings that gradually became General Chapters. The drawing up of our new Constitutions, in which the nuns took part as actively as the monks, provided an occasion for devising a new structure allowing the nuns and the monks to remain a single Order while respecting their differences and taking the best advantage of their complementarity. Here again the Order remained faithful to its basic general orientation since 1892: the search for a broader and deeper union.

OUR PRESENT

Before looking toward the future it seems opportune to recapitulate some of the above stated key points and add some others with the aim of delineating the main characteristics of our experience today.

The present moment in the life of the Order is characterized by some positive realities and by others that present themselves as challenges. Among the first we can mention:

- a clear constitutional affirmation of our monastic contemplative identity in the heart of the Church.

- a conscientious and programmed effort in the field of initial and permanent formation.

- efficacious collaboration and interdependence among the pastoral organs of the monks and the nuns.

- an emphasis on the Regions as associative intermediary forums, without detriment to local autonomy or to the system of filiation.

- an increase in foundations, especially among the 'Young Churches', in the form of small communities.

- a healthy pluralism among the different houses, above all among those in different geographical and cultural regions, yet at the same time respecting the unity of the Order.

- an authentic desire to grow in the vocation to which we have been called.

- a discreet openness toward a sharing of the cistercian gift, be it in an advisory capacity toward monastic programs that envision possible incorporation, or by an attitude of listening to requests of those who wish to share in the cistercian grace and vocation.

The challenges to be confronted are different and are of differing degrees of urgency. Among these we point out:

- the aging of some communities, the lack of vocations, and the reduction in numbers due to deaths and exits.

- the difficulty of finding suitable persons able to serve in positions of authority.

- the diffusion of a certain individualism and activism that endangers the cenobitic and contemplative quality of our life.

- the necessity of an anthropological model that will integrate individuality and mutual relationship, as well as the masculine and feminine present in the human psyche.

- discernment of the values and counter-values of local cultures and universal culture, in the midst of which our existence develops.

- the difficulty of earning one's living by one's own labor and maintaining large properties and economic structures on a *horarium* of five working hours.

- the possibility of the incorporation of monastic vocations leaning toward a simpler prayer life and with a greater inclination toward work.

Each of the above mentioned points would merit a detailed examination, but this is not the time for it. We could, however, point out the relationships among them and show how some others are also the causes of further realities of no slight importance.

The new Constitutions of the Order, after twenty years of intense work, allow us to reflect on our experience in an articulate way, while at the same time providing us with a solid footing and an objective reference as well. Such a firm basis, together with discretion and consultation, also allows us to be open to monastic programs of cistercian life conceived outside the Order, as well as toward other forms of spiritual association without running the risk of a loss or diminution of our own identity.

The increase in the number of foundations, despite the decrease in personnel, brings with it, consequently, the existence of smaller communities. This, in its turn, has repercussions on life style, interpersonal relationships, and kinds of work and forms of celebration, giving rise to a monastic life characterized by simplicity.

Given that the majority of these foundations are to be found in the so-called 'Young Churches', the Order's leading and programmatic center has undergone a shift: we have moved from being a Eurocentric Order to a pluricentric Order. To look at it in another way, we could also say that from a universal Order we are becoming a pluricultural Order.

Aging, exits, and lack of recruitment can be reasons for the lack of capable persons when it comes to electing superiors, hence the importance of the efforts made, and to be made, in the field of initial and ongoing formation.

Likewise, aging and the lack of capable persons to serve in roles of direction and authority, a challenge that often surpasses the resources of the motherhouses, could be addressed at the regional level.

An anthropological model of personal and cenobitic stamp could be an answer and an alternative to the ideological individualism inherent in our western society, and in the developing universal culture.

The acceptance of genuine cistercian vocations more orientated toward work, as a way of service and search for God, could be an alternative more coherent with our monastic profession, rather than the hiring of seculars to attend to our work and economic needs.

Reaching out toward the future

To celebrate is, above all, to commemorate; that is, to make present and actual the event celebrated. To celebrate is to live.

To celebrate the birth of the Order is to allow it to become a living and operative reality in our present-day experience, and to find there a fount of inspiration and a stimulus to reach out toward the future.

Without forgetting from where we come and where we are, we can ask ourselves how far we wish to go, how far is God calling us to go.

The objectives we are about to present are intended as a general response to the challenges we face. Moreover, they would appear to be realistic since they take into consideration our present experience.

- First and foremost, to take a step forward in the process of the spiritual renewal of each person and each community.

- Second, to sink our roots more deeply into the cistercian tradition and the charism of our Fathers.

- Third, to revitalize and readapt the structures and pastoral organs of the Order, beginning with the local community.

- Finally, proceeding prudently in a process of inculturation, to open new channels for the expression of our patrimony.

For the moment, we present these objectives as proposals or statements of purpose. The time will come for converting them into operative programs. We hope that they will draw the attention and motivate the reflections of each member of the Order.

There remains, however, one final word. The most important challenge of our Order remains that of unity. Unity among the various Regions first of all, but also unity between the male and female branches of the Order, while at the same time fostering respect for cultural differences and the complementarity of the sexes. There is also need to learn how to integrate into the Order's unity the many forms that the cistercian charism is taking on nowadays within our communities and at times among the lay people who have spiritual ties with the lives of our communities. Finally, this centennial celebration of the Chapter of Union should remind us of the need to seek out ways that will some day allow us, along with our brothers and sisters of the Common Observance, to arrive at what was the ultimate aim of the Capitulants of 1892—one day to bring about the full unity of the great cistercian family.

LECTIO DIVINA

Circular Letter to the Members of the Order, January 26, 1993

My dear Brothers and Sisters:

I trust that this New Year will be a year of grace for all of you. The Lord gives himself without measure to those who have infinite desires. Let us pray for one another that the divine action may not be in vain in us.

In my circular letter of last year, I presented the Good News of the *Schola Caritatis* in the context of the New Evangelization. My intention was, at the same time, to say something about monastic contemplative identity; or, better yet, attempt to conceptualize my own experience in order to communicate it to you.

Once again, I wish to thank those who have written to me sharing their reactions and reflections. I renew, through this letter, my invitation to dialogue and to a sharing of the gifts the Lord gives us.

I would like today, in the context of the Gospel of the School of Charity, to offer you some thoughts concerning *Lectio Divina*.

I consider that the pillars of our contemplative life are: the Eucharist, *Opus Dei, Lectio Divina,* and *Intentio Cordis;* and these pillars are set upon the foundation of asceticism, work and solitude; all being energized by the prudent alternation of these *exercitia,* within the framework of a communion of love and convergent pluralism. Not being able to include everything in one letter I will focus on *Lectio.*

I am very much aware that two of my predecessors have written on this most outstanding exercise of our monastic *conversatio,* and I would not be able to improve on what they wrote. Nor am I sure I will differ from my predecessors in any way, though I can assure you I will not contradict them.

In his 1978 letter Dom Ambrose said to us: 'If we succeed in developing the practice of *lectio* it will have far-reaching effects on the quality of our monastic life and the contemplative dimension of our monasteries will be enriched'. When I read those words then, I could sense all the truth contained in them. Today, being more convinced than ever, I am their spokesman.

Well, enough of preambles, I want to spare you the fatigue and annoyance of a long and wide-ranging document. For this reason I have written what follows in the form of brief maxims or *sententiae.* I trust that this will prove more profitable and, perhaps, more pedagogical.

I follow in this the examples of the ancient spiritual writers. Many of them were accustomed to draft their works in sentence form, each conveying a central theme. The sentence is a brief and succinct saying offering advice and a rule for living, or shows forth doctrine, morals, and good sense, and, in the best examples, wisdom. However, for the sentence to convey wisdom, it is necessary that he who writes and they who read feel and savor the taste of what they do and live.

PRELUDE

1. The Spirit inspired the Scriptures; therefore, it is present and speaks through them. If it breathes in, it also breathes out.

2. The Scriptures breathe life by the inspiration of the Spirit; that is why they are the breath of the christian monk.

3. All of this living book converges on Christ. The Divine Scriptures are one book only: Christ. He is the concise, living, and efficacious Word.

4. All Scripture points to the mystery of Christ: prefigured in the Old Testament and present in the New, internalized by each Christian, and consummated in glory.

5. Because God is Infinite, his Word is also Infinite; Scripture enshrines infinite mysteries, its meaning is unfathomable.

6. The literal meaning of the text is always the point of departure; the letter reveals the deeds and presents the persons; history is the foundation.

7. The Spirit takes us beyond the letter; our theological life opens the doors of meaning to us:

- Allegorical, building faith through the discovery of Christ and his Church.

- Tropological, teaching us to act in the truth of love.

- Analogical, showing us and drawing us toward that for which we yearn.

8. The Gospel is the mouth of Christ, ever ready to offer to us the kiss of eternity.

9. The Gospel is the body and blood of Christ, to pray and live it is to eat and drink it.

10. The Gospel is the power of God because it shows us the way and gives us the strength to follow it.

11. Herein lies true life, and my spirit neither has nor desires anything but the prayerful reading of these mysteries!

12. The Church is the only sounding board of the Word of God. Because she is the Body of Christ, she herself is also the Word. Scripture gives us life in the Spirit, when received in the framework of tradition and *magisterium*.

13. Our *Lectio Divina* should prolong the Word beyond the Liturgy in order to prepare us for a more fruitful celebration of the same.

14. The cenobite understands the profound meaning of the Word only when living in communion and concord with his brothers.

15. Monastic *conversatio* should create a biblical climate allowing each and all to be protagonists in the dialogue of salvation.

16. The *humus* of humility is the good soil in which the Word produces abundant fruit.

17. Only in recollection can one receive; only in silence is heard the beating of the heart of God.

18. We speak to God when we pray with love; we hear God when we read his Word with faith.

19. When we are 'nailed' to the Book through our perseverance

and diligence in *Lectio*, then we will comprehend the folly of the good God.

20. To know Christ crucified, we must be crucified to the world.

21. 'Here I am, may God write in me what he wills', said Mary. When the heart is a letter written by God, all of God's letters resound in the heart.

22. He who lives the Good News offers the world reasons to live and die.

FIRST MOVEMENT: *riposato*

23. *Lectio Divina* is:

- a meditated reading, above all of the Bible, prolonged in contemplative prayer.

- a reading about God with the eyes of a spouse and the heart of the Church.

- a reading gratuitously made in order to receive gratuitously the Author of grace.

- a transformative reading that evangelizes us, making us evangelizers.

- an interpersonal relationship in faith and love, with Christ who speaks to us, in the Spirit who teaches us, and under the gaze of the Father who regards us.

- a pilgrimage of words toward the Mystery of the Word.

- a slow assimilation of saving Truth whilst in dialogue with the Savior.

- an enamored faith that seeks the Face of God in order to anticipate what is yearned for.

- immersion, co-penetration, divinization, emersion.

24. *Lectio* is *divina*:

- for God is read in his Word and with his Spirit.

- because we are brought before the Mystery and it is made present in the heart.

- when God who speaks is heard and his presence tasted.

25. *Lectio Divina* is dialogue; it is therefore reception, self-gift, and communion: reception by attention and reflection, self-gift through our response, communion through encounter.

26. Miriam of Nazareth, in dialogue with Gabriel, offers us a captivating example of *Lectio vere divina*.

27. Because *Lectio Divina* is life, it is also movement—movement in which different moments or experiences can be discerned: reading, meditation, prayer, and contemplation.

28. Reading, then meditation, prayer, and contemplation—is what normally occurs when we give it time to happen.

29. The gratuity of *Lectio Divina* is different from the utility of study. Study endeavors to master the word; *Lectio Divina* surrenders and yields before it.

30. *Lectio Divina* also differs from spiritual reading. The last can have as its end the acquisition of knowledge, the formulation of

convictions, or the stimulus for generous self-giving. The aim of the former is union with God in faith and love.

Second Movement: *coraggioso ed ampio ma non troppo*

31. *Lectio Divina* is not, as a rule, immediately gratifying. It is an active and passive process of long duration. One does not reap the day following the sowing! The worm is not instantly transformed into a butterfly!

32. There is nothing so purifying as enduring the silence of the Word. However, all who know how to wait reap the reward.

33. If you allow yourself to be possessed by the Word, you will hear even his silence.

34. In *Lectio Divina* there is also room for the Fathers of the Church and Cîteaux, their writings confirm and amplify the biblical message; because of their christian spirit, they are sure guides of correct interpretation; and by their holiness of life, they teach us how to live, and help us to commune in the Holy Spirit.

35. Other books are helpful in the measure that they allow us to assimilate the Mystery and be transformed by it.

36. When the beginner says, 'For me, everything is *Lectio Divina*', it is to be understood that for him *Lectio Divina* is meaningless.

Third Movement: *adagio però continuo*

37. Pay attention: it is God who wishes to speak to you and awaits your reply!

38. The various experiences or moments of *Lectio Divina* come together in one movement of the spirit. They can coexist and mutually overlap; they can even alternate in an ever-changing order. The pedestrian makes many movements, but all come together in one action: walking.

39. Assiduous practice lessens rigidity. He who exercises little increases rigidity and makes slow progress. He who does not exercise does not advance.

40. *Lectio Divina* is a daily practice for the monk and nun at a privileged hour—the time that is necessary to bring about a dialogue with the most faithful of friends.

Reading

41. Reading is a form of listening that allows of always being able to return to what was heard. Listening is being and letting be; without listening, there is no interpersonal relationship.

42. If you read to read and not to have read, then your *lectio* is serene, restful, and disinterested.

43. Do not waste time in looking for a text that is pleasing; choose your text beforehand, perhaps the day's liturgical readings, or follow some theme, or a consecutive reading of the whole Bible.

44. The fool falls into the temptation of saying, 'I already know this text!' The wise man knows that it is one thing to know the chemical formula of water and another to savor it by a spring on a summer's day.

45. If you do not comprehend what you are reading, ask the Lord to help you to understand. You can help the Lord by reading the

text in its context, comparing it with parallel texts, finding the key words, determining the central message, and so on.

46. If you have read well, you will be able to say what the text means.

Meditation

47. To meditate is to chew and ruminate, for it is to: repeat, reflect, remember, interpret, penetrate, etc. One who thus meditates on the Word is transformed according to the Word and becomes a mediator of the Word.

48. If the text read means nothing to you, love the Word beyond the words and do not hesitate to surrender yourself without reserve. If the text is a hard saying and you apply it to your neighbor, try rereading it in the first person.

49. There is no meditation without distraction. Return, then, to the reading. Concentrate on the key words.

50. When the text speaks to your heart, you have reached and received a precious fruit of meditation.

Prayer

51. Prayer during *Lectio Divina* can take many forms: praise, petition, thanksgiving, compunction, etc.

52. Having listened by reading and meditation, you can now speak in prayer. If you know what the text says and what it says to you, what do you say to Him?

53. Silence can also be a response, as much for the one who prays, carried out of himself, as for Him who knows all.

Contemplation

54. To contemplate is to take silent delight in the Temple, which is the Risen Christ.

55. To contemplate is to encounter the Word, beyond words.

56. To contemplate is to live in the Risen One, rooted in the now of this earth, reaching out to the beyond of the heavens.

57. Contemplation is vision. The contemplative sees the resurrection in the cross, life in death, the Risen One in the Crucified.

58. Contemplation is the thirst caused by the seeming absence or the satiety of mutual presence.

59. The contemplative is at a loss for words, simply because he knows.

FOURTH MOVEMENT: *codetta*

Collatio

60. *Collatio* is contribution or provision, confrontation or dialogue. It is to provide fuel for meditation, fire for prayer, light for contemplation, and motivation for acts.

Action

61. Action refers, before all, to the conversion of one's heart, behaving as a disciple and under the discipline of the Truth revealed for our salvation.

Collaboration

62. Every good work is in collaboration with the One who does all things well. He who collaborates with him works and prays with all.

POSTLUDE

63. The Bible is not intended only to tell us about God but to transform us according to the form of Christ.

64. Scripture is the word that informs, giving us the form of Christians.

65. The virginal conception of the Virgin Mother is a mystery of redemption and a model for imitation; conceiving the Word in the womb of the heart, embracing the will of the Father, makes us brother, sister, and mother.

66. The words are for us, not us for the words, because we are for the Word.

67. Those who have progressed in *Lectio Divina* experience the need for fewer words and more of the Word.

68. Those who have been transformed by the Word can read it in the events of each day, and in those signs of the times that are voices of God manifested through the deepest human aspirations.

69. Those who have revealed truth engraved in the innermost depths of their hearts, do not depend on the sacred text and are for others living bibles.

70. If you want to know and reach Christ, you will arrive much sooner by following him than by reading about him.

Having arrived at this point in the letter, I realize that I have written more than I had intended to, but certainly much less than the subject deserves. There are many aspects of *Lectio Divina* that have been left out, and others that I have never experienced.

We all know that one of our capital 'vices' is activism. Dom Gabriel had already mentioned this in 1955, and in the house reports of the last General Chapter, it appeared with great frequency. We are dealing with a pernicious vice, for it unsettles monastic *otio*, shatters the desire for eternal life, interferes with the continual search for the face of God, and alters, finally, the very nature of contemplative life.

I know of a powerful weapon with which to attack and conquer this most unnatural activism: the equilibrium and alternation between *Lectio Divina,* liturgy, and work. The best way to safeguard this equilibrium is to give *Lectio Divina* a place of priority. *Credete expertibus!*

Allow me to share some words of Gilbert, abbot of Hoyland, that challenged me deeply during my first years of monastic life, and have preserved for me until the present all of their prophetic weight.

> *You, who pray on the run but dally with books, you, who are fervent in reading and lukewarm in praying—reading should serve prayer, should dispose the affections, and should neither devour the hours nor gobble up the moments of prayer. When you read you are taught about Christ, but when you pray you join him in familiar colloquy. How much more enchanting is the grace of speaking with him than about him! (Serm. Cant. VII:2)*

Actually, however, the great master of *Lectio* is William, abbot of Saint-Thierry. His prayed meditations are an eloquent testimony to his application to lectio and to his heart, full of desire and divine contemplation. Put yourselves under his tutelage and he, as a good disciple of the one only Teacher, will make masters of you.

This letter has no conclusion. It is for each of you who must continue it. Please, however, let no one bring it to a close. Let us leave it unfinished, as a sign of the search that is to continue until it ends in Infinity.

THE EUCHARIST

Circular Letter to the Members of the Order, January 26, 1994

Very dear Brothers and Sisters,

Once again, I draw near to each one of you through the medium of a circular letter. I know that it is better to circulate than to write circulars, but one does not impede the other. I trust, then, that this will find you all well: persevering in fraternal unity and in the breaking of the bread with joy and simplicity of heart.

The present letter is a continuation of the preceding one. By means of the other, I invited you to join me at the table of the Word; with this, I intend to say as much again, but this time at the table of the Eucharist. This double and unique banquet has only one aim: conformation according to the model of him who died and rose for our salvation.

The Eucharist is the fount and summit of the school of christian and monastic love. We are, therefore, in the very heart of the *Schola Caritatis*.

The Eucharist is the sacrament of the dialogue of sacrificial love between God and humankind. God sacrifices and gives himself so that we can offer ourselves as victims—living, holy, and pleasing to God. This is the spiritual worship that we are invited to offer.

There is no doubt that through the centuries eucharistic doctrine has accented different aspects of the mystery. Nor is there any doubt that other aspects hidden today will be uncovered tomorrow. Moreover, the same is valid for eucharistic devotion; history is witness to its different manifestations.

Tradition underscored the essential, the Eucharist as: sacred celebration, sacramental sacrifice, sacrificial banquet, and the real presence of Jesus Christ. Our own century rediscovered others aspects: the 'memorial' of the Pasch, the building up of the Church and of ecclesial communion, the eucharistic priesthood of all the baptized, as also the *epíclesis*, or invocation, of the Spirit. More recently other dimensions have come to light; participation in the Resurrected One, the divinization of the cosmos, the anticipated *parousia,* and social commitment.

Not wishing, nor being able to say it all, it is necessary to circumscribe the theme, but leaving unlimited openness to the mystery in order to lose ourselves infinitely in it. Permit me, then, a word concerning the Eucharist as the mystery of union with Christ and fraternal communion.

THE EUCHARIST AND UNION WITH CHRIST

We must understand with total realism the words of Jesus at the institution of the Eucharist: 'Take, eat, this is my body' (Mt 26:26). The subject 'this' (the bread) is identified with the predicate 'my body' (the person of Jesus). Moreover, if we believe that Jesus was and is the Only Son of God, who can neither deceive nor be deceived, we must conclude that the consecrated bread and wine is Christ really present. Our ecclesial faith has been constant and unanimous in this respect.

Risen and Present

The Eucharist is above all a sacrament of presence, for it is the sacrament of the Pasch and of the salvation that is Christ himself, in person. That is why the first Christians spoke of the 'table of the Lord', 'the supper of the Lord' (1 Co 10:21; 11:20). He who had eaten with the apostles made himself present and presided at the meal. The story of the disciples at Emmaus is clear testimony to this reality: Jesus appeared to them in the breaking of the bread. Today Jesus says to us: 'Behold, I am at the door and knock; if anyone hears my voice and opens to me, I will enter his house and take "the supper" with him and he with me' (Rv 3:20).

Our eucharistic celebrations actualize the apparitions of the Risen One, allowing him to fulfill his word: 'I will come back to you' (Jn 14:18–22). We believe that he comes back today as he came that first day of the week, and came for the second time on the first day of the following week (Jn 20:19,26).

It is above all, through the Eucharist, that each of us is put into real contact with Jesus Christ, dead and risen for our sakes. Each time we celebrate the Eucharist, the Lord makes himself present in several different ways.

- First through the very community gathered in his name and oriented toward him. When the Risen Christ appears in the midst of his disciples, shut up in a room for fear of the Jews, we can believe that he came not from without but from within the one heart that united them.

- Christ also makes himself present when the evangelical Word is proclaimed. That is why, at the invitation of the deacon, 'The Word of the Lord', we respond, 'Glory to you, O Lord'.

- Above all, Christ makes himself present in the consecrated bread and wine. He himself is hidden under appearances of bread and wine, in order to be eaten and drunk. His own divine person humanly incarnated, historical and inculturated, crucified and resurrected, and bursting with divine glory, makes himself present in order to consume, as he is consumed.

- In the same way, Christ makes himself a transformative presence when we eat and drink him at communion. We consume him in order to be converted into his own body; we assimilate him in order to be assimilated.

- All these ways of presence make ever more present the one who is always present, the Present One.

The motivating force of our contemplative life can be seen as search-encounter. Jesus presents himself to us in the Eucharist where he seeks and finds us; he thus invites us to seek and to find Him. Our life, oriented toward contemplation, consists in seeking the Presence and making ourselves present. Christian contemplative life is unimaginable to me without the Eucharist, and without a deep participation in it.

Spouse and Bride

The Eucharist is the sacrament of the coming of the Lord in person. The desire for this coming motivates our daily celebration of the Eucharist. With the Spirit and the Bride, we cry: 'Maranatha! Come Lord Jesus' (Rv 22:20). Recognizing ourselves as Church-Bride and wishing to prolong the presence and communion, we do not hesitate to preserve the consecrated Bread after the celebration. We thus make use of our right over the already glorious Body of our

Spouse and Lord: 'The Groom does not have authority over his body but the Bride' (1 Co 2:4).

However, what relationship can we establish between the Eucharist and the matrimonial union, in reference to the union of Christ and the Church?

Fathers of the Church were not lacking who likened the Eucharist and matrimony to Christ and the Church, basing themselves on the text of Ephesians 5:22–32. The celebration of nuptials between Christ and the Church occurs in the nuptial banquet of the Eucharist: here the Lord as Spouse makes the Church his own and incorporates her into himself as his body and blood, that is why 'he feeds it and looks after it, because no one hates his own body' (Ep 5:29).

The Church, for its part, as a New Eve, becomes 'flesh of his flesh and bone of his bone'. In effect, in the Eucharist, 'Christ loves the Church and sacrifices himself for her' (Ep 5:25). To this sacrifice of the Lord and Spouse corresponds the total sacrifice of his Bride, the Church.

The 'new and eternal matrimonial covenant' that is wholly eucharistic, becomes reality for us in our monastic consecration. This covenant and consecration occur precisely in the eucharistic wedding banquet and is called to be renewed in each celebration of the supper of the Lord. Only thus can we represent Christ united to his Bride, the Church, by indissoluble bonds. Only in this way can we persevere in the fidelity of love until the coming of the Lord.

Prayer and Mysticism

Thanks to the celebration of the Eucharist, the Church is a praying community. It is precisely in speaking of the Eucharist that Paul says to the Corinthians: 'When you meet together as *ekklêsia* . . .' (1Co 11:18).

If prayer is entering into communion with God, we can understand why the Eucharist fosters prayer. Even more, we can say that the Eucharist was instituted to make the ecclesial community a praying body.

The eucharistic celebration reaches its height in the words of the Lord: 'Take and eat, take and drink'. To take is to receive, not only to receive, but also to be received. Eucharistic prayer is communion in mutual giving and mutual receiving. In this way, the word of Jesus is accomplished 'You in me and I in you' (Jn 14:20).

The eucharistic Christ is the glorified Christ who is in full communion with the Father and the Spirit. To eat him is to partake of the trinitarian communion. When we pray, eating and communing, we become a dwelling of God, dwelling in God. When any one of us approaches the Eucharist with a loving faith, Jesus says, 'The Father and I are One' (Jn 10:30).

'And he is forthwith gathered up to God in love through the Holy Spirit and receives God coming to him and making his abode with him, not spiritually only but corporeally also, in the mystery of the holy and life-giving body and blood of our Lord Jesus Christ.' (William of Saint-Thierry, *Meditations* X:8, cf. XIII:5)

Is it too much to say that eucharistic communion is the true door by which to enter into the mystery and be mystically transformed? Can we maintain that the eucharistic mystery is the privileged place of the mystical experience? If Christ is a consuming fire, is it not normal that our hearts should burn in the obscurity of faith when the broken Bread has been shared and eaten?

EUCHARIST AND FRATERNAL COMMUNION

The simple reading of the eucharistic texts of the New Testament tells us clearly that the Eucharist is the sacrament of solidarity between Christ and the brethren, the sacrament of shared life. It expresses and produces communion in solidarity with the life of Jesus and with all believers who partake of the same Bread. At the same time, it commits us to the sharing of this life.

If the monastic community is above all a community of faith, then the Eucharist, sacrament of unity, has in it a supreme function to fulfill. Celebrating the sacrament of unity together allows us to manifest already existing unity and to nurture it in order that it may grow to its eschatological fulfillment.

Together toward God

The evangelist, in Matthew 18:20, speaking of the search and encounter with God in the liturgy says, 'Where two or three are gathered in my Name, there am I in the midst of them'.

Those gathered are not simply 'in' but, according to the Greek text, 'moving toward'; that is, oriented toward an intense search of the Name—that is, the Person. This once more explains why, in the eucharistic assembly, the Spirit and the Bride cry: 'Come! Maranatha!'

In the Eucharist, we seek Jesus, as a community, in a tension toward the eschatological, toward the ultimate and definitive. In it, we live the first commandment of love of God within the ambience of the second commandment of love of neighbor, in the person of our community, brothers and sisters.

The Gospel of John is fully Eucharistic (cf. above all in Chapter 6). However, it happens that when the time comes to speak of its institution, John omits it. And so, you know what he does? He puts in its place the new commandment: 'Love one another as I have loved you' (Jn 13:34–35)! Thanks to this mutual love, Jesus tells us: 'He who eats my flesh and drinks my blood lives in me and I in him' (Jn 6:56).

At the end of his *Rule*, Saint Benedict gives us his spiritual testament: love one another ardently. He then expresses one last desire: may Christ bring us all together to eternal life! The Eucharist is a volcano of incandescent love that makes ardent love possible. In each celebration, the Lord returns to bring us all together into his glorified and eternal life.

The Body of the Kyrios

In the Eucharist, Jesus is present, immolated, and risen, that is to say: the *Kyrios*. That is why Paul speaks of 'the supper of the *Kyrios*', the 'cup of the *Kyrios*', and 'the table of the *Kyrios*'. Now, the title of *Kyrios* carries with it a reference to the community. It means the *Kyrios*-Lord of the universe, the world, the Church, the community.

'None of us lives for himself and none of us dies for himself. While we are alive, we live for the *Kyrios*; when we die, we die for the *Kyrios*. Therefore, alive or dead, we belong to the *Kyrios*. It was for this purpose that Christ both died and came to life again, so that he might be *Kyrios* of both the living and the dead' (Rm 14:7–9).

When Saint Paul, writing to the Corinthians, says the bread we share is a participation and a being in the body of Christ (1Co 10:16–17), he is referring also to that body of Christ that is the community. That is why, afterwards, he will state that the unity affected among all is a constituent part of the celebration; anything contrary to this, 'is not the supper of the Lord' (1 Co 11–20).

Further on, in 1 Corinthians 11:29, we read, 'A person who eats and drinks without recognizing the body is eating and drinking his own condemnation'. What does the word 'body' signify in this context? We can say that it refers to the Church, without overlooking the reference to the eucharistic Body of the Risen One. In effect, that is how the whole structure of the passage brings it out; furthermore, the Apostle had already said: 'We are all one body who partake of the one bread (10–17); and a little later, he will affirm: 'You are the body of Christ' (12:27).

Benedict invites the superior to say the Lord's Prayer aloud, twice a day. In this way, all can renew the commitment to mutual pardon and remove the thorns of discord. It presupposes the Lord's invitation: when you approach the altar to offer your gifts. With a certain trepidation I cannot avoid asking myself: When the Lord presents himself to us, besides being reunited, does he also find us united? Are we more preoccupied with the legality of the celebration (conformity to ritual), than for authenticity (the concord of the assembly)?

Communing and Sharing

The primitive community of Jerusalem tells us about the fruits of the 'breaking of the bread in the homes and the eating together, praising God' (Ac 2:46–47). That is, 'the believers were united and held all things in common (2:44), all thought and felt the same, possessing all in common and no one considered anything he possessed his own' (4:32).

Concerning the preceding, the abbot of Ford, Baldwin, doctor of the Eucharist and of the common life, gives us the fruit of his life and meditation in the following:

> *Charity knows how to convert individual ownership into communion; not by doing away with individual property, but so that property may lead to communion, that communion may not be lacking, nor its good impeded. But diversity or property that impedes the good of communion is contrary to charity.*
>
> *The gifts received are reduced to unity, to communion, in two ways: when the gifts given to individuals are possessed in common by the sharing of love and when they are loved in common by the love of sharing. A gift is always common to the one who has it and the one*

who does not. If he who has it shares it with another, he has it for the sake of another; and he who does not have it actually does have it in the other because he loves him! (*Tractate* XV, on the cenobitic life).

Even more, the most profound sense of this shared meal is only understood when we are in solidarity with the poorest and most dehumanized members of the body of Christ. In effect, he himself tells us: 'When you give a banquet invite the poor, the crippled, the lame, and the blind; and happy are you because they are unable to repay you; you will be repaid when the just are risen' (Lk 14:13–14; cf. 14:21).

Our evangelical and monastic poverty also invites us to solidarity with the impoverished and to prefer those humans broken by our inhumanity. The generous response to this invitation is not a work of flesh and blood. It is a gift of the Father who grants us a deep solidarity through the Body and Blood of his Son.

★　★　★

The previous Mixed General Meeting had as its central theme 'contemplative identity'. Reading the reports of the houses, as well as the 'synthesis of the important themes and common challenges', I do not find the Eucharist mentioned very often; however, it was not missing in the 'conferences' presented by several superiors. True, the references are few but necessary to help us not lose sight of what is evident.

On the other hand, I am certain that we are all in accord with what is maintained by the *Magisterium* of the Church:

> *The celebration of the Eucharist and the intense participation in it, as fount and summit of all christian life, forms the irreplaceable and animating center of the contemplative dimension of all religious communities* (SCRIS *Contemplative Dimension* 9. 1980).

No community can be built if it does not have its roots and core in the celebration of the most holy Eucharist, from which should spring, consequently, all education in community spirit (Vatican II, *Presbyterorum Ordinis* 6).

It is for this reason that I had wanted to dedicate this circular letter to the Eucharist. I trust that it will also serve as a bridge and preparation for the central theme of the next Mixed General Meeting: 'The Community, School of Charity'.

Visiting the catacombs, I found a very ancient image: a woman with her arms extended in an attitude of prayer. It represents Mary, the Church, each one of us. Like Jesus with his arms spread on the cross, through him, with him, and in him, we should offer ourselves in the eucharistic sacrifice so that all the dispersed sons and daughters of God may be brought together in communion.

THE CONSTITUTIONS

Circular Letter to the Members of the Order,
January 26, 1995

Dear Brothers and Sisters,

A new year in our pilgrimage toward the Father's House has just begun and those who are formed in the School of Charity (*Schola Caritatis*) cannot remain idle—still less when they desire to renew themselves day after day according to the image and likeness of Christ who is the only true image of God.

The present letter is motivated by a particular event. An event in our small history that is inscribed in the great Salvation History of humanity by a God who became one of us.

Ten years ago, the General Chapters of Holyoke and Escorial took place. Our new Constitutions saw the light of day in these capitular assemblies. It is fitting to celebrate this event in order to rekindle in each and everyone the fire and light experienced at that moment.

This very special circumstance moved me to write you, with the Permanent Councilors, this letter on the new Constitutions. We are confident that the same Spirit who inspired our constitutional text, will again inspire a new breath of life in our hearts, using these words that are the reflection and mirror of our lives as cistercian monks and nuns.

HISTORY

Fifteen years of work preceded the General Chapters of Holyoke (1984) and Escorial (1985). The Mixed General Meeting of 1987 did not bring any substantial changes except in what concerned the nature of the relationship between the two 'Branches'. The years 1994–1995 can thus be considered the tenth anniversary of our renewed Constitutions.

During the fifteen years that preceded Holyoke, after several consultations, three successive projects submitted to the communities and Regional Conferences for study, and orientations and decisions of various General Chapters, we were able to arrive at a common understanding and an expression of this in a text voted almost unanimously both at Holyoke and Escorial.

The presence and action of the Holy Spirit were truly felt at the General Chapter of 1969. Some of the basic choices that we find in the Constitutions come from this Chapter. Moreover, we cannot doubt that the same Spirit assisted the Order during the following years of preparation and work.

Furthermore, we can affirm that even the purely juridic elements of our Constitutions are the fruit of a wisdom acquired by the Order and the Church through the centuries. The fidelity, or infidelity, to these same elements has been a source of grace and misfortune. History teaches us this.

MEANING

The question is valid and pertinent. What is the meaning of the recent Constitutions, renewed according to Vatican II? Meaning here signifies a path that gives us joy, a life turned toward eternal happiness.

Our Particular Way of Following Christ

Before everything and first of all, we can say that the Constitutions are the concrete expression of our particular way of following Christ according to the Gospel and the *Rule* of Saint Benedict.

This means that the approval of the Constitutions by ecclesiastical authority is the guarantee that they express the Gospel, that they help and incarnate its exigencies, and that they always lead toward it.

Consequently, our cistercian charism can be considered as a form of 'exegesis of the Gospel'; it brings out and reveals certain aspects of the Gospel. Because of this, the Constitutions, as medium and incarnation of our charism, are an instrument of evangelical interpretation; they clarify our reading of the Gospel as Cistercians.

Plan of Salvation for Us

We can also say that the Constitutions present the plan of salvation and evangelical and monastic sanctification for us, Cistercians.

Because of this, our monastic life does not run parallel or in juxtaposition to our christian life; it is the same christian life brought to fulfillment thanks to a way inspired by the Spirit of God.

We are not first of all Christians and then monks. It would be more correct to say our monastic fulfillment is our christian fulfillment.

It is in being monks that we are Christians; monasticism is our way of being Christian, and our way of being Christian is monasticism. For us, because of God's call, there is no other way of identifying ourselves with Christ. The Constitutions present this mode of identification with the Lord and are thus our monastic path of christian salvation.

Our Book of Life

All of the above helps us to understand why the Constitutions are not a simple 'code of regular discipline', but much more: a book of life. Indeed, they proceed from life and lead to life. Similarly, they can also be considered as:

- a vocational guide: in the words of the Constitutions, it is possible to hear the call of God to follow Christ as a Cistercian.

- a spiritual guide: in the words of the Constitutions, we are able to find an orientation and a stimulus, a motivation and a meaning as the works of the unique Guide who leads us toward the complete truth.

- a guide for the discernment of individual charisms: in the Constitutions, we meet objective words that confront our aspirations and our personal ways of living the common charism.

Expression of Our Charism

Let us say, finally, that the Constitutions are the lasting expression of our cistercian charism of the Strict Observance. They express the consciousness that the Order has of itself in this moment in its history. They are, therefore, our letter or our card of ecclesial identification, with all that can signify for unity and formation in the grace that the Spirit has given us for the building of the Body of Christ and the service of humanity.

And because they are a concrete expression of our charism, they are also a harmony of means and ends, of observances and values, in order to live the christian life in all its radicalism, centered on the search for God. Precisely because of this, we also find in them a two-fold complementary aspect:

- normative aspect: prescriptions of a juridical character at the service of persons and communities.

- didactic aspect: motivating principles that promote life in the Spirit.

USEFULNESS

What has just been said about the meaning of our Constitutions speaks to us also about their usefulness. We want to clarify, however, even more what has been said. For this we now ask the question. Of what use are the Constitutions? The answer to this question could take several volumes!

We assume that everyone accepts the juridical usefulness of the Constitutions. Those who want to live together and in society must agree on several things—norm and law precisely, make for affability. A city without stoplights and full of cars runs the risk of chaos. In addition, it is equally evident that the cars do not run because of the stoplights but because of their motors. We do not walk in the Spirit because of the Constitutions, but we need them to coordinate our walking together animated by the Spirit.

Then, without fear of repeating ourselves and avoiding making usefulness a principle and norm of everything to the point of depriving the text of its meaning, we will limit ourselves to the three following points of interest.

At the Service of our Historical Identity

Every group, or human organization, needs a text that expresses its particular culture—that is, its manner of understanding life, its perception of the meaning of existence, its particular way of being in relationship with God, with others, with the cosmos, and with itself.

A culture, however, is also a living reality. Each generation needs to re-express it. A religious institute expresses its understanding of its particular vocation and its manner of living the Gospel in its time by its Constitutions. Saint Benedict and his first disciples did it in the Holy *Rule*. Our Fathers of Cîteaux did it in the *Exordium Parvum* and the *Charter of Charity*. Our immediate predecessors, in this century, did it in the Constitutions of 1927.

Our new Constitutions, in their introduction, link us to the age-old tradition that unites us to Cîteaux, without any doubt. Even beyond Cîteaux, they put us in line with the great Eastern and Western monastic tradition that is rooted in the Gospel itself.

The cistercian vocation is always an appeal for a concrete and real community. This community is, together with all the other communities of the Order, co-responsible for the cistercian patrimony. We are not the owners of this patrimony. We are only its guardians. It is a common possession of the People of God, the Church. When the hierarchy of the Church approved the Constitutions, it officially attested that the form of life described in them is not only an authentic way of living the evangelical call to a life of perfection, but also a faithful incarnation of the cistercian patrimony in the context of the Church and world today.

At the Service of Formation

New people entering our monasteries are gradually formed to the cistercian life, above all, by concrete daily life.

Nevertheless, it is necessary to be able to present them with a text where our spirituality and the concrete way of understanding and living it today are expressed. Doubtless, during the time of the novitiate, it is necessary to present the *Rule* of Saint Benedict and the *Charter of Charity* to the novices. It is also of prime necessity, however, to present the Constitutions to them.

All the Constitutions, and not only the section referring to formation, are formative—that is, putting them into practice conforms us to a form of life. Moreover, it reforms us in order to conform us to the form of Christ, cistercian monk. The entire process of formation is oriented toward the progressive transformation into the likeness of Christ, by the action of the Holy Spirit, and the maternal care of the Mother of God.

At the Service of Belonging and Unity

Modern hermeneutics remind us that a written text, once drawn up, has its own existence, which evolves with each reading of it. Familiarity with a text creates a family spirit among all those who cultivate this familiarity. Familiarity with the Gospel, with the Fathers of the Church, with the authors of the great monastic tradition, is exactly what makes us feel that we belong and are united to the great christian family and the great monastic family. It is not for nothing that our old Usages prescribed the annual reading of the complete text of the Constitutions in community.

Our new Constitutions are well known and used frequently in certain communities of the Order. They are presented during initial formation; they are commented on by the abbot or abbess in Chapter; each monk or nun has a personal copy of them or can have easy access to numerous copies available for the use of the community. In general, in these communities, it is easy to find a love of the Order, a sense of belonging to a monastic family, a desire to deepen the essential elements of the cistercian life, and a creative fidelity in the manner of living pluralism.

In other communities, it must be said, the Constitutions are scarcely known. Many brothers or sisters hardly know where to find a copy in the library. Some have never seen them or, at least, have never read them in their entirety. They seem to think that the Constitutions are a collection of norms and rules that the superior must consult when there is a canonical problem to solve. We can ask ourselves: is not all this explained by the fact that the sense of belonging is weak in these communities and, weaker still, the sense of belonging to an international and pluricultural Order?

The Constitutions present our life as a response to a call to consecration to God through monastic profession. They remind us of the constituent elements of monastic *ascesis* lived in a community of brothers or sisters. They present us with the norms that should govern daily life at the local level so that the community is truly a 'School of Charity'. Finally, they describe the mechanics, which allow the various autonomous communities of women or men to form a single great community of communities, the Cistercian Order.

KEYS TO READING

A key to reading is a way of interpretation, i.e., an orientation for reading a text and interpreting it correctly. A key to reading, if it is really this, consists in a reality underlying the entire text and that enlightens the whole text as well as each of its parts.

We offer here three keys for reading in order to understand correctly our Constitutions: Jesus Christ and his Gospel, the cenobitic *Rule* of Benedict, and the contemplative charism of Cîteaux.

Jesus Christ and the Gospel

Jesus Christ and the Gospel are, without any doubt, the first and principal key of interpretation for the entire constitutional text. The

Constitutions are at the service of the search for and encounter with Jesus Christ following the way of the Gospel. Our hope consists in entry into the Kingdom of Heaven, all together, guided and led by him.

All this implies the renunciation of our own will, following the example of the Lord who was obedient even unto death. It is in renouncing ourselves that we participate in the passion of Christ. In order to prefer nothing to Christ, we must become strangers to the ways of the world.

By the profession of solemn vows, we hand ourselves over to Christ. We continue the entire length of our monastic life by learning the 'philosophy' and the mystery of Christ, at the school of Christ, until he attains the fullness of maturity in us.

Because of this, we can say without hesitation that our entire life is a participation in: the passion, the compassion, and the mission of Christ, the priesthood, thanksgiving, peace, hope, and coming of Christ. In a word, our entire life is a participation in the mystery of Christ. In addition, if our life is dedicated to Mary, it is in order to grow in perfect communion with Christ.

We seek Christ—this is true. Nevertheless, it is also true that Christ himself comes to meet us especially in the person of the abbot and abbess, the seniors, the sick, those in need, and guests.

The entire life of the local community must be conformed to the supreme law of the Gospel. And all the organization of the monastery, of the school of divine service, has as its end: the formation of Christ in the heart of each one and the intimate union of each one with him in order to form all together a single Body, the Body of Christ.

Without the good news of the Kingdom and the constant reference to the King, our Constitutions lack meaning and are incomprehensible.

Cenobitic Monasticism

Cistercians today seek God in following Christ, guided by the Gospel, interpreted and mediated by the *Rule* of Saint Benedict. For this reason, the abbot and abbess ought to explain the *Rule* often, our on-going formation and our monastic profession are made according to the *Rule*, and the General Chapters must watch over its observance.

Just as Saint Benedict wrote a rule for cenobites, so our Chapters of Holyoke and Escorial did the same in drawing up our Constitutions. Precisely because we follow the *Rule* of Saint Benedict, our Constitutions declare that our form of life is cenobitic.

In our Constitutions, we find a 'law of the common life', made up of observances, communitarian structures, and a quality of relationships based on love. Without all that, it would be unthinkable to speak of the community as a school of fraternal charity, and still less, without the Eucharist, as source and summit of the communion of all in Christ.

Our cenobitic life tries to reproduce the model of the first christian community of Jerusalem in which everyone owned everything in common and had only one heart and one spirit. This is, evidently an ideal. However, we cannot speak of idealism: the Gospel, the *Rule*, and the Constitutions offer us the means to promote the Spirit so that the ideal is converted into reality.

In a word, our Constitutions have been written by cenobites and for cenobites. They can only be understood if we read them and live them with the eyes and hearts of cenobites.

Contemplative Orientation

Our cenobitic identity is fully understood when we affirm at the same time the nature and contemplative goal of the Cîteaux of yesterday and today. Without the light of our total orientation to contemplation, we cannot understand our constitutional text. The contemplative purpose and project underlie all the Constitutions.

Our contemplation and our contemplative life are incarnated and expressed in all our actions and in every moment of our life. Indeed, at every moment and in each action, we seek God who seeks us, moved by the loving desire to see his Face and to hear his Voice.

Because of this, we can say that all the ordinances of the Constitutions lead us to perceive an aspect of this Face and make us attentive to his Voice. However, this does not prevent certain determined ordinances from being explicitly destined to protect, favor, and develop our contemplative experience of the Lord and his mystery.

The contemplative orientation, which defines the nature and goal of the Order, is expressed by constant prayer in a climate of solitude and silence, and by cultivating simple relationships with the very simple God. It is thus that purity and simplicity of heart produce the fruits of peace, and deep and constant stillness, at the same time as continual remembrance of the presence of God.

Everything, absolutely everything, in the house of God, should favor silence, peace, and recollection. Even the construction of the monastery should completely safeguard the recollection and solitude of those who live there. The ultimate criterion of an authentic contemplative vocation is the search for God by means of continual prayer; to this, superiors must be attentive so that each and everyone can make good use of their free time in order to give themselves to reading and prayer.

Silence, *ascesis*, and fasting, under different forms, are at the service of the contemplative search for the Lord and spiritual desire. The *Liturgy of the Hours* and *lectio divina* are the school of continual and contemplative prayer. The relations with the outside world and even the reception of guests are discerned according to the particular character of our contemplative life.

Spiritual desire is the soul of the contemplative orientation of our life. This desire allows us to live in heaven while still being on earth and to make the Mother of God present in our heart. This desire, during the hours preceding sunrise, expresses itself by waiting for the coming of the Lord in hope.

Contemplative orientation and spiritual desire incite us to learn, day after day, the philosophy of Christ, a philosophy that is learned only in conforming oneself to Christ.

The contemplative life itself is our particular way of participating in the mission of Christ and of the Church, and of inserting us into the local churches. Above all, a foundation ought to be understood as the gift of a contemplative presence to a local church.

Finally, if in our life or in the Constitutions that express it, we cause the disappearance or impoverishment of Christ and his Gospel, Benedict and his *Rule* for cenobites, Cîteaux and its contemplative orientation, nothing remains but ashes at the mercy of the wind.

★   ★   ★

Ten years ago, Dom Ambrose, in writing to the Order regarding the new Constitutions, presented several general considerations, made some concrete suggestions, and treated certain difficulties. The objective of his circular letter in 1984 was to stimulate the monks and nuns of the Order to make the best possible use of the text of Holyoke.

The present letter is in continuity with that of my predecessor. The same desires animate it. Already, at the last General Chapter, I referred to the Constitutions as one of the privileged instruments with which to pursue the conquest of the gift of spiritual inculturated renewal and the gift of new life that the Spirit gives to whoever has the courage to die to self in order to live to a God who became flesh.

At the beginning, in indicating the aim of this letter, I also formulated, with the Councilors, the desire that the Spirit inspire in our hearts a breath of life by using the words that the same Spirit had inspired when we drew up our renewed Constitutions. In conclusion, it only remains for me to say:

> *May God grant that by the breath of his Spirit the brothers and sisters may observe them in a spirit of fraternal charity and fidelity to the Church, and so joyfully make their way to the fullness of love with the help of the Blessed Virgin Mary, the Queen of Cîteaux.*

DE UTILITATE ALIORUM

Circular Letter to the Members of the Order, January 26, 1996

My dear Brothers and Sisters,

A year has ended and a new year has begun. It is another opportunity given to us by the mercy of God in order for us to continue the conformation of ourselves to his son Jesus Christ. There is something in particular this year for each of us; we will celebrate another Mixed General Meeting and the two interdependent General Chapters. It will be an occasion, this time, for evaluating and enriching our community experience of the *Schola Caritatis*. Thus, the central theme of the next meeting is: 'The Community, School of Charity'.

In my last letter, I said that the Eucharist is the font and summit of the school of christian and monastic love. It is not possible for us to love as Christ loved us if we do not nourish ourselves at this divine font. This present letter is to be understood in the light of the preceding one; there is no Eucharist without love and there is no love without the Eucharist.

The *Schola Caritatis* is built upon the precept of the love of God and neighbor and it is wholly orientated toward this end. The goal of the 'school of divine service', which is the *Rule* of Benedict, is the 'preservation of charity' (*RB* Prol.47); or as the abbot of Clairvaux would put it: 'to increase and preserve charity' (*Prae* 5). For our cistercian fathers, the school of the *Rule* is a school of Christ, and in it, one learns the love of neighbor, effect and proof of the love of God (Cf. Bernardo, *Div* 121; William of Saint-Thierry, *Nature of Love* 24–26). That is why our Constitutions present the cenobitic life as a school of fraternal charity (*Cst.*3,1).

Our whole monastic formation can be summed up in learning how to love: to stir up one's capacity for being by the gift of oneself and receiving from others, by being both the subject and the object of love. All teaching methods presuppose a doctrine and a practice. Saint Benedict, a practical man, does not linger over theories; he teaches us that one learns to love by loving. Chapter 72 of his *Rule* can be understood in this light: maxims on love to be put into practice.

The fourth precept of good zeal stands out among the rest for two reasons: its structure is different and it seems to occupy a central place. It says, 'No one is to seek what is useful for himself, but rather what is useful for the others' (72:7). We have here a characteristic expression of cenobitic love. That will be the subject of this letter. First, I must state a presupposition.

Cenobitic Personalism

Each of us has his own theory about the human being. It matters little if we call it anthropology, a theory of personality, or principles of human and personal development. Knowingly or unknowingly, we have all formed a set of ideas concerning our own human reality. Numerous and varied factors have contributed to this end: our reading, experiences, relationships, significant persons, personal interests, successes and failures, the flow of life.

It matters little if our 'anthropology' is implicit or articulated, whatever it be, its influence is everywhere in our lives. What is more, I almost dare to say that 'anthropologies' float about in the very air we breathe. Can we doubt then the influence of depth psychology, and behavioral, humanistic, and existential psychologies, in North Atlantic countries and beyond?

Cistercian spirituality, from its very beginnings, had a solid doctrine on the human person as foundation and support for the search for God and union with him in love. Numerous treatises '*de anima*' attest to this truth.

At various times and in other contexts I have called attention to the necessity for an anthropological model of a personalistic and cenobitic stamp in which to situate our monastic life in the times in which we live. Some persons and regions have already offered theoretical and experiential answers concerning this need.

In a simpler form I, too, offer a first response in the form of thoughts. They may have little appeal but are not lacking in meaning; if you wish, they can be called sentences. They will labor under a double deficiency: they are lacking a more feminine vision of reality, and the indispensable contribution of multiculturalism. All this may serve as an invitation to continue reflecting on this theme and to enrich it. I would like them to undergird the evangelical and cenobitical doctrine of the good zeal that seeks the good interest of others rather than its own.

Person-personalization

It is proper to God to be a tri-unity of persons; personhood (the fact of being a person) is an eminent sign of the image of God in the human being.

To be a person in the image of God involves existing in relationship, as a unity of two or more people, one for the other.

Only God and the human person are capable of life in communion; the divine WE is the eternal model of the human we.

God is not an 'Other' but a 'You' to us, which is the basis of every other relationship.

The human person finds his/her model in Christ, the incarnated and humanized divine Person.

The person is:

- someone in relationship to others.

- an autonomous being called to interdependence.

- a self-awareness that communicates and is open to the presence of others.

- conscience and free in order to love in truth.

- one for all and all for one.

- the one who:

  - is master of himself in giving himself to others, receiving, and sharing existence.

  - is capable of communion and community with God and with others.

  - predisposes himself in order to make himself available and puts himself at the disposition of others.

The 'I' is personalized by the 'you' and the 'they'. This takes place in concrete and definite historical, social, cultural, political, and religious contexts; if it were not for others, we would not be anyone or anything.

Our personal being acquires depth in the calm of intimate dialogue, free converse, and united action; love, speech, and cooperation create and sustain reciprocal and personalized relationships.

The process of personalization is founded on our personal autonomy that is open to interdependence with others.

We are autonomous through our individuality (I as a social being) and our authenticity (I being myself in relation to others).

We are interdependent through the gift of ourselves in the service of fellowship and to a common project.

Interdependence allows you and me to be an us, and for the mine and the yours to be converted into an ours; this is strengthened and enriched through:

- obedience: free setting aside of autonomy in favor of communion with God and the brethren—losing oneself in order to find oneself.

- re-ordering: free relinquishment of what is ours in favor of divine filiation and human fraternity—dying in order to live.

Women seem to be more open to interdependence than men, the latter being more inclined to autonomy; this difference of emphasis is also found between cultures.

Liberty-liberation

Authentic liberty is also an eminent sign of the divine image in the human being; it is rooted in our personal human condition and in it is rooted our dignity as human persons.

No one is freer than Christ, who lived spending himself to bring together the dispersed.

Freedom is founded on truth and tends toward the good and to communion; it implies the capacity to give ourselves in order to:

- be ourselves and find our identity.

- actualize ourselves and shape our own destiny.

- tend toward the goal by free election of the good.

- build communion on four different levels and between the levels themselves:

  - with God as sons.

  - with our neighbor as brothers.

  - with creation as lords.

  - with history as co-protagonists.

Our freedom is characterized by being a reality:

- in a situation: geographical, historical, cultural, generic, social, economic.

  - Our freedom is real but conditioned by its context and not unconditional and absolute.

  - It only exists in dialogue with circumstances. That is why it can be responsible.

- before God—all free acts have reference to the ultimate end.

  - The most liberated freedom is that which tends most strictly toward the final goal that is God.

  - Freedom relates to good naturally and by its very being, and to evil by defect and corruption.

- Only the divine omnipotence of the Creator can create a being capable of saying yes or no to its Creator.

• toward the definitive—the unrepeatable and irrevocable.

- To come to be 'someone', one must opt freely and definitively for something and someone.

- We are merely 'something' when we do not opt loyally for someone.

- The more faithful and lasting a commitment is, the more human and personal it is.

- Without commitment and fidelity, there is no mature freedom.

• holistic—aside from being free we have freedoms and the need for all to be free and have freedoms.

- I am free if I also have religious, moral, political, and economic freedom.

- Personal freedom decreases when social freedom diminishes.

- I am less free when each and all are less free.

- The struggle for my freedoms is authentic when it includes the struggle for the freedoms of others.

- The renunciation of some freedoms is justified by the strengthening of the freedoms of others.

- Freedom without order is anarchy and order without freedom is dictatorship.

- under tension—consisting of pairs of tensions.

  - Freedom is a gift; it is a grace of existential openness to all that is.

  - It is also a task; we have to arrive at freedom by freeing ourselves continually, overcoming the opposition between determinisms and capabilities, limits and possibilities.

  - We are free—capable of operating by inner conviction, knowing and willing what we do.

  - What is more, we have freedoms: religious, moral, political, and economic as part of being free.

  - We are free from absolute determinisms.

  - We are also free to build communion practicing the truth in love.

Full freedom is always a freedom of consent and not of option; he is not more free who chooses more but rather who is more committed.

Women seem to be more committed than men are; the latter seem more focused on the breadth of options.

Love-loving

God is Love for he is total and eternal gift and acceptance; created in the image of God, we have been created to love.

In the death and resurrection of Christ, we find the most telling example of the love for the Father and from the Father.

There is nothing more important than to love; it is more important to love than to live, because to live without love is not life but death. One lives because of love and one lives to love. Love is the life of the dying and the death of the living.

In loving, the human beings discover themselves in their deepest identity as lover.

To love is:

- to extend the limits of the 'I' in order to be reborn as persons: 'I', 'you', 'we'.

- to affirm that one plus one is one and that the 'I' and the 'you' are not added together but are multiplied.

- to know that conviction and selflessness matter more than emotion.

- to give and receive what cannot be bought or sold but rather is given as gift and freely received.

- a self-gift, a giving of self more than just a gift, giving oneself in giving . . . and with no end to the giving.

- to desire the good of the other and to do good to him.

- to affirm the other as worthy, unique, and unrepeatable.

The affirmation of love differs in its manifestations, it can be:

- maternal: merciful and naturally unconditional, predominantly affective.

- paternal: reliable and spontaneously conditional, with an accent on the effective.

- fraternal: universal and friendly, emphasizing the developmental.

- erotic: heterosexual and tending toward the carnal, predominantly unitive and possessive.

- divine: absolute and free gift; in God the offering is uppermost, in us the receiving.

Fraternal love is basically a developmental love; it is born of three attitudes in relation to others:

- caring: affective and effective dedication to the life and well-being of the neighbor.

- responsibility: a free, generous and prompt response to the needs of others.

- respect: an attentive and delicate attitude toward others as they are and not as I want them to be.

Fraternal love includes maternal mercy and effectiveness, paternal reliability and effectiveness, and can have unlimited growth in gratuitousness and unconditionalness, almost in the way that God loves us.

Woman reveals to man, more than he does to her, that we are human in the measure we love and are loved, in the measure we give and receive.

THE CONCERNS OF OTHERS

I hope that the thoughts or sentences above help to encompass anthropologically the doctrine of cenobitic love that I want to present to you. Let us now turn to the teaching of Benedict: 'No one is to pursue what he judges to be better for himself, but instead, what he judges better for someone else' *(RB* 72:7).

This maxim on disinterested and selfless love, as well as the other eight maxims, incarnates concretely the good zeal or most fervent love proper to a heart overflowing with the inexpressible delight of love. It also allows the heart to expand, burn, and boil with fervor. This love is quite different from new or first fervor. And what is more, it is compatible with the fact of feeling and judging oneself 'a poor monk or nun', 'just one of the community'; however, this love is not practiced or experienced by those who simply vegetate or waste their days in mediocrity.

The practice of this specific kind of good zeal, as well as the practice of humility, purifies from vices and sins. Moreover, it leads to God, as does the practice of obedience and the *dura* and *aspera* of the monastic *conversatio*.

What is more, given that Christ alone takes us to heaven, we can say that the exercise of most fervent love, that only looks to the good of others, conforms us to Christ, who strove for our good and not for his own, and brings us all together to the kingdom of heaven.

The cenobitic Patriarch also finds a model in the apostle Paul: 'I try to please all in any way that I can by seeking, not my own advantage, but that of the many, that they may be saved' (1 Co 10:33). The same apostle who sang *'Caritas non quarit quae sua sunt'* (1 Co 13:5), never tired of urging: 'Each of you should look to others' interests rather than to his own; your attitude must be that of Christ Jesus' (Ph 2:4–5).

It is easy to see that beneath this teaching lies the model of the primitive community of Jerusalem: 'Those who believed shared all things in common . . . The community of believers were of one heart and one mind' (Ac 2:44; 4:32).

The maxim that occupies us has no direct parallel in the *Rule*; nevertheless, we can say that the entire *Rule* is meant to educate us in how to live this disinterested love.

The more significant parallels would be: 'to deny oneself in order to follow Christ' (*RB* 4:10); 'to hate one's own will' (*RB* 4:60); 'they are to obey one another' (*RB* 72:6); and 'prefer absolutely nothing to Christ' (*RB* 72:11; cf. 4:21). Perhaps there is also a connection with what is said of the abbot: 'Let him know that his duty is rather to profit his brethren than to preside over them' (*RB* 64:8).

Without any pretense of playing the exegete, let us look with greater attention at what seems to me to be four key words in the benedictine text:

- *Nullus (no one)*: Absolutely all are involved without exception; Benedict uses the same term in 3:8 where it seems to exclude the Abbot.

- *Utile (useful)*: Referring to a physical-material good profitably useful, but also to moral-spiritual goods (cf. *RB* 33:2; 42:4).

- *Sequatur (follow, seek)*: Connotes the choice of a value (cf. *RB* Prol. 7, 17; 3:7; 4:10; 5:8) or the non-following of a counter-value (*RB* 3:8).

- *Magis (even better)*: Appeals to a value and a conscientious and free option, proper to a responsible person who uses his reason (and is not moved by passion only). The school of divine service is a place in which to grow in personal freedom and conscience.

Let us listen to the words of an authentic interpreter of Saint Benedict and of his *Rule*: Saint Bernard, abbot of Clairvaux. Bernard tells us that because God is Love, and precisely because of this, he has loved us first. And because he loves us first, he loves us freely and disinterestedly. This is how we are to love one another (*Dil*)!

It is not to be marveled at, then, that Bernard quotes the pauline texts mentioned above more than ninety times in his works.

In greater detail, the abbot of Clairvaux teaches us that: charity is the unblemished law of the Lord because it does not seek what is useful for itself but rather for others (*Dil* 35). For this reason charity is 'light' and 'purity' (*SC* 63:8). The 'pure of heart' are those who do not seek after their own interests but Jesus Christ's, nor what is useful for themselves but for others (*Conv* 32). Consequently, purity of heart consists in:

- seeking the glory of God and serving neighbor (*Mor* 10 = *Ep* 42:10).

- pleasing God and saving souls, benefiting others more than presiding over them (*ad Abbat* 6; cf. *Div* 45:5).

This free and disinterested love, pure and just, characterizes the third degree of love in which God is loved for his own sake and not for our sake (*Dil* 26):

> *This is the charity that does not seek after its own interests. She sees that the son does not preoccupy himself with his own affairs, but rather in loving his Father. Fear, on the contrary, forces the servant to seek after his own comforts, and ambition impels the mercenary toward greater gain* (*Div* 3:1).

But he who is imprisoned in his 'self will', through which he seeks only personal benefit, does not give glory to God nor is he useful to the brethren (*Pasc.* 3:3), and can only be healed through the love that does not seek its own (*Asspt* 5:13).

Mary is the most sublime model of this love. She made herself, with 'boundless love', 'all in all' and surety for all (*OAsspt* 2). What Bernard says with respect to those who are dead to themselves and alive to others applies to no one more than to her.

Happy the mind that has been wise enough to enrich and adorn itself with an assortment of spices such as these, pouring upon them the oil of mercy and warming them with the fire of charity! Who, in your opinion, is the good man who takes pity and lends, who is disposed to compassionate, quick to render assistance, who believes that there is more happiness in giving than in receiving, who easily forgives but is not easily angered, who will never seek to be avenged, and will in all things take thought for his neighbor's needs as if they were his own? Whoever you may be, if your soul is thus disposed, if you are saturated with the dew of mercy, overflowing with affectionate kindness, making yourself all things to all men yet pricing your deeds like something discarded in order to be ever and everywhere ready to supply to others what they need, in a word, so dead to yourself that you live only for others (SC 12:1).

SOME CONCLUSIONS

I trust that I have not wearied you with the preceding passages. I realize that they were dense and I hope that they have also been rich, not because they are mine, which they are not, but because they come from the Fathers.

I would now like to offer some conclusions on the doctrine expounded; I say some because I want you yourselves to draw out the rest. To summarize:

- the practice of love restores the image of God in us and allows the community to become an icon of the trinitarian community.

- the maxim of Saint Benedict on 'seeking the interests or good of others' encapsulates the meaning of fraternal charity in its practice and exercise; as in the same manner, the ultimate meaning of the benedictine-cistercian *ascesis* as a way toward the contemplation of God.

- the vision of God is the blessed reward of the pure of heart; that is to say, those who seek not their own interests but those of Christ and of neighbor.

- without the reality of freedom and disinterestedness exercised for the benefit of the neighbor no common life is possible; we are here at the very font of cenobitic life.

- the process of personalization and personal liberation goes through a deliberate, conscious, and free setting aside of ourselves in order to serve and benefit others.

- unfortunately our hearts are never free of 'mercenaries' who traffic selfishly with God and with neighbor, nor are there any lack of 'bachelors and old maids' who have made themselves the center of their universe displacing God and neighbor.

- worse still: 'In all monasteries . . . there are sarabaites, the self-interested (*seipsos amantes*, 2 Tm 3:2) who ever seek their own' (Bernard, *3 Sent* 31).

- to seek after the interests of the others is the most efficacious and practical remedy for the disease of depersonalization, and the disintegration of a community afflicted with individualism.

- it means a love that liberates and decentralizes us from ourselves in order to center us on the Other and the others, putting us at their service. However, be aware of subtle forms of self-centeredness: what can I do to love others more? It would be better to ask oneself: what do my brothers or sisters need, or how can I best serve them?

- there is no greater happiness than to make others happy; that does not mean inventing needs to satisfy and so self-satisfy oneself. It is in losing oneself that one finds oneself: one finds one's life through others!

We are approaching the end of the letter, but not of love! May the Lord give us his Spirit so that the renewal of our spirits will shout out the news of the Gospel, as the cistercian contribution to the new Evangelization, on the threshold of the ninth centenary of the foundation of Cîteaux and the third millennium of the birth of Christ. Let us pray:

O Lord my God, why do you not remove my sin, and why do you not take away my iniquity? So that having cast away the heavy load of my own will I may breathe under the light burden of charity, that now I may not be encompassed with servile fear nor seduced by mercenary cupidity, but that I may be led by your Spirit, the Spirit of liberty by which your sons are led and may it give testimony to my spirit that I am one of your sons since the same law is mine as is yours, and as you are so may I also be in this world (Bernard, *Dil* 36).

THE NINTH CENTENARY OF CÎTEAUX

Circular Letter to the Members of the Order,
January 26, 1998

Dear Brothers and Sisters,

We are celebrating the ninth centenary of the founding of Cîteaux.
Moreover, in less than two years' time, christian history will turn a
page to enter a new millennium.

The present letter falls within this time frame. I wish to look respectfully, from where we are today and from my own limited perspective,
at the world, the Church and the Order. It is important to know
the living context in which our life is unfolding. The adage that,
'Every point of view is only the view of a point,' is universally valid,
but without points of view we lose the view of both the present
and the future.

The accelerated changes of recent years point to the fact that we
are not only in an age of change—that is, the chronological shift to
the year 2000—but also in a change of age, with very deep cultural

shifts. Moreover, we live in a culture of change as a characteristic of life, since we live in the midst of change, with changes all around us and in a continual expectation of more changes.

These deep mutations are a time of both crisis and grace. They are moments of apocalyptic discernment—God's hour in which he wishes to intervene with a greater display of his saving will. Similarly, but on a more spiritual level, the celebration of the nine hundred years since the founding of Cîteaux, mother of us all, is a reminder to live time as a Liturgy, that is, as an act of thanksgiving and as an occasion for conversion.

The intention of this letter is to help us all reflect, pray, and act. I would like to contribute to your understanding of our times and its signs, knowing that your reactions and replies will also help me.

A WORLD IN MOVEMENT

Our monasteries are scattered on all five continents. Wherever they are, they find themselves within a worldwide process of:

- neo-liberal modernization with its rejection of the poorer classes.

- a universal extension of this culture provoking the affirmation of cultural pluralism.

- a search for new gods, a thirst for the true God, and the need for a new Evangelization.

A closer look at the worldwide situation lets us see, among other things, a series of mega trends clearly typical of today's world. The following ones constitute a frame of reference, something like a road, the end of which we cannot see nor do we know where it will lead.

- The cold war has ended and so has the arms race between the two hegemonic blocks: Russia and its communist block on one side, the United States with its Western allies on the other. Russia has ceased to exist as a superpower. We now live under a **mono-polar geopolitical system**. No one doubts the worldwide control of the United States. It is still too soon to predict what can happen when China finishes emerging from within the ocean of this worldwide situation.

- The disintegration of the block of countries formerly controlled by the Soviet Union has meant the eruption of **nationalisms and nationalities**. In some places, this has occurred at the price of the shedding of blood. We can recall what happened in the former Yugoslavia. The same phenomenon is taking place in the ethnic wars of Central Africa, which are fed by interested parties on the outside.

- The industrial revolution has given way to the **technological revolution**. We are beginning to see what this means for labor relations and the production of goods: manpower is no longer the primary factor. The same can be said of raw materials and the countries that export them. Science and technology rule the work force. Consequently, the gap is widening between the developed North and the developing South.

- Related to the foregoing is another significant change that has occurred: **interdependence**, globalization, or the appearance of a 'single worldwide system', in which everyone affects everyone else on a planetary scale. Although this is basically a structural and technological phenomenon open to many possibilities, it is now producing its fruits on the economic and regional levels. This explains the birth of the European Economic Community, the North American common market (NAFTA), the block formed by Japan and the South-East Pacific countries, and the common market of the southernmost American countries.

- The debate between socialism and capitalism has come to an end. The hegemony of the capitalist system—under its neo-liberal form—is a fact. **Economic neo-liberalism** has taken advantage of planetary interdependence and is attempting to globalize the world economy to convert the world into an immense free market. For Third World countries, the dilemma is whether to be included in, or excluded from, this new, obligatory, socio-economic system that fosters both development and exploitation. In either case, the poorest thirty percent of the world's population is excluded. Such is the price of inclusion in this new system! The impoverished masses of humanity have become the world's human garbage! This neo-liberalism shows a deep concern for productive economic efficiency and a remarkable inefficiency and lack of concern for the social distribution of the goods it produces. Not only does it not resolve the problems that previously existed in this regard, but it also increases them.

- We are also facing a **cultural change** of deep consequence, where we are witnessing:

  – the growth of a culture 'of the masses', an invasive, universal culture born in and exported from North America.

  – the predominant influence of the means of communication that transmit cultural forms in such a way that the mass media are conditioning and even determining the culture.

  – the fading away of 'modern' culture as lived in the Western world of the North Atlantic, into a 'postmodern' culture.

  – the growing influence of women in terms of their increasing roles of service, authority, and power.

  – the de-christianizing of christian Europe with the multiplication of Christians not linked to any church and for whom Christianity is a frame of reference, but not a religion to join. At the same time, there is the rapid growth of african Catholicism and the slow christianizing of Asia's pluralistic religiosity.

CHURCH IN MOVEMENT

The Church of today is not withdrawn from the joys and sorrows of the world in which it lives and which it attempts to serve with the light and strength of the Gospel. It is not removed from the deep changes and accelerated transitions that today's world is living.

Some people speak of a new springtide for the Church; others see it more as winter. The global project of a new inculturated evangelization would be a sign of spring. Rigid Catholic uniformity governed from the center would be an indication of winter. A more detailed analysis allows us to speak of basic tendencies, analytical categories, or theoretical **models** that help us to understand and describe the present-day Church scene. The different local churches in their historical realities—just like religious orders and congregations—may express more than one of the different models, with the emphasis or dominant model differing from one place to another. We can distinguish three models of the Church:

- a **traditional** model emphasizing the Church as an institution that communicates truth to a distant world alienated from God.

- a **modern** model putting the accent on the Church as an organization that presents a doctrine in response to the questions of secularized persons and societies.

- an **incarnated** model that stresses the following of Jesus, preaches the Good News to everyone, and tries to embody the Gospel in poverty, through the more impoverished people of this world.

If we place ourselves in the center of the christian world, that is, Rome and the Vatican, we can discern two programs, the features of which are becoming clear at the end of this millennium. Once again, it is a question of programs that do not mutually exclude each other. In a certain sense, they characterize the College of Cardinals:

- a **religious and political program** that assures the political visibility of the faith to strengthen the ethical and political function of the Church in society. The enemy of this program would be the darker side of modernity and a secularism that blocks the implementation of christian social models.

- a **dialogical and reforming program** that, in order to promote a more collegial system, stimulates dialogue with the other great religions, openness in ecumenical dialogue, changes in how the papacy functions, and reforms in the structure of the Roman *Curia*.

There is no doubt in anyone's mind that the Church at the end of this millennium has been strongly marked by the pontificate of John Paul II. Here is a person who is both multifaceted and strong in his sense of identity: a man who is sweet and firm, compassionate yet resistant, with a great gift of leadership, good qualities as actor and communicator, facility in learning languages, ease in the rhetorical arts, an artist and a poet. However, any '**portrait**' of John Paul II must necessarily go beyond the Pope himself. It will tell us much about the Church of today, and perhaps of tomorrow, too. His pontificate of over nineteen years lets us point out the following characteristic features of this pope.

- He is a philosopher and a theologian whose formative years were influenced by Thomism and personalism. He is clearly christocentric, which explains his strong attraction for a philosophy of man.

- He is deeply devoted to the Mother of Jesus and Mother of the Church. He is thus the pope who consecrates to Mary different persons, cities, countries, and even the whole world.

- He often acts on two different levels: looking outward, he is the pope of ethnic minorities, human rights, world peace, the dispossessed, and the poor; looking inward, he is the pope who defends traditional doctrine, keeps Church discipline, and devises new pastoral plans.

- He is the pope who has opened wide the door of ecumenical and interreligious dialogue.

- He is the traveling, missionary pope, more than any of his predecessors; twenty percent of his time has been passed traveling.

- His appointment of bishops has given rise to a particular type of bishop: orthodox, with a solid theological formation, and a strong Catholic identity, faithful to Rome, centered on spirituality.

- He is the pope who has condemned both communism and classical capitalism to 'humanize' the meaning of work. When he stood up to communism he was applauded by the West. The other side tried literally to assassinate him. Now that he criticizes capitalism and its cultural consequences, he is crossed off by many in the West as morally meaningless.

- Never in history has there been a pope with such worldwide political influence. He has been mediator of conflicts over the Beagle Canal, Lebanon, Panama, and, above all, Poland, along with being an active participant in various meetings held under the auspices of the United Nations: Cairo, Beijing, Río de Janeiro, and elsewhere.

- More than anyone, he is the deep friend and champion of women's rights in today's world. It is most curious that very many women, who only know the opinions of the pope through what they read in the press, consider him anti-feminist.

Now let us look at **consecrated religious life**, since it is the immediate, living context in which our monastic life is located. According to the different geographical areas, we can see the following typical situations:

- **Africa** is a virgin who has been repeatedly violated but always remains faithful to herself. Consecrated life there is marked by a strong spirit of celebration and community, a deep sense of what is autochthonous to the region and thus a need for inculturation.

- **Asia** is harmonious through its centuries-old sensitivities, but is tense today because of an uncertain tomorrow. Consecrated life in Asia is a significant minority searching for new forms based on monastic models, open to temporary religious experiences as a preparation for life in the world.

- **North America,** in its technological, secularized, and religious grandeur, is the defender of liberties and the melting pot of many races. Consecrated life there shows an exquisite sensitivity in favor of cultural pluralism and the role of women in society and the churches.

- **Latin America** is the continent with a Catholic majority, the home of many martyrs, deeply desiring a social justice that has been long in coming. Consecrated life there is searching for new life styles with a greater sense of history and for greater insertion into the poorer, marginalized levels of society.

- **Western Europe**, wise in its old age, has exported its classical culture and structures. Consecrated life in Western Europe now tries to re-dimension its activities, overcome its vocational crisis, and be a prophetic voice crying out in the desert of bourgeois society.

• **Central and Eastern Europe**, separated from their western sister for many years, are rich in lasting traditions. Consecrated life there features the central place given to monasticism, the glorious stigmata of its fidelity to the Lord, and an updating that does not betray its own nature and history.

• **Oceánia** is not a continent of water, but of a vast multitude of islands that give joy to the Pacific Ocean. Consecrated life in Oceánia has difficulties in the formation and stability of its members due to the immense distances involved. At the same time, there is great hope for the future because of its youthful character and its faithfulness to the Gospel.

THE ORDER: NOW AND IN THE FUTURE

There are many ways to look at the Order in its present historical situation and with an eye to the future. One possible way is from the perspective of values, challenges, and utopias. During the last General Chapter, I spoke of utopias or dreams. Now seems to be the moment to look more closely at the values and challenges, though not forgetting the importance of creatively dreaming while awake.

The Gift and Value of Monastic Identity

Values are 'attractive goods'. That is why they are powerful forces motivating our behavior, helping us to advance and persevere in the way of life we have embraced. Values are constitutive elements of the cistercian grace that motivate persons in their personhood, galvanize whole communities, and touch the whole Order. We can say that these values are like gifts after a victory. They are graces, gifts from the Lord, the acceptance of which implies not a little sweat and tears so that they may become life and growth.

In our Order, we find many valuable realities that can be thought of as relatively acquired, or in the process of being so. They thus motivate the journey of the Order today. However, this does not mean that we can rest on our laurels. On the contrary, we must know how to examine ourselves to continue advancing in our journey.

I would like to discuss at greater length one of these valuable victory gifts that characterize our life today. It is the clear, existential, and juridical statement of our monastic and contemplative **identity** in the heart of the Church and in confrontation with today's world. The fact of being able to make this statement after so many years of renewal, *aggiornamento,* and institutional reform should make us thank the Spirit of the Lord, who has always guided us and been with us.

We can understand the importance of a clearly defined identity if we consider that, without it:

- there cannot be a sense of self, of continuity in time or of consistency at any given moment, either as a human person or as a monk or nun.

- nor can there be any continuing existence, in the midst of changes in the concrete living of monastic observances or in the Order's pastoral structures.

- any sense of community, of shared ongoing existence together, would also be impossible.

I realize that there are many ways in which personal identity can be understood. For our present purposes, we are only speaking of identity as a significant mode of existing, with the dynamic relationships flowing from this mode. Let me explain. The identity of the different forms of life within the People of God emerges from the relational process of existence in the Church. The distinction of the different charisms takes place in the context of the tension between their convergence and their divergence, between communion and separation.

We can thus say that our identity is a reality that lets us define ourselves in terms of what makes us meaningful within a network of relationships, but without inauthentic inclusions or falsely narrow exclusions. That is how we can say that we identify ourselves as meaningful followers of Jesus in the heart of the Church community. However, this is obviously not enough. The years after the Council have taught us to go back to the origins and to go deeper in depth. Remember how we had to consult the founding fathers of Cîteaux in order to describe our own identity more clearly? Let us return now and recall the lesson we learned.

In the first place, we should remember the intention or 'purpose' of our founding fathers. It is clear that the reform that they undertook was above all a movement of spiritual renewal. Such a renewal project could only be carried out based on precise, well-defined ideals. What were these ideals? What characterized the founding charism that our fathers received from the Lord?

The primitive documents from Cîteaux, quite apart from any problems they may present to historians, clearly present us with the following ideals:

- **authenticity** in monastic observance, in the spiritual life, and in liturgical life.

- **simplicity** and poverty in everything, to follow, and to be poor with, the poor Christ.

- **solitude** so as to be able to live for God while building up a communion of brothers.

- **austerity** of life and of work, to promote the growth of the New Man.

- **conformity** to the *Rule* of Saint Benedict, a conformity that is absolute, that is, without additions contrary to the *Rule's* spirit and letter.

Actually, these ideals were very similar to what all the reformers and renewers of the eleventh and twelfth centuries were trying to accomplish. Nevertheless, the accent in the New Monastery on the *Rule* of Saint Benedict, to be observed with 'greater strictness and perfection'—*artius atque perfectius*—seems to have been the key to their success. In fact, the first fathers found the monastic identity they wanted in their conformity to the *Rule*. Above all, they found there the balance and harmony needed for seeking God over a long period.

There is no mention in the primitive documents of a literal observance of the *Rule*. It is a question of keeping it in all its basic demands and of following it in its purity and probity. The probity and purity of the *Rule* is what constitutes its essence as a practical monastic way to live the Gospel. The *Rule* offered our founders a proven way of evangelical perfection thanks to its prudent balance of the traditional monastic observances. The *dura et aspera*—the hardships, difficulties, and observances—are mediating realities, instruments, and expressions of purity of heart and unity of spirit: *puritas cordis* and *unitas spiritus*.

Here, then, are the basic convictions concerning the *Rule* of Saint Benedict that the first cistercian fathers wished to incarnate in their lives:

- The search for God is the purpose of monastic life (*RB* 58:7).

- God is found in Christ (*RB* 4:21; 72:11).

- The cenobite carries out this search under a rule and an abbot (*RB* 1:2).

- The *Opus Dei* occupies a primary place in the monastic day (*RB* 43:1–3).

- Private prayer is a preparation and prolongation of the *Opus Dei* (*RB* 4:56; 52:1–5).

- Reading and meditation alternate with work to balance the monastic day (*RB* 48).

- Obedience, taciturnity, and humility are the pillars of ascetical life (*RB* 5–7).

- Fraternal charity, under the form of good zeal, governs the morality of the *Rule* (*RB* 72).

- The monastery is a workshop within which the monk labors throughout his life under the orders of the Lord and is himself worked upon by God (*RB* 4:78).

- Discretion is the essential virtue for having peace in the house of God (*RB* 64:17–19).

- Stability is required for this life to be fruitful (*RB* 4:78; 58:9, 17).

Moreover, the *Rule* taught our fathers—just as it teaches us today—to lead an integral, harmonious, balanced, *holistic* life. There are in the *Rule* a series of paired elements that are complementary to each other and act like balanced magnetic poles (see table).

The first disciples of Cîteaux's founders and the second cistercian generation—Bernard, William, Guerric, Aelred, Isaac, Amadeus, Gilbert, Baldwin, John, Adam—all think of the *Rule* as a text offering direction and advice for the interior life. Benedict offers abundant teaching on humility, obedience, love, and the fear of God. Moreover, he invites the monk to drink directly from the Gospels and the Church Fathers. Our teachers of the twelfth century reread the *Rule* in the light of this previous monastic tradition, without

Prayer: *Listen readily to holy reading, and devote yourself often to prayer. Every day with tears and sighs confess your past sins to God in prayer* (4:55–57).

Work: *Idleness is the enemy of the soul. Therefore, the brothers should have specified periods for manual labor as well as for prayerful reading* (48:1).

Common Good: *No one is to pursue what he judges better for himself, but instead, what he judges better for someone else* (72:7).

Personal Good: *If there are artisans in the monastery, they are to practice their craft with all humility* (57:1).

Prayer in Common: *Nothing is to be preferred to the Work of God* (43:3).

Private Prayer: *If someone wishes to pray privately, he may simply go into the oratory and pray* (52:3).

Discipline: *Discipline your body; do not pamper yourself, but love fasting* (4:11–13).

Dispensations: *There should be consideration for weaknesses* (34:2; 55:21).

Silence: *Monks should diligently cultivate silence at all times* (42:1).

Communication: *The brothers are to express their opinions with all humility* (3:4).

Enclosure: *No one shall presume to leave the enclosure of the monastery without the abbot's order* (67:7).

Hospitality: *All guests are to be welcomed as Christ* (53:1).

Disappropiation: *No one may presume to give, receive, or retain anything as his own, nothing at all* (33:2).

Needs: *In order that this vice of private ownership may be completely uprooted, the abbot is to provide all things necessary* (55:18).

Older monks: *The younger monks must respect their seniors* (63:10).

Younger monks: *The seniors must love their juniors* (63:10).

Seriousness: *A monk speaks gently and without laughter, seriously and with becoming modesty* (7:60).

Joy: *No one may be disquieted or distressed in the house of God* (31:19).

neglecting the signs of their own times. They thus developed some aspects of life in the Spirit that are hardly to be found in Saint Benedict: for example, their teaching on the human soul and the image and likeness of God, their emphasis on self-knowledge, their treatment of love and mystical contemplation. The *School of the Lord's service* also becomes a *School of charity*.

The founding charism of our first fathers, which is the charism that establishes our cistercian identity, was embodied in the primitive documents. Obviously, however, the documents are neither the charism nor the identity. The charism, as the experience of the Spirit configuring the monk with Christ in a special way and giving a specific identity, resides in human hearts: those of our founders and in our own.

Now let us look at our present situation. The cistercian charism as a specific form of evangelical life—a dynamic and transforming gift of the Spirit—resides in the heart of each one of us. In fact, our vocation to a cistercian monastery can be thought of as the discovery of our true spiritual identity. We find within us the seal imprinted there by the charism and the desire that this grace, this seal of the Spirit, reach its full potential. Although it can sound like an exaggeration, we must say that, when we arrived at the monastery, we already had the cistercian identity and the founding charism of Cîteaux in their pure and original state, as seeds ready to grow.

The charism of the founders and the consequent identity have been transmitted to each one of us to be constantly lived, preserved, deepened, and developed. This process takes place in communion with the Body of Christ that is in constant growth. The good of both the Church and the world require our fidelity to the gifts we have received. The cistercian charism and identity are a gift of the Spirit to the Church and, through her, to the world. The Order's new Constitutions are our identity card, letting us identify ourselves within the Church community. All our efforts for a new step in spiritual renewal rest on these convictions.

Once again, let me present in a synthetic format the guiding principles of this new stage of inculturated spiritual renewal. It is taking place within the context of a deeply changing world and of a Church inviting us to share in the process of a new evangelization. Its principles are:

- **following** Jesus.

- **orientation** toward his Mystery.

- **formation** for cenobitic living.

- **belonging** to an Order.

- **communion** in and with the Church.

- **solidarity** with all men and women.

- **discernment** of one's culture.

- **inculturation** of our Patrimony.

- **dialogue** with other churches and religions.

The foregoing might seem to be somewhat abstract, but it is easy to make it more concrete if we look at ourselves. Let us contemplate respectfully—the only way to look at human beings—the 4,350 monks and nuns who make up the Order today. There is no doubt whatsoever that we ourselves are the great value, the great mutual gift that constitutes the spiritual wealth of the Order at the present time, after nine centuries of pilgrimage through history, guided through it all by the Lord.

It is true, our wealth, the motive of our song of thanksgiving, are the one hundred sixty-five communities of persons of every age and social condition called by the same Lord. In some communities there are up to four or five different generations, which is immensely precious in today's world.

Our riches are all the many older monks and nuns, so full of wisdom and dedication to their neighbor, so joyful to have lived and to still live united to the Lord Jesus during their years of silent fidelity. Our riches are also the younger brothers and sisters called by the Lord to be configured to his monastic image. They are today's vital enthusiasm and the hope for the future. Our riches are also all the middle-aged members of the Order who are carrying the weight of today's burdens. They have the joy of knowing that they are strong links between the past and a future full of promise.

Moreover, how could we fail to mention, among so many people who are known, or perhaps unknown, to us, the saints who give joy to God's house? In our own century, now ending, the Lord has given us the splendid witness of the martyrs of China, Spain, and Algeria. There are many reasons to think also of Blessed Gabriella Saghedu of Grottaferrata-Vitorchiano, Blessed Rafael Arnáiz Barón of San Isidoro de Dueñas, Blessed Cyprian Michael Tansi of Mount Saint Bernard, and Venerable Marie-Joseph Cassant of Our Lady of Désert.

The theme of identity will become more important in the immediate future. The deep changes that are taking place in the field of communication and human interaction, plus the growing awareness that all life is interconnected, will result in new replies to the traditional question of identity, on the personal, group, and social levels. Increased pluralism and the global nature of environmental issues will require us to specify more clearly the core elements of our vocation, which we cannot renounce. We will have to discern what can be assimilated from outside, then renounce what is accidental or accessory so as to give to others what is most valuable in our charism and thus enrich them and ourselves.

Challenges and Stimulants

The noun 'challenge' comes from the verb 'to challenge', the meaning of which is to defy or provoke. The noun is synonymous with 'incentive', 'stimulant', something that pushes us to face difficulties with courage and fortitude. Sociologically speaking, it is the set of characteristics of a given historical, social, and cultural context that question the behavior of human groups.

From a theological viewpoint and in relation to the Order, it is important to see that challenges are not simply historical facts, but also words of God for us here and now. We can think of them as invitations from the Lord to act in conformity with his plan of salvation for us as Cistercians at this end of the twentieth century and beginning of the twenty-first. Thus, in their deeper meaning, the challenges that face the Order today are also 'signs of our times', or signs from God for this historical moment.

From among the different challenges that confront us, let us concentrate on just one: the need to spell out a new doctrine and vision of man, that is, a new **anthropology** at the service of our cenobitic life. This is something closely linked to the theme of monastic and contemplative identity. Every change of epoch requires an adjustment in the meanings and visions of reality. The very first reality that requires an adjustment is anthropology, that is, the vision that a human being has of him or herself. Every change of anthropology brings with it a change of spirituality. Although this is not the time or place to elaborate on this theme, which I wrote to you about in a previous letter, it does seem to be the moment to present some suggestions.

Anthropology—the question of what it means to be human—has experienced a series of important shifts in recent years. These new approaches cannot be ignored when we ask questions about ourselves. To put it briefly, we can speak about shifts:

- from a masculine-centered approach to a **human-centered** one. Anthropology must be about man-woman humanity, not just about males. Nor is this because of women's rights, but rather in order to recover the fullness of humanity.

- from duality to **unity**. The human spirit can be thought of and experienced only within the limits of material reality. We are not spirit and body, but incarnated spirits.

- from idealism to **realism**. We only discover what it means to be human from what exists in the historical framework of times, places, and cultures.

- from a one-dimensional vision to **multi-dimensional** one. What is essential, simple, and well defined is not the only thing that is important, but also what is existential, complex, and unlimited.

- from what is immanent and closed in on itself to what is open to **self-transcendence**. The human being is characterized by going beyond itself. It can only be understood from its own interiority and from outside itself.

I would like to pause for a moment and explain the first shift mentioned above, the shift toward an integral vision of humanity. More specifically, let us look at the new awakening, growing importance and increasing leadership of women in the world and Church today. It is something that can greatly contribute to the enrichment of our human and monastic identity. We are especially sensitive to it since we are an Order formed of both monks and nuns. It is increasingly clear to more and more people that male and female identities are not established separately from one another. On the contrary, their establishment is achieved precisely through the relationship of man and woman within a wider network of relationships and in a continual process of growth toward maturity. As a result, **relational ability** is the essential feature of either form of personal identity, and is therefore an absolutely necessary component in the development of an anthropology. If such a development is not achieved, we will fall into the stereotyped models promoted by the mass media of communication.

Focusing our attention now on the man-woman relationship, we can see three general models used to describe it:

- the model of **absolute difference** (bipolar dualism). This model does not see the difference between personhood, which is a reality common to all human beings, and the male or female condition that is specific to each gender. For those who think this way, the biological, psychological, and social characteristics of each gender determine everything else. Thus, they conclude that there is an absolute difference between man and woman.

- the model of **total equality** (emancipated uniformity). This model emphasizes the similarities so much that it makes the differences disappear. What is proposed is thus an androgynous, unisexual existence.

- the model of **interdependence** (equivalent, differentiated reciprocity). This model emphasizes the reciprocal otherness of man and woman within their personal equality. It rejects both an equality based on the lowest common denominator between the sexes and a complementarity based on subordination of one sex to the other. It states that the person is transformed in relationships and in community.

The third model—that of **interdependence**—integrates what is positive in the two other models and avoids their disadvantages and limitations. Thus, it is the best for rethinking our situation in a full, complementary way.

Perhaps the most interesting element of present day anthropology is the discovery of woman as **archetype** of humanity. As surprising as it may seem, this vision does not come from radical feminism, or from any of its better-known advocates. It comes from Christianity, from Catholic tradition. More precisely, it comes from the official Church *magisterium* as expressed in the teaching of Pope John Paul II. A renewed awareness of what it means to be female cannot be just a question of roles to be regained or rights to be obtained. It is much more a matter of rediscovering a human dimension that deeply touches both women and men, though in different ways.

A woman is a representative and archetype of the entire human race. In other words, she represents the humanity that is proper to all human beings, both men and women. The feminine gender is a living symbol of all that is human. A woman's female qualities have a prophetic character, since they show man's own identity. It is impossible to achieve an authentic interpretation of man—that is, of what is 'human'—without an adequate reference to what is 'feminine'. Human identity is marked by 'being for the sake of another' (John Paul II, *Mulieris Dignitatem* 4, 7, 22, 25, 30).

In this sense, a woman represents humanity in three different but complementary ways at the same time:

- by her condition as **spouse**, which is both reciprocity and the demand for it. This spousal quality is the consciousness of possessing an exclusive yet complementary gift to be shared with another person. It is the capacity to move and enable a man so that he, too, may show reciprocity, self-manifestation, and acceptance of another.

- by her condition as **mother**, that is, her feminine priority in the area that is most distinctly human, that of life, pain, and care. Her maternal quality is a free gift of self to another and a fullness that is reached through self-loss and acceptance of the other with all that person's limitations. It is the natural capacity to know how to wait for what needs time to come to fruition.

- by her **femininity**, which is a general mode and feature of 'being woman'. It implies being centered on caring for, and remaining present to, the other. It is the capacity to foster, by sympathy and adaptation, the other person's self-manifestation. Life is conceived as the possibility of meeting another person 'face to face' in such a way that each one's personhood will grow from it.

Mother Church and our Order within her still have much to learn about how to live and act as mother, spouse, and female caregiver, as these qualities are lived and experienced by a woman. To ignore one half of humanity is the most appalling form of lack of self-knowledge!

We can no longer doubt that one sign of our times is the strengthening of the role of women in our present society and culture. This fact leads us back to a fundamental element in the teaching and life of Jesus; something we should never have forgotten. It affects not only women, but also men: 'The new awareness on the part of women helps men to revise their own mental criteria, their way of understanding themselves, of judging and interpreting their place in history, of organizing their life, whether this be on a social, political, economic, religious, or Church level' (*Vita Consecrata,* 57).

If we look at our own situation, we find that many nuns of the Order understand themselves and the charism inside them in terms of 'fecundity'. They have chosen the better part and it is to be mothers and sisters of Jesus, listening to his word and putting it into practice. Their whole being beats to the rhythm of welcoming others, being fruitful, giving life. They join Guerric of Igny to tell us: *Oh faithful soul, open wide your bosom, expand your affections, admit no constraint in your heart, conceive him whom creation cannot contain! Open to the Word of God an ear that will listen. This is the way to the womb of your heart for the Spirit who brings about this act of conception* (*Second Sermon for the Annunciation* [27], 4).

We long for the hour when our nuns will teach us to read sacred Scripture from their own contemplative heart. With their eyes transformed by love, may they reread for us the tracts of theology, morals, monastic spirituality, and the cistercian charism and identity. When they reformulate our formulations, there will be born a new, inclusive form that will create many new formulas. Moreover, all this will flow from the riches of Christ, even though for many of us it implies a challenge of conversion. It will not come from easy accommodation to the spirit of our times.

Just as 'in the fullness of time' (Ga 4:4) everything depended on the consent of a human creature—Virgin, Spouse, and Mother—in a similar way at the threshold of the third millennium, the hope of a new humanization depends on the 'feminine genius'.

Nine centuries of cistercian history come to an end at the same time as the first twenty centuries of christian history. A new millennium opens before our eyes: not only a new age, but also the change of an age. What will the face of the Order be in the near future? How will it serve the Church and the world? Will everything we have held as essential until now remains so? What surprises does the Spirit have in store for us? Questions such as these—and many others—do not have a reply at the present time.

Nevertheless, we do know the gift we have received: our vocational charism. It is for the sake of serving many others. We ardently want this charism to be fruitful according to the divine favor and our own poor collaboration. Our hope is unconquerable because God is faithful and shares his fidelity with us.

Creative fidelity to our own identity—and the desire to enrich it by integrating all the capacities and gifts received—prepares us to strengthen the communion existing in the cistercian family. And may they weave a network of friendship with the immense number of baptized who recognize the same gift in their hearts.

CULTURE AND MYSTICISM

Circular Letter to the Members of the Order,
January 26, 1999

Dear Brothers and Sisters,

In my circular letter last year on the occasion of the Ninth Centenary of the founding of Cîteaux, I wrote you about our monastic identity as Cistercians. I also invited the nuns of our Order to interpret and explain the cistercian charism from their own hearts as women. I also offered you my vision of the world, the Church, and of consecrated life at the present time.

Now I write you again, just as we are about to leave the twentieth century. First, I wish to present here a view of **contemporary culture**, although I realize that my vision is limited to the flow of culture in the western countries of the North Atlantic. It seems to me, however, that in one way or another, the present cultural changes in this part of the world are affecting the large majority of local cultures. Due to the worldwide process of globalization, different elements of this North Atlantic culture are now found everywhere, either as friendly 'guests' or as unfriendly 'invaders'. Everything indicates that, in a not too distant future, this culture will tend to replace many other forms of cultivating human life. It is destined to be the existential framework in which we live. It will also be the context in which we will have to develop what is the central theme of this present letter, that is, the **mystical dimension** of our cistercian life.

You have already heard me say, on many occasions, that our in-culturated spiritual renewal depends on three basic realities: our following of Jesus, our formation as cenobites and our orientation to the Mystery. However, these realities do not exist in a vacuum. They can only be real within a specific cultural context. That is why it is so important for our inculturated spiritual renewal to discern the world's cultural environment.

As cistercian monks and nuns, we are following the poor Christ in communities where communion is *totally oriented toward an experience of the living God* (General Chapter 1969, DCL). Translated into the language of our Constitutions, this means that: Our *Order is a monastic institute wholly ordered to contemplation* (C.2).

From its very beginning, the cistercian charism has been able to respond in an inculturated way to the needs of the Church and the world. The phenomenal success of cistercian life can only be explained by what was at its very roots, that is, the **spiritual and mystical experience**. The deepest needs of the moment in which we are living are not too different from those of the twelfth century, which explains why our medieval mystics turn out to be so relevant to humanity today, to men and women who thirst for mystery and experience. However, it is not enough that they were mystics. *We* have to be, too. We will be, if we open our heart to the work of the Spirit and collaborate with him, knowing that:

> *This* [mystical] *way of thinking about God does not lie at the disposal of the thinker. It is a gift of grace, bestowed by the Holy Spirit who breathes where he chooses, when he chooses, how he chooses and*

upon whom he chooses. Our part is continually to prepare our heart
by ridding our will of foreign attachments, our reason or intellect of
anxieties, our memory of idle, absorbing or even sometimes necessary
business (William of Saint-Thierry, *Golden Epistle*, II,14).

So let us look at the panorama of today's changing culture and at
the place religious awakening has in it. Then we will understand
more easily the importance of mystical experience for humanity's
future and the challenge that this represents for us.

CULTURES

The reality of culture is always a subject of controversy, especially
at times of transition like our own. Nevertheless, it is absolutely
necessary to look at culture, especially when it is a question of
making a diagnosis of it. It helps to realize that the **structure** of
reality is considered today from three points of view. There is:

- its infrastructure: the economic dimension.

- its superstructure: the political dimension.

- its omni-structure: the cultural dimension.

We can add something more; during the last fifteen years, the world
has been experiencing a downturn of the political dimension and an
increase in the cultural dimension. This return to culture is principally a return to culture's religious dimension. The upswing applies
to the great traditional and historical religions as well as to the other
innumerable manifestations of mysticism and of the religious spirit.
In the past, the different crises of religion favored political activity,
but now it is the reverse: the political crises of our day favor religion.

All human beings—and monks and nuns are no exception—live,
choose, and act in a particular cultural universe. Any change in

this cultural world causes changes of behavior, due to the change in one's general perception of reality. The mass media of social communication has created a 'cultural industry', that is, it produces symbols, values, and meanings that change the way we see ourselves and how we relate to ourselves, to others, to *the* Other, and to other things.

We are all aware that we are living in a period of history that is not only an epoch of changes, but also a change of epoch. Any such change of epoch is experienced in a complex fashion, since it is a process of unknown implications without a timetable and without any foreseeable end-point. Such a historical transition, or change of epoch, explains why our culture at the end of the twentieth century is one of transition. Our moment in history marks the end of modern culture and a passageway to . . . we know not what!

Perhaps we can characterize the present western culture of the North Atlantic—and that of the rest of the world influenced by it in different degrees—like this.

- There is radical *modernity* in the scientific and technological sphere.

- In the cultural sphere, there is a *postmodernism* that has no alternate goal in view.

Before going any further, I should say a brief word about the facts of modernity and postmodernism. The broad meaning of the term **modernity** is in relation to the last five centuries of western history. Modernity can be broken into periods as follows: the sixteenth and seventeenth centuries were preparatory; the so-called 'Enlightenment' in the eighteenth century was central, followed by increasing development in the nineteenth and twentieth centuries. Modernity in the strict sense would run from the French Revolution up to the student revolution of May 1968 or until the energy crisis of 1973. Among the causes of modernity, the following should be pointed out:

- the geographical discoveries that put Europe into a global context.

- the Protestant Reformation, which favored the development of the personal conscience, with its defiance of the principle of authority alone.

- the copernican and galilean revolution, which removed us from the center of the cosmos.

- the growth of the experimental sciences, which has led to modern technology.

- reflexive philosophical thought, which questioned the accepted vision of the relationship between the human person and material things.

- capitalism as a rational means for producing goods.

In synthesis, the two main characteristics of modernity are the autonomy of the person in relation to any form of subjection, and the use of reasoning in opposition to any form of religiosity or faith. Though running the risk of excessive simplification, we can describe the modern point of view with five key words:

- **reason**: which was deified during the French Revolution.

- **humanity**: as something more than just the sum of all peoples, states, or nations.

- **history**: that is, time lived as a unit of continual progress.

- **emancipation**: from ignorance, dogmas, authorities, powerlessness, and so forth.

- **progress**: as an optimistic and limitless development in which utopias can flourish.

Not everyone has lived this process of modernity as something personal, but all have shared in it to the degree in which it has been exported by the Western countries of the North Atlantic. However, there still exist a few human groups who are rooted in a type of pre-modernity. There are others who 'modernize' their culture without necessarily assimilating the spirit and values of modern North Atlantic culture.

It is not easy to speak about **postmodernism,** for the simple reason that it does not exist, but is in a state of becoming. Without yet being a fixed point of view, postmodernism is a 'mood', a frame of mind alive in the average person, especially among the youth in western countries. It is a mood that is gradually expanding throughout the world. Here is a case that shows the truth in what someone has said, that philosophers are simply notaries who have arrived late on the scene and make official note of what has already happened.

Some such commentators tell us that postmodernism is a worn out modernity that has not been replaced. A worn out modernity means that it can neither produce nor create anything new, since the principles that inspired it are themselves worn out. However, modernity has not been replaced, since postmodernism still seems like modernity without the latter's great, optimistic myths. Postmodernism would be a one-sided reaction to modernity's one-sidedness, caused by a desire for light and stability after modernity's relative fiasco.

Others are more nuanced in their analysis and distinguish three types of postmodernism, namely:

- **neo-conservative** postmodernism, which is, above all, a defense reaction on the part of the consumer-oriented production system in order to protect itself in time of danger. It is the western capitalist system reacting against its own crisis. The accent is put on economics: cleansing of the economy, capitalization of companies, production increases, or selling off state-held companies. On the level of the

average person, this type of postmodernism is characterized
by a set of slogans, such as, 'Life consists in elbowing through
the crowd and pushing'. 'He who does not compete does not
succeed.' 'You have to get ahead in the world.' 'If work is not
productive, competitive, and profitable, it serves no purpose.'
'Time is money.' 'Professionalism means excellence.' The
postmodern heroes among the neo-conservatives are those
who succeed by speculating on the stock market, or the
financiers who author books like, 'In Praise of Benefits' or
'An Apology for Success'.

- **contentious** postmodernism would be a vast movement of
  deconstruction governed by a rejection of any underlying
  ideal or any thought of globalization. It is a process of
  'unmaking' starting from a basic metaphysical doubt. It
  stresses pluralism, decentralization, differences, happenings,
  breaking with the past, openendedness, and immanence.
  The leaders of this postmodern trend are still 'rebels with
  a cause'. Some of them describe their position in words
  like this: 'Instead of uniformity, differentiation; instead of
  absolute values, a plurality of standards; instead of efficiency,
  communication; and, instead of lasting commitments,
  conditioned agreements.'

- **disenchanted** postmodernism emphasizes the reasons for its
  disappointment with modernity. It points out that human
  reason has not opened to truth, but rather to knowledge
  for the sake of controlling others; progress has become
  retrogression by going against human rights and natural laws;
  equality is based on one-sided agreements that are broken
  for any reason; and the happiness that was promised is late in
  coming: right now everything is unhappiness. Most of these
  disenchanted postmodernists are 'rebels with nausea'. One
  of them has said that, 'In the world in which we live, there
  is only one thing that keeps me going: my next vacation'.
  Another one of them said with a smile, 'The goddess of
  reason wants to get me, but I run faster than she does'. A

third one described the situation like this: 'Yesterday it was yoga, tarot cards, and meditation. Today it is alcohol and drugs. Tomorrow it will be aerobics and reincarnation.'

We should be aware that our moment in history, like every time of change, is a time of **crisis**. We are at a critical moment, similar to what the christian West experienced during the fourteenth and fifteenth centuries. That period of the 'Renaissance' was, at one and the same time, the end of the Middle Ages and the dawn of the modern age. We are indeed living at a critical time, one open to a new birth, but marked right now by a pervasive crisis of life, identity, ideologies, and models by which to live.

From the **religious** point of view, we are also experiencing a deep change and a crisis of transition. Simplifying the situation to an extreme, we can say that we are passing from a **pathological** conception of religion to a **therapeutic** one. As we know, for some key representatives of modernity, religion was either:

- a human disease, according to Nietzche.

- an abnormal social phenomenon, according to Marx.

- an immature psychological condition, according to Freud.

It is worth recalling the Freudian concept of religion and its influence on his interpretation of spiritual, religious, and mystical experience. It is an approach that has deeply marked the twentieth century. Religion would be the desire to return to the protection originally offered by one's father in infancy. This desire is then projected onto an imagined God, since that is the only God that exists. Mystics are therefore undervaluing reality. They are deluded about the world they perceive, which they unconditionally submit to as a result of grief flowing from their pain. In other words, mystics suffer from psychic infantilism. Even more surprising then, that in the context of postmodern culture, religion turns out to be the best of therapies, which fact has thrown the Freudian approach into crisis. Something similar is happening in relation to absolute Being, or God. Some spokespersons for modernity proclaimed in different ways the **disappearance** of God:

- God is dead: the death of God.

- God is silent: the silence of God.

- God is an ideology, either socialist or capitalist: the impersonal God.

- God is progress: God only exists for those who think everything is going wrong!

- God does not exist: the result is that we are saints!

- God is a game: let's play God!

On the contrary, in postmodern thought we find that the divine has **reappeared**, although accompanied by a de-institutionalization of religion. We can ask what the causes of this phenomenon are, and there are many different answers:

- the recuperation of our traditional mystical heritage.

- the encounter of Western culture with cultures of the East.

- exasperation with the dictatorship of mere reason.

- the need for mystery to counteract science's pretense of explaining everything.

- the need for self-denial and self-giving to counteract the monopoly of efficiency, consumerism, waste and violence against nature, mother earth and the environment.

- amazement at, and fear of human power, which can transform nature by genetic engineering and atomic science, but cannot control the ongoing consequences of this transformation.

Different **sacralizing** or 'mystical' tendencies correspond to these causes of postmodernism. Thus, there is an ecological current of spirituality, a sectarian current, an esoteric current, and an eclectic current. Other forms of a sacred secularity should also be mentioned, such as the sacralization of a nation or race; the worship of, and fascination for musical experience as in rock concerts; the weekend football liturgy; or turning the sanctuary of the human body into a place of worshipful exposure. All of this is telling us that, alongside the process of desacralization of religion, there is a parallel process going on, which sacralizes nature and the secular world. These two processes have different faces according to their geographic location and local culture. It is hardly necessary to point out the ambiguity that dominates this whole field of attitudes and behavior.

In this new postmodern cultural environment, it is easy to understand and accept the fact that a clinical experience of depth psychology cannot be allowed to determine what beings should or should not exist. Modern reason knows very well that there is a serious error of method in jumping philosophically or theologically from sense knowledge to abstract metaphysics or from what is psychological to what is spiritual. A young psychiatrist once said, 'What a shame that Freud never had the chance to psychoanalyze a true mystic, and it's also too bad that he is not living today to help all the little scientific mystics we have'.

Everything seems to show that the western culture of the North Atlantic, marked as it is by the postmodern shift, is **thirsting for mystery,** wearied of ideologies, moralisms, dogmatics, and ritualism. Such a cultural context lets us reevaluate genuine religious experience. Faith needs the experience of conversion and prayer so that it can produce a theology that respects mystery. It knows that, when compared with the Mystery, all our knowing is approximate and all our talking is a stutter. It is because of this transcendence of the Mystery that we must avoid falling into a type of mystical fideism, or heresy of feeling that all are already one without conversion. That is also why we *are in duty bound to offer a generous welcome and spiritual support to all those who, moved by a thirst for God and a desire to live the demands of faith, turn* to us (*Vita Consecrata*, 103).

Mystical Experience

I wish to speak now about mystical experience, not about mysticism. 'Mysticism' refers to a perceptible cultural phenomenon characterized by an opening to religious values. The mystical experience, about which I now wish to speak, concerns the direct apprehension of one's interiority, the experience of deep presence and communion from within one's own depths. More concretely, I wish to speak about christian mysticism, understood as an experience of faith through the interiorization of the christian Mystery.

Let us say at once that the 'Mystery of Faith' sums up and contains in itself the whole of christian life and existence. *The Church professes this mystery in the Apostles' Creed and celebrates it in the sacramental liturgy, so that the life of the faithful may be conformed to Christ in the Holy Spirit to the glory of God the Father. This mystery, then, requires that the faithful believe in it, that they celebrate it, and that they live from it in a vital and personal relationship with the living and true God. This relationship is prayer* (Catechism of the Catholic Church, 2558).

Mystery

The human person, as an intelligent and free being, is oriented to mystery from within, by a need that will never disappear. This orientation, which springs from the person's deepest roots, is what constitutes him or her precisely as a person. Men and women of all places and times tell us that the mystery is reflected in all of *nature*. Thus, they speak of '*that other*' reality. Artists and poets go further and intuit that this bewitching and seducing *I-know-not-what*, is something that goes beyond all beauty perceived by the senses or understood by human reasoning. Philosophers, for their part, know that in the depths of *all being* there is something that has always been known yet remains always *unknown*. Through the centuries, anthropology has taught that the human being should not wander far from *itself* in order to find the *mystery*. Yet, to designate it, different religious traditions speak of '*the totally other*'.

What concerns us now is the biblical and New Testament meaning of the mystery. Saint Paul tells us that the mystery is that divine secret that can only be known through revelation. It is identified with divine wisdom and the divine will (1 Co 2:7; Ep 1:9). What we as human beings could not have known by our own powers has been revealed through *sheer grace* by:

- God himself (Ep 1:9; Col 1:26).

- God's Spirit (1 Co 2:10).

- the prophetic Scriptures (Rm 16:26).

In particular, the mystery consists in the divine plan of salvation achieved by the paschal death and resurrection of Christ, together with all the good gifts promised to those who are saved. In this way, the mystery of God (Col 2:2) is equivalent to the mystery of Christ (Col 4:3; Ep 3:4). It is:

- Christ himself (Col 1:27).

- Christ crucified (1 Co 1:23).

- *Christ in you* (Col 1:27).

The best pauline text on the mystery is the following one: *He* [God the Father] *has given us the wisdom to understand fully the mystery of his will, the plan he was pleased to decree in Christ, to be carried out in the fullness of time: namely, to bring all things in the heavens and on earth into one under Christ's headship* (Ep 1:9–10; cf. the entire hymn of Ep 1, as well as Col 1:25–26).

Actually, the whole life of Christ is mystery, not just his Incarnation and Passover. His humanity itself is the primary sign of what divinity is. What is visible in his earthly life leads to the hidden, invisible mystery of his divine sonship and universal mission of salvation. Jesus himself during his public life told his followers: *Knowledge of the mysteries of the kingdom of heaven has been granted to you* (Mt 13:11, and parallels). The granting of this revelation was a cause of great joy for him: *I give praise to you, Father, Lord of heaven and earth, for although you have hidden these things from the wise and the learned you have revealed them to the childlike. Yes, Father, such has been your gracious will. All things have been handed over to me by my Father. No one knows the Son except the Father, and no one knows the Father except the Son and anyone to whom the Son wishes to reveal him* (Mt 11:25–27, and parallels).

In the light of all this, it is easy to understand what we read in the Catechism of the Catholic Church: *Spiritual progress tends toward ever more intimate union with Christ. This union is called 'mystical' because it participates in the mystery of Christ through the sacraments— 'the holy mysteries'—and, in him, in the mystery of the Holy Trinity. God calls us all to this intimate union with him, even if the special graces of extraordinary signs of this mystical life are granted only to some for the sake of manifesting the gratuitous gift given to all* (*CCC*, 2014).

Epígnosis

The words of Jesus quoted above tell us that there is no *full-knowledge (epígnosis)* of God without the mediation of divine grace. It is a gift meant for all, but undelivered to the proud and given to the humble. Once again we find that Saint Paul has an interesting instruction on *full-knowledge*, a doctrine that is one of the foundations of the christian teaching on contemplation (cf. Ph 1:9–10; Ep 1:15–19; 3:14–19; Col 1:3–5, 9–12; 2:2–3; 3:9–14; Phm 4–6). We can see here that Paul prays for the gift of *full-knowledge* on behalf of all his hearers and readers, not just for a select group from among them. In his own life, *full-knowledge* and the apostolic ministry are mutually necessary; Paul preaches what he lives (Ep 3:1–3; Col 1:24–29).

This type of knowledge is closely related to the theological virtues. It is based on faith, but differs from it by a certain dynamic quality. It goes hand in hand with charity, which is both its source and its fruit, and it opens the way to the promised treasures of hope. *Full-knowledge* is an integral part of faith, hope, and charity, being an experience of faith and charity that lets one touch what is hoped for.

The object of *full-knowledge* can be summed up as the intimate life of God and his saving will given by Christ in the Spirit. Its immediate result is an authentically christian life. At the same time *full-knowledge* of Christ requires the practice of virtue, counter to the teaching of some gnostics! Virtue bears fruit in *full-knowledge*; there is no *theoria* without *praxis*, no contemplation without ascetic self-denial (cf. II Pet 1:5–11).

The text of Saint Luke about the disciples of Emmaus (Lk 24:13–35) shows us something more about *full-knowledge*. Divinely revealed Scripture lights the fire of love and, in the eucharistic banquet that follows, *full-knowledge* communes with God by knowing him through a communion of love.

In the final analysis, the charism of *full-knowledge* is similar to the gift of *wisdom* (1 Co 2:6–16) and to the *understanding* that John talks about in his first Epistle (1 Jn 5:20; cf. 2:3–5; 4:7–8, 13, 16; Jn 14:21–23).

Experience

The richer the objective revealed reality, the deeper and more trans-forming will be its subjective experience. It is dangerous to forget that moral life needs dogma and that spirituality—the *existence of faith*—needs theology, which is the *understanding of faith*. In any case, is not mystical experience the flowering of revealed truth, just as revealed truth is the root of mystical experience?

Throughout the twelfth century, the cistercian century, there reigned a beautiful balance between the objective and subjective aspects of christian mystical experience. Revelation was not thought of as a series of truths that were external to the human person, but rather as life that transforms and fulfills the person, since it satisfies the deepest longings of the human heart. Personal experience re-mained always subject to the objectivity of the revealed fact: *Follow the dictates of faith and not those of your own experience*, because it is only through faith that you can hold fast to what you cannot grasp with your mind (Bernard, *Quad* 5:5; *SC* 76:6). Mystical experience is thus a reality of grace that accompanies the entire life of the one who believes, transforming it from light to clarity and from glowing embers to blazing fire.

Experience is a basic building block in the teaching of the first Cistercians. The reason is simple: all their spirituality is based on love. Therefore, it is not strange that they invite us to spiritual experience and desire it ardently.

> *Let your voice sound in my ears, good Jesus, so that my heart may learn how to love you, my mind how to love you, the inmost being of my soul how to love you. Let the inmost core of my heart embrace you, my one and only true good, my dear and delightful joy . . . I pray you, Lord, let but a drop of your surpassing sweetness fall upon my soul, that by it the bread of her bitterness may become sweet. In experiencing a drop of this may she have a foretaste of what to desire, what to long for, what to sigh for here in her pilgrimage. In her hunger let her have a foretaste, in her thirst let her drink. For those who eat*

you will still hunger and those who drink you will still thirst (Aelred, *Mirror* I,1;2).

The most frequent use of the word in the works of Bernard and Aelred is in their teaching on the most common spiritual experience, namely that of spiritual searching and growth, the experience of love on the way to God as it passes through different stages or degrees. This experience of love is shown at its clearest and strongest in one's free consent to God's will: *You must seek the Word, in order to consent to it. He himself will achieve this in you* (Bernard, *SC* 85:1).

Obviously, our cistercian fathers and mothers are aware of specifically mystical experience even though they do not always distinguish its more or less extraordinary features. They use a wide vocabulary and many symbols to speak of it, like: rest, Sabbath, ecstasy, visits, rapture, kisses, embrace, union, elevation, leisure, marriage, unity of spirit, and deification. For them, ascetical and mystical experiences are two realities that are joined together in a single supernatural thrust of the human person toward God.

Then, beginning with the fifteenth century, the subjective aspect begins to predominate in mystical writings. Mystical experience refers to the personal, affective, conscious experience of the Mystery through knowledge and love, thanks to a special divine gift. Its different elements are emphasized and analyzed: God's action increasing the capacity of the subject; the new light of knowledge and love; active passivity; the intuition of the divine Presence; mutual union and communication. These experiences can refer either to the mystery of the inner life of the triune God or to the mystery of his saving will. It all comes through Christ in the Spirit.

It is not hard to distinguish different types of experiences within the almost infinite number of possibilities for dialogue between God and his human creatures. A simple reading of the spiritual classics lets us speak of mystical experiences that are:

• **substantial**: such as infused contemplation, loving

knowledge, warm light, bright flame, hidden presence. Emphasis is put either on knowledge, in the affirmative or *kataphatic* way, or on love, in the negative or *apophatic* way.

- **ordinary**: with presences and absences, consolations and desolations, desire and love.

- **accidental**: with a variety of phenomena, such as ecstasy, raptures, visions, locutions, revelations, touches, and the like.

- **apostolic**: characterized by acting with Christ who saves in history.

- **cosmic**: finding God through nature, which can reveal him or make his presence known.

Substantial and ordinary mystical experiences are a normal part of the life of grace and of growth in the theological virtues. It is in this sense that every baptized person is a mystic. That is why a mystic is not a special person. He or she experiences the same things as any other Christian, but in a different way. Similarly, the grace of God acts in a mystic as in any other person, but the mystic knows that grace is at work.

In our monastic context, marked as it is by the cistercian tradition, the most common experiences of the Mystery usually have to do with compunction of heart, God's liberating goodness, the *alternatio* of spiritual states, the desire of the infinite or absolute, the desert with its fascinating and transforming darkness, serving the community with the Beloved and resting in him.

Obviously there are an infinite number of degrees of intensity in these experiences. It will depend on the torrent of God's generosity and on the receiver's capacity for them. They are usually more intense at moments of change or transition, such as a conversion or a decision that will affect the future. Times of intense desert aridity also cause a greater sensitivity to God's action. On the other hand, it must be said that such experiences can often happen without the help of any known or appropriate cause, even though they are helped by a climate of faith, hope, and charity lived patiently in daily life. Often they become more habitual and result in an underlying state of *chiaroscuro,* somewhat like predawn or dusk, in which you can speak of neither light nor darkness. In any case, these experiences often accompany us throughout our life in the Spirit. They play an important role in our process of ongoing conversion and their final purpose is to conform us to the image and likeness of Christ the Lord.

I will briefly elaborate here three of the experiences just mentioned. You will easily see that they are closely related to each other.

The Desert

Few persons pass much time in a monastery without experiencing the fact that growth along the way leading into the Mystery implies a deep process of purifying simplification. This process is usually a disconcerting one and makes us enter into crisis. The truth is that our superficiality is blocking a deeper level and our complexity is fighting God's simplicity. We are floating corks that are hard to sink and wrinkled raisins whose skin resists being smoothed, so when the Lord does this, it hurts.

What is most disconcerting, however, is that penetrating into the divine Mystery is usually experienced as dryness or a desert. In practice this means that there is great difficulty in freely using our faculties—intellect, will, memory, emotions—during the times dedicated exclusively to prayer. This difficulty seems to have little to do with *epígnosis,* mystical experience, or contemplation, at least with our ideas about such things.

Such relative inability to use our faculties can last for months or years. What is happening? It is simply a greater infusion of faith-hope-love. It is a purification of our reception of the faith and a simplification of our love so that we can become more capable of receiving God.

In this theological desert, which lets us enter into the Mystery, the inability to use our faculties is accompanied by other common experiences, such as the absence of sensible enjoyment from both the realities of God and the things of the world; an eager remembrance of God that is at the same time painful; a feeling of going backwards yet with practical fruits of progress; some type of deep, hidden peace in God and a desire to rest quietly in him. There is no sensible consolation in this desert, but there is fidelity—on the Lord's part to us and on ours to him.

It is important to distinguish between the desert experience and an experience of depression; and between feeling 'depressed' and a real clinical depression. In the desert, despite possible feelings of being 'depressed', we sense that we are going forward toward . . . something we do not know. Now and then we become aware of the fruits of our conversion and can use our faculties normally in daily life outside of prayer. It is different in a clinical depression, where one goes around in circles with a general loss of meaning in daily life and no positive fruit; one's attention is so centered on self that it blocks every other type of activity.

Whoever is mysteriously entering through the desert into the Mystery need not do much, since he or she is being remade. One's cooperation with the divine work of grace is reduced to:

- persevering with humility and submission to the Lord.

- abandoning oneself in peace and love into his hands.

- cooperating when possible with simple acts of faith, hope and love.

Perhaps the best that can be done is to pray in confidence with William of Saint-Thierry:

Forgive me, Lord; forgive my heart's impatience for you. I seek your face; by your own gift, I see your countenance, lest you should turn it from me at the last. I know indeed and I am sure that those who walk in the light of your countenance do not fall but walk in safety, and by your face their every judgment is directed. They are the living people, for their life is lived according to what they read and see in your face, as in an exemplar. Lord, I dare not look upon your face against your will, lest I be further confounded. Needy and beggared and blind, I stand in your presence, seen by you though I do not see you. And, standing thus, I offer you my heart full of desire for you, the whole of whatever I am, the whole of whatever I can do, the whole of whatever I know, and the very fact that I so yearn and faint for you. But the way to find you, that I do not find (Meditations, 3:3).

Unfortunately, not all monks and nuns are like William; many of us abandon the way that is leading us through the desert to the deep, restful valleys of the Mystery.

The dark, transforming experience of the desert is usually intensified during thanksgiving after Eucharistic Communion. This is very understandable, since the Eucharist is the mystery of faith that mystically transforms the person who enters into it. No moment of the monastic day is more mystical than the time immediately following the celebration of the Eucharist.

May the Lord grant that nothing take us away from the *secret of intimate contemplation* or from *friendship with solitude (amica solitudine)*. May we know how to let go of everything that is useless, unnecessary, or disturbing to our *friendship with quiet (amicam quietem)*, due to its incompatibility with our way of life. (Bernard, *Letters* 237:3; 143:1).

Desire

Bernard of Clairvaux, as a student in the school of Saint Augustine, teaches us that desire is undifferentiated psychic energy that searches with increasingly insistent urgency for what we need. Desire expresses a feeling of absence and is a movement that drives our entire being toward the absent good: *Every rational being naturally desires always what satisfies more its mind and will. It is never satisfied with something that lacks the qualities it thinks it should have* (*Dil* 7:18; cf. *SC* 58:2; 31:4; 32:2).

Desire for the infinite shows both the finiteness and the fullness of the human being. It is a precious footprint of the Creator in the human soul. In this sense, desire is a basic thrust of the spirit, a psychic sigh, in which the desire for God can take root. Desire is the underlying source and root of love. When it bursts into consciousness and becomes the willed search for God, it is converted into the love and desire for God. God is touched by *desiderii digito, the finger of desire*, as Saint Bernard says (*SC* 28:10). When the *soul* has nothing of its own, nothing in its exclusive possession, but has everything in common with God, it is called a *spouse*. This spouse, who whispers, *Let him kiss me with the kiss of his mouth*, is a *soul athirst for God* (*SC* 7:2). It boils down to saying that we are desire, because God is Desire in us. He arouses our desire in order to awaken and to satisfy our hope. That is why desire is grace.

Our desire for God refers both to God himself and to our own entrance into communion with him. What is paradoxical about this experience is that the desire for God implies that he is absent yet, at the same time, we cannot desire him unless he is present. This alternation between presence and absence awakens our desire and keeps it burning. Saint Bernard says, *Unless we use the utmost vigilance in attending to these gift-laden visits of the Holy Spirit, we shall neither desire him when he seems absent nor praise him when he is present* (*SC* 17:1–2). The abbot of Clairvaux speaks again from his own experience when he says, *As long as I live, the word 'return', the word of recall, will be on my lips to recall the Word. As often as he slips away from me, so often shall I call him back. From the burning desire of my heart I will not cease to call him, begging him to return, as if calling after someone who is departing. I will implore him to give back to me the joy of his salvation and give himself back to me* (*SC* 74:7).

The cistercian nuns of the thirteenth century exemplified in their lives the spiritual teaching of the cistercian fathers of the preceding century, especially the teachings of Bernard and William about the soul as spouse, thirsting in burning desires for love. In her work, *The Seven Manners of Loving (which come down from the highest place and which return again to the summit from which they came)*, Beatrice of Nazareth presents seven experiences of love that are to be expected in the context of growing in christian life. The experience of desire, in its active and passive forms, is the key to her whole work. In the fourth manner of loving, Beatrice offers us a description of the soul's first passive experience of the power of God's love. The experience is simply a restoration of God's likeness that had been lost.

> *In the fourth manner of loving, Our Lord is also accustomed to give other manners of loving, at one time with great pleasure, but at another with great sorrow. I wish to speak of this now. Sometimes it happens that love is sweetly awakened in the soul, rising up with joy, and flows in the heart without any human collaboration. And then the heart is so touched with tender love, is drawn toward love with such desire, is so strongly held by love and so passionately embraced by love, that it is totally conquered by love. In this the heart feels a great closeness to God, a substantial clarity, a wonderful delight, a noble freedom and a strict necessity of obeying love. The soul then experiences fullness and superabundance. It feels all its senses sanctified in love, its will turned into love and so deeply immersed and absorbed in the abyss of love that it is made wholly into love.*

Closer to our day, Blessed Rafael Arnáiz Barón (1911–1938) exemplifies perfectly that *cor inquietum*, that restless heart burning with infinite desire for God. Everything in Rafael's life is explained by his desires for God, for the Absolute and for eternity:

> *I long for eternal life . . . I long to fly to true life. My soul longs and groans to see God, tied as it is to the body . . . Life will be space and light where this little spark of love which I carry in me will expand, catch fire, see your Face and give out more light than the sun . . . I am giddy, sick from the love of God. I long for Christ! How can I*

help it? . . . The thirsty deer looks frantically for a hidden spring of water where it knows it can rest from its exhaustion and the water will calm its thirst . . . Lord, Lord, as the deer yearns for running streams . . . I yearn to love divinely. I suffer from living here . . . I long for eternal life (Writings, Dec. 9, 1936)!

Moved by his great desire and after a period of deep suffering, Rafael passed his final days longing for Christ, *whom I love and adore above everything else, whom I sigh for, suffer for and weep for, and for whose sake—you know it, good Jesus—I would gladly lose my mind (Writings,* March 20, 1938).

In other words, desire is the living impulse that, together with truth and action, constitutes the deepest orientation and drive of a human being toward something more complete, final, and absolute. Without desire for God, there is no communion of love with God. Desire is, therefore, hunger and thirst for the infinite, a life process unable to be satisfied, and an existential groan of hope.

I have spoken of 'desire' in the singular to distinguish it from 'desires' in the plural. The latter are explosive fragments of true desire that have become misdirected toward something finite, toward illusions or simply toward self-satisfaction. These so-called 'desires' are what psychoanalysis is speaking of when it tells us that desire is a regressive phenomenon that prevents self-gift and self-fulfillment, and that, as separate beings, we are full of desires to recover our lost fusion.

Zeal

The person who has entered into the mystery of divine fire burns for the salvation of the world. This salvation is the manifestation of the glory of God and itself gives God glory. If our life is hidden with Christ in God, we cannot help burning with zeal for good works, that is, for the salvation of all people, which is what gives God glory. When the Lord sends someone in a mission of service, he actually goes with that person. Moreover, for the person who loves, being with Christ and serving him are almost the same thing.

> *When the Bridegroom perceives, as he always does, that the bride has taken her rest for some time on his bosom, he does not hesitate to entice her out again to what seems more serviceable. It is not that she is unwilling, or that he himself is doing what he had forbidden. But if the bride is enticed by the Bridegroom this is because she receives from him the desire by which she is enticed, the desire of good works, the desire to bring forth fruit for the Bridegroom, for to her the Bridegroom is life, and death is gain. And that desire is vehement. It urges her not only to arise but to arise quickly for we read: 'Arise, make haste, and come'. It is no small consolation to her that she hears 'come' and not 'go', knowing from this that she is being invited rather than sent, and that the Bridegroom will be coming with her . . . She is not therefore aroused against her will when what happens is already her will, for it is no other than an instilled eagerness for a holy profit* (Bernard, SC 58:1–2).

Gratuitous, oblational love, that seeks not its own benefit, knows how to sacrifice its own good for the spiritual good of one's neighbor. *Love which seeks not its own benefit*, as Saint Bernard says to his monks, *has long since convinced me not to prefer my own cherished desires to your gain. To pray, to read, to write, to meditate, or any other gains that may result from the study of spiritual things; these I consider loss because of you* (SC 51:3; cf. 52:7). However, the primacy of service is authentic only when it is based on the desire and deep joy of always being with the Lord.

> *The spirit is affected in one way when it is made fruitful by the Word, in another way when it enjoys the Word. In the one it is considering the needs of its neighbor; in the other it is allured by the sweetness of the Word. As a mother, she is happy in her child, but as a bride, she is even happier in her bridegroom's embrace. The children are dear, they are a pledge of his love, but his kisses give her greater pleasure. It is good to save many souls, but there is far more pleasure in going aside to be with the Word* (Bernard, SC 85:13).

Charity, or 'communion of wills', synthesizes being a spouse and being a mother, prayer and action, mystical experience and social commitment. This brings me back to placing mystical experience within the framework of our cenobitic—not to say simply christian—life. For Saint Bernard love, or charity, is a *common will* shared with God and those with whom we live (cf. *Pasc* 3:3; *VNat* 3:6). When this will is not common to the persons we live with, it is very probably not shared by God either. Love of neighbor nourishes and purifies the love of God that already exists, while love of God crowns love of neighbor (*Div* 121; *I Sent* 21).

This love of neighbor, or *social love*, plays a decisive role in the growth of the spiritual life toward mystical love. The schemata and vocabulary can vary, but the doctrine remains the same.

- There are three grades of *truth*: in oneself, by *judging oneself*; in one's neighbor, by *having compassion on him*; and in God, by *contemplating him* (Bernard, *Hum* 6; cf. 19–20).

- There are four degrees of *love*: love of self for oneself but open to social love of neighbor; love of God for oneself; love of God for himself; and love of oneself for God (*Dil* 23–33, 39–40).

- There are three *sabbaths*, or periods of rest: love of self, love of neighbor, love of God (Aelred, *Spec car* III:1–6).

In the last analysis, *No one has ever seen God. Yet, if we love one another, God remains in us, and his love is brought to perfection in us* (1 Jn 4:12). Let us rest, then, in the shade of the love of God and neighbor. *Both loves are mine when I love you, Lord Jesus, my neighbor because you are a man and showed mercy to me, and nevertheless you are God over all, blessed for ever* (Bernard, *SC* 60:10).

If we monks and nuns of the third millennium are not mystics, we will not be cenobites either. In such a case, we will mean very little, or else we will be a counter-witness and—perhaps for some, God forbid—a cause of scandal. Therefore, at this hour of human history, at this moment of cultural transition, we monks and nuns must turn our lives with a new decisiveness toward the Mystery, so as to be mystically transformed by it. Our christian mystical experience is, in the last analysis, an experience of being reformed and conformed to Christ. This is the only way we can offer guidance for the dawn of a new age and provide religious witness for the secular world of today. This alone is how we can give the help that is so vitally necessary in the dialogue with other religions and in our contemplative service to the christian Churches.

Although it may seem paradoxical, what is needed today are prophets who announce that the God of Christians was more dead than what a certain modern atheism affirmed. It was death from the cerebral, masculine theological rationalism of some 'believers'. However, God is much less dead than what some were saying, thanks to the feminine intuition springing from the heart of many unknown mystics. Among the latter is she who loved with all her heart, with all her soul, with all her strength, and was full of grace. She thus became Mother of Love, whose Father is the God of Love.

THE TWENTIETH CENTURY
AND THE RISEN JESUS

Circular letter to the members of the Order,
March 20, 2000

Dear Brothers and Sisters,

We have left the nineteen–hundreds behind and begun the two–thousands. This does not yet mean a change of century, only of numbers. Only when we begin the year 2001 will we be able to say we are in the twenty-first century. In any case, this is of little importance. Our way of measuring time is not the only one; there are other calendars and other cultures besides our own.

The human being is a time-bound being whose life is measured by succession: before, now, and after. As *homo viator*, we can only come to maturity by going on pilgrimage through time, letting ourselves be shaped by events while at the same time participating in them and contributing to the task of history. Yet this is not all, as Christians we affirm that time has come to a certain *fullness and completion* (Cf. Gal 4:4) by the very fact that God has entered into human history, eternity into time.

In this sense, the year 2000 has a very particular meaning for us. Exact chronological calculations aside, we are celebrating the 2000 years since the birth of Christ, a cause for special rejoicing and gladness. In order to sanctify this moment and help us to celebrate it better, the Church has summoned us to the Great Jubilee of the year 2000.

Though the Great Jubilee retains its connection with the three dimensions of time and with our hope in eternity, it also involves looking back to the most basic and permanent foundation of our life and history, and opening ourselves to it once again. In this sense, the Jubilee means orienting ourselves toward the future and at the same time opening the prison of time in order to gain free access to the one who remains forever: Jesus, died and risen for our glorification.

I would like to begin this circular letter with two conciliar texts taken from the Constitution on the Church in the Modern World, *Gaudium et Spes*:

> *The joys and the hopes, the griefs and the anxieties of the men of this age, especially those who are poor or in any way afflicted, these too are the joys and hopes, the griefs and anxieties of the followers of Christ. Indeed, nothing genuinely human fails to raise an echo in their hearts . . . That is why the Church realizes that it is truly and intimately linked with mankind and its history* (GS 1; cf. 4).
>
> *The Church believes that Christ, who died and was raised up for all, can through his Spirit offer man the light and the strength to measure up to his supreme destiny . . . She likewise holds that in her most benign Lord and Master can be found the key, the focal point, and the goal of all human history. The Church also maintains that beneath all changes there are many realities that do not change and that have their ultimate foundation in Christ, who is the same yesterday and today, yes and forever* (GS 10).

These words invite us to cross the threshold of the Millennium, arm in arm with all of humanity, following the Risen Jesus, the Lord of all time. As the Cistercian Order of the Strict Observance, we are aware of being in deep fellowship with the twentieth century. Since we came to birth at the same time, its pain and joy, its progress, its lapses and vicissitudes were also our own.

In two previous circular letters, we have already contemplated together on the worldwide and ecclesial context and on present-day culture, all of which served as a framework to help us understand our cistercian identity, intimately bound up as it is with the mystical dimension of christian life.

I now invite you to recall the past in order that we may walk securely in the present and project ourselves into the future. Let us contemplate the **twentieth century** and look behind its many people and events in order to discover the **Risen Jesus**. Let us awaken our faith in the Lord of history, the faith of yesterday, today and always, and let us work accordingly.

OUR TWENTIETH CENTURY

A first look

There was no lack of **contradictions** in the nineteen–hundreds. It was at the same time a century of great massacres and of great economic development, a century of mass democracies and of totalitarian dictatorships, of globalization and of aggressive nationalism, of technology at the service of both life and death, of nuclear peace and innumerable wars.

Various key **words** were coined and often heard. Each of them characterized a complex reality in a simple way. Not everyone today will know all of them, but they are worth recalling: nation, psychoanalysis, liberalism, protectionism, socialism, communism, democracy, totalitarianism, popularism, progress, modernization, radicalism, development, secularization, atomic, genocide, peace, ecology, technology, cybernetics, bioethics, globalization . . . the list could continue.

Already at the beginning of the 1960s, it was being announced that: *Today, the human race is passing through a new stage of its history. Profound and rapid changes are spreading by degrees around the whole world* (GS 4). This statement proved to be even more true in the years that followed. It is safe to say, then, that history has never before undergone such acceleration. Never have changes been so rapid and far-reaching. Never have the agents of change been so varied.

A few dates appear to have signaled irreversible **transitions**: the war of 1914–1918, the Bolshevik revolution of 1917, the economic and commercial crisis of the 1930s, the great war of 1939–1945, the de-colonization of Asia (1946–1948) and Africa (1957–1967), the Second Vatican Council (1962–1965), the conquest of the moon in 1969, the collapse of communism along with the fall of the Berlin Wall and the end of the Cold War in 1989, the world-wide commercial 'boom' of the early 1990s and the new world order following the 'Gulf War' in 1991.

Relative to all that has been said, there is also need to mention certain barriers that have been overcome, the kinds of **development** or progress that years ago seemed impossible or unthinkable: the elimination of age-old diseases, interplanetary voyages, nuclear research, manipulation of human genes, nearly instantaneous communication around the globe, the rise in population, increased life-expectancy, rapidly rising literacy rates, the new mega-cities, and so on.

In spite all of this we also note another characteristic of our twentieth century, namely the **inequalities** of the past that have continued into our own day. The transformations just mentioned have not altered the hierarchies that were in place at the beginning of the century. The nations of North America and Western Europe are still the wealthiest, even though Japan and a few countries of eastern Asia and the Arab world have attained a greater level of prosperity than ever before. The inequalities that already existed are now abysmal: a rich one-fifth of the world population controls eighty percent of the resources, while yet another one-fifth made up of the poor has access to barely one percent of the resources. The other three-fifths make do with nineteen percent.

From the 'gender' point of view, the inequalities are even more noticeable. Women carry out sixty-three percent of the work done in the world but possess only one percent of the cultivated land and receive only ten percent of the world income. Seven-five percent of the world's poor are women, as are seventy percent of the world's illiterate.

Most historians and critics agree that the twentieth century has been marked both by **violence** and **war** on the one hand, and by **notable progress** on the other: that is to say, the scientific progress (developments in computer science, communications, and medicine), civil progress (the spread of democracy, the new social role of women, the development of international organizations) and ecological progress (care for the environment) that stand out over the last one hundred years. Our present pope, in just a few words, makes an intuitive synthesis of our century's situation: *Our times are both momentous and fascinating* (*Redemptor Missio* 38).

General features

The characteristic features that give our century a particular face and a well-defined identity are many. Most likely, if we take them together as a whole, we can come up with something concrete. Looking to the past and then centering our attention on the present, we can say that the twentieth century was:

- the century of **freedom**: both because of the end of colonial imperialism in Asia and Africa, and because democratic systems, overcoming various totalitarian regimes, have gained over half of humanity.

- the century of **capitalism**: political freedom usually goes hand in hand with economic freedom. With the overthrow of the communist system, the economic structure of over half the world's societies is capitalistic.

- the century of **electronics**: if printing reduced the cost of communication and information to one-one thousandth, the transistor radio brought it down to one-one millionth. The result has been a shift from the industrial era to the era of technology and computer science.

- the century of the **massive market and the market of the masses**: everything is produced in the greatest quantities possible for the greatest possible number of consumers.

- the century of **genocides**: from the dramatic genocide of the Armenians hidden beneath the euphemism 'necessary military evacuation of the war zone' (1915), to the 'holocaust' of the Jewish people, to more recent versions such as 'ethnic cleansing', 'crimes against humanity', and 'forced evacuation.' The numbers vary, but the brutality of the deed remains the same.

- the century of the **'new barbarians'** (from the Third World): who make peaceful invasions by emigrating to the technological-industrial countries of the First World, thus modifying the make-up of these societies and giving rise to the reactions of racist minorities.

- the century of the **unforeseen**: quite simply because so many unexpected things came about, which confirms the statement: history is given new direction by the unexpected.

We can add to this another characteristic that left its mark on the twentieth century, namely that it led to a **new era of revolutions**:

- the **digital** revolution: we are moving from 'voice recognition' to 'artificial intelligence'.

- the **biotechnical** revolution: which will end up either performing miracles or creating new monsters.

- the revolution against the **democratic system**: either in the form of tribalism (minorities that gain strength), fundamentalism (the manipulative simplification of society), totalitarianism (the rejection of individual freedom), or others.

- the revolution against the **capitalist system**: as advocated by ecology (to defend the health of the planet against the threats of 'progress'), or through various forms of socialism (since a few live at the expense of many and since many are excluded from the prevalent world-order), or by radical feminism (with its more global view of the human person and its project of significantly transforming the current system of relationships).

Is it possible, then, to make a unitary interpretation of the twentieth century? That is to say, is it possible to find **one feature** that in itself embodies our century's identity? Many historians have tried to meet this challenge. They would all agree that the study of history has to seek to understand events in terms of individual and collective responsibility, in terms of human motivations and consequences. It is an attempt to make a unitary synthesis of the most fundamental orientations. Contemporary historians would also agree that, with the year 2000, it is not only a century that is coming to an end, but also an historical epoch, that is, a period with a character all its own, represented perhaps by an emblematic figure or a particularly eminent personage.

230 Circular Letters to the Members of the Order

There are several such synthetic interpretations of the twentieth century. From a northwestern point of view it might be called:

- a **'short century'**: the central meaning of the century is to be found in the events that took place between the First World War and the end of the Soviet Empire.

- the century of the **'great illusion'**: the illusion consisted in thinking that human history is based on an intrinsic rational necessity, leading to Bolshevik communism.

- the century of the **'end of history'**: with the end of the ideological conflict and the victory of capitalism over communism, history has reached its culmination and, consequently, its end.

- the century of **'fear'**: fear of war, of hunger, of robbery, of terrorism, of dictatorships, etc.

- a century of **'civic passions'**: movements of women's suffrage, human rights, or colonial independence.

- a **'failed'** century: since the phantoms that haunted its beginning are still there at its end: nationalism, racism, violence, lack of respect for the human person, etc.

- the century of **'ideological wars'**: between 1914 and 1945 two bloody wars took place in Europe and around the world, while between 1945 and 1991 there were yet other conflicts on the national level in Korea, Vietnam, Afghanistan, etc.

- the century of a **'bipolar world'**: centered on two great superpowers, the United States and Russia, with their respective spheres of influence and satellite countries.

This diversity of answers clearly shows us that it is not easy to make a single evaluation and synthesis of one hundred years of human history. Moreover, what would it look like if our point of view was the East or the South?

The primacy of shared responsibilities.

A half-century ago, more precisely in 1945, the liberal and capitalist democracies of England, France and the United States, together with the Union of Soviet Socialist Republics, overcame the totalitarian and imperialist threat of Germany, Italy, and Japan. Following the war, there began the silent confrontation between Russia and the United States. At the same time, the defeated former powers were given help to reconstruct democracy and economic well-being. The new nations Asia and Africa, freed from the colonial yoke, did not create new social, political, and economic alternatives; instead, nearly all of them fell in line with the communist or capitalist systems. The fall of Russian communism demonstrated the **superior efficiency** of the liberal capitalist economy and greater adaptability of democratic systems.

Consequently, from the geo-political and socio-economic point of view, everything seems to indicate that the Euro-American west has come out as the winner in a century marked by so many conflicts. More precisely, we can see that the United States of North America currently exercises the **greatest influence** on the economic, social, political, and cultural world order. The globalization of industrial and technological capitalism is due to its uncontested supremacy. In the 'global village' of our contemporary world, North American culture so dominates languages and communications that everyone depends on it in one form or other.

Nevertheless, the Euro-American west has not been the only leading actor in the century ending. **Other important influences** have played and are playing their part, perhaps increasingly so. Global capitalism is unthinkable today without the self-determination of the Latin American, Asiatic, and African countries. This has imposed a more democratic character on international exchanges. Likewise, the inclusion of players who were formerly excluded from the democratic game—such as women, workers, racial and religious minorities—has become possible, thanks to their struggles to recover their rights. Moreover, such phenomena as China's resurgence, Japan's wealth of tradition and technology, India's reserve of human and spiritual values, Africa's deep sense of identity with the land, southeast Asia's capitalism, and the Islamic world's growth remind us that the world's future is not only in the Euro-American West.

We are all more and more aware that the 'poly-centric' world of the twenty-first century—even though a single superpower acts as 'international policeman'—requires a **joint effort** toward peace and universal concord by means of dialogue, the recognition of the dignity of all parties, and a strengthening of international institutions. Above all, we must also recognize that universal concord can come about only by means of efforts for reconciliation and mutual forgiveness.

Let us listen to someone who has been a traveling companion for several generations during the century we are now concluding, someone who has a sense of being invested with a *universal fatherhood*, who embraces all men and women of this age, without distinction:

> *But one question can be asked: was this century also the century of 'brotherhood'? Certainly an unqualified answer cannot be given. For this reason, it seems to me that the century we are beginning ought to be a century of solidarity. We know one thing today more than in the past: we will never be happy and at peace without one another, much less if some are against others. . . . Never again must there be separation between people! Never again must some be opposed to others! Everyone must live together, under God's watchful eyes! . . . We are all responsible for all* (John Paul II, Address to the Diplomatic Corps, 10 January, 2000).

The Church and the ocso

This is not the place to show how the great political, social, economic, and cultural events of the past century have affected or are
affecting our own monastic cistercian history. Nor will I attempt
here to chronicle the life of the Church and the Order over the
century, since this would take us beyond the scope of a letter such
as this.

It does seem, however, opportune to remember that our interpretation of history cannot be just a history, be it secular or sacred. As
dwellers on the frontier between this world and the next, we
must read history as a place of grace-filled and saving encounter
between God and humankind, as well as a place of the disgraceful
encounter between the City of God and the city of Satan.

We might say, then, that the **history of humanity** is not what we
see and read about everyday in the newspapers and the latest reports.
None of these takes into account the hand of divine Providence
guiding the ultimate course of events. *That the earthly and the heavenly
city penetrate each other is a fact accessible to faith alone. It remains a mystery
of human history* (GS 40). What really orients and directs the path of
humankind's history is the radical search for the Kingdom of God
and his justice, following the Risen One, trusting that all the rest
will be given as well.

Concerning the **history of the Church**, then, there is even more
reason to affirm that the human and divine dimensions are at work
simultaneously. Revealed mystery is received with faith and lived
out in specific times and places. Since the Order's history is part of
the Church's history, what is said of the Church also applies to the
Order. The history of the Order is a humanly conditioned history
and, at the same time, is caught up in the saving plan of the God
of Love. There are two active forces working and cooperating in
our history: the Spirit of Christ and each one of us. While it is easy
to make out the footprints we ourselves have left over time and in

various places, it is difficult to perceive traces of God since they elude any 'when' or 'where'.

In the history of the Church, and of the Order as well, each **Jubilee** or anniversary is prepared by divine Providence. It is an invitation to each of us—according to each one's grace and at the appropriate time—to look over the history of the Church and the Order with the eyes of a believer, especially over the last one hundred years, in order to give thanks, to convert ourselves, to assimilate it all, and to give praise.

To give thanks and praise especially for all the **signs of hope** shining in the ecclesial sky at the end of the second millennium: the welcoming of charisms and the Church's promotion of the laity; the recognition of the role of women in the Church; the flourishing of various movements within the Church; dedication to the cause of christian unity; openness to interreligious dialogue; dialogue with modern or contemporary culture; catholicity or universality that respects the different cultures; unconditional support for peace, justice, and the dignity of human life; the emergence of the Church's 'Marian profile'.

To give thanks and praise also because **glimpses of resurrection** are not lacking in the Order today. These are the fruits of faithfulness to grace in the past: numerous martyrs who sealed the offering of their lives with their own blood, a body of legislative documents that are both inspiring in their spirit and clear in their norms, fidelity to the point of heroism in extreme situations, the inculturation of the patrimony in new cultural contexts, foundations in the young churches, desire for gospel and monastic radicalism as a contribution to the new evangelization, increasing collaboration between monks and nuns at the level of authority, affective and effective openness to the cistercian family, the participation of lay groups in the cistercian charism, and so on.

A contemplative look at our own history also brings to mind these words of Benedict, our patriarch: *To attribute to God, and not to self, whatever good one sees in oneself. But to recognize always that the evil is one's own doing, and to impute it to oneself* (RB 4:42–43).

THE RISEN JESUS

Let us now open our eyes to the *deifying light*, to that *light of life* that enlightens our steps and allows us to run forward without being caught off guard by the darkness of death (*RB* Prol. 9–10, 13).

Jesus Christ, *the fullness of time*, is the Lord of the ages and, perhaps even more so, of our twentieth century. It is he who gives all of history its definitive meaning, transforming it into a **history of salvation**, that is to say, into a succession of divine acts and human responses in order to carry out God's plan. When God becomes man and rises from the dead, the divine breaks into human history as never before. Therefore, God-made-man and risen from the dead by power from on high:

- gives meaning to the past, of which he himself is the fullness.

- transforms the present into the acceptable time.

- gives meaning to the future by opening it to the hope that vanquishes death.

A meta-historical event

The witnesses of the resurrection present it as a borderline event: the things that preceded it are incarnated in history, but this history itself and what follows leaps beyond the limits of history. The Risen One is met in a state of life that surpasses the coordinates of time and space. In this sense, he is 'trans-historical'.

On the other hand, the witnesses of the Risen One with their testimonies about the resurrection can be placed and dated. The same can be said of the impact and consequences of this event throughout human history. The centuries-old presence of the Church is proof of it. This is the great paradox of christian faith; though based on a meta-historical event, it has revolutionary historical consequences.

Everything would have come to an end after Calvary had not Jesus, raised up by the Father, begun to *let himself be seen, show himself, reveal himself, appear* (Lk 24:34; Ac 7:2.30; 13:39; 1 Co 15:5–8). It is something that imposes itself from without and flies in the face of the objectively verifiable experience of his cross and death. In other words, the **initiative** is his, Jesus'. His followers, both men and women, welcome him and receive him.

Jesus, then, lets himself be seen, or is shown in a **new state** of *glory* (Ac 22:11; 2 Co 4:6). It is an *apocalipsis* (revelation) of Jesus Christ (Ga 1:12.16). The revealed glory is an anticipation of the eschatological, that is to say, of what is final and definitive.

The **experience** of meeting the Risen One is unique in its kind, having no point of comparison with other spiritual experiences. It gives rise to 'knowledge', though not of a simply objective kind that remains apart from the one who has the experience. Whoever meets the Risen One is totally affected and taken over by the life of the Lord. Although it is not independent of faith, this knowledge is not a consequence of faith. Rather, the Risen One is the foundation of our faith: *If Christ has not been raised, our faith is futile* (1 Co 15:17).

Our **faith** in the Risen Lord is based on the testimony of the Apostles, concerning which we have no doubts. However, this is not all. Our **testimony** of the Risen Jesus, in order to be truly such, cannot be based simply on something we have heard, but must also be supported by our own '**experience**' of the Risen Lord, through the mediation of the Holy Spirit within the believing Church.

*We know God by faith as if by hearsay, but through contemplative
love he reveals himself to us in a kind of manifestation of his presence.
He who was made known by hearsay is now found to be really present,
as it were, the very one who before seemed a stranger to us, of whom
we had only heard, and who had not shown us his presence* (Saint
Gregory the Great, *Commentary on the First Book of Kings*,
Sch, 391).

The Church also, at each moment in its history, *experiences Christ in
itself and blossoms with the fullness of life.* It can therefore bear witness
to the message of salvation with confidence and boldness (Paul VI,
Ecclesiam Suam, 6).

This experience is possible only when faith accepts Christ, *seated at
the Father's right, no longer in lowly guise, but in his own flesh transformed
with heaven's beauty.* This faith purifies the heart and makes it possible
to experience the Risen One: *with the hand of faith, the finger of desire,
the embrace of love, with the mind's eye* (Saint Bernard, SC 28:10).

The community, as a fraternal communion of love in the Spirit, *is
a God-enlightened space in which to experience the hidden presence of the
Risen Lord* (*Vita Consecrata* 42; Mt 18:20). The abbot of Clairvaux
has something to say in this regard: *You are mistaken, holy Thomas,
you are mistaken if you hope to see the Lord when you are apart from
the company of the apostles. Truth has no love for corners; roadside lodging
places do not please him. Truth stands in the open and delights in discipline,
the common life, and common undertakings* (Saint Bernard, Asc 6:13).

These experiences take absolutely nothing away from our life of
faith. Rather, they make it possible to accept all the self-stripping
and self-forgetfulness involved in living a life of faith and love. Anyone who has touched the Risen Lord with the hand of faith can
state: *It is enough for me that Jesus is still alive. If he lives, I live, for my
spirit acts through his. Yes, he is my life, my all in all. For what can I lack
if Jesus is still alive? Rather everything else may be taken from me, nothing
else matters to me so long as he lives. If he wishes then, let him take no*

account of me. It is enough for me that he still lives even if he only lives for himself (Guerric, *Sermon* 33:5).

Lastly, it must be said that our experience is similar but not identical to that of the first witnesses. Our experience presupposes theirs, whereas their experience is rooted in their years of living with the Master. In any case, had we only the experiential witness of the apostles, the Risen Lord would be a figure of the past, inoperative for us in the present, and could hardly give us cause for future hope.

I remember saying a few words at the close of the 1990 General Chapters concerning my 'weak and strong points'. Among the latter, I mentioned the following: 'the ability to **bear witness** to the constant, active presence of the Risen Christ and his Mother at the heart of the Church'. Can I say the same now, ten years later? Thanks to the gospel witness of our seven Brothers of Atlas, I answer with even more conviction and boldness than before: Yes! This statement is an act of faith by which my freedom and my conscience are once again converted under the influence of divine grace. It will be a credible and acceptable statement if I embody it in a docile and fruitful life in the Holy Spirit.

An inexpressible event

For our forebears in the faith it was not easy to find appropriate words for the new reality they experienced. Beginning with their very first account, the witnesses used a **varied vocabulary** that could be said to fall into three categories: resurrection, exaltation, and vivification, as illustrated in the following texts.

- *If you confess with your lips that Jesus is Lord and believe in your heart that God raised him from the dead, you will be saved* (Rm 10:9).

- *Therefore God has highly exalted him and bestowed on him the name that is above every name* (Ph 2:9).

- *Put to death in the flesh but made alive in the spirit* (1 P 3:18).

Clearly, the first witnesses communicated the event by means of **formulas** that soon became public and fundamental. These formulas arose in various contexts: preaching, catechesis, liturgy, and mission. Here are two others, both very primitive, taken up by Saint Paul years later in his letters.

- *For I delivered to you as of first importance what I also received, that Christ died for our sins in accordance with the scriptures, that he was buried, that he was raised on the third day in accordance with the scriptures, and that he appeared to Cephas, then to the twelve* (1 Co 15:3–5).

- *Descended from David according to the flesh and designated Son of God in power according to the Spirit of holiness by his resurrection from the dead, Jesus Christ our Lord* (Rm 1:3–5).

There then followed the composition of the **Easter narratives** we find in the Gospels, which refer to the empty tomb, the witness of the women (absent in the early accounts or *kerygma*), and the apparitions of the Risen Lord (with differences of time, place, recipients, and reactions). These accounts are an apologetic complement to the *kerygma* (the corporal nature of the resurrection).

Finally, we have the ***kerygmatic* discourses** of Peter and Paul included in the Acts of the Apostles (Ac 2; 3; 4; 10 and 13). Luke's elaborations aside, these speeches reflect a primitive kernel (the presence of semitisms) belonging to the accounts given to the early community. They contain three typical elements: the contrast between the failure of the jewish leaders and the efficacious action of God in raising Jesus; the transformation of the disciples, thanks to the apparitions, into witnesses of the wonderful eschatological events with which God has brought about salvation; and the testimony of Scripture as a confirmation of God's action.

Though formulated in a variety of ways, these texts communicate to us a **single message** of vital importance, on which our christian faith is founded.

- Jesus appeared to certain disciples after his death.

- He was announced as risen from the dead.

- He who is Risen is the same as he who was Crucified, even though he is no longer the same.

- His physical body is now a spiritual and glorified body.

Moreover, it is not only our faith that is founded on this truth. Our monastic life, as a life of faith, would lack christian identity and would be absolutely devoid of meaning without Jesus Christ glorified. Our monastic life is a *progressive resurrection* in the Risen Christ (cf. Guerric, *Sermon* 35:5).

An event full of meaning

All of the New Testament writings are a 'rereading' of the fact of the resurrection and of the reality of the Risen Lord. This means that the resurrection and the Risen Lord are in themselves a synthesis of all reality. This basic kernel of the christian fact and the christian message is of unfathomable wealth. Let us try to enter into this mystery and seek its meaning.

The resurrection of Jesus Christ, considered in a **global** way, might be understood as the irruption of what is eschatological (i.e., ultimate, unsurpassable, definitive) into our human history. In other words, the Spirit irrupts into mortal flesh, and life totally absorbs death. It is the definitive revolution in cosmic, human, and historical evolution.

From the point of view of **the Father and the Holy Spirit**, though it perhaps seems bold, we might say that the virginally fertile fatherhood of God reaches its fullness in a way unforeseeable on the human plain, in the resurrection of the only-begotten Son. It is the supreme work of creation and spiritualization; whereas the first creation sprang from nothing, the second springs from death! The resurrection reveals the self-giving love of the Father and of the Spirit in response to a life given, even to the point of total emptying on the cross. The prophecy of the Psalms thus finds its completion: he did not allow his Holy One to experience corruption, he did not abandon him to Hades, and he showed him the path of life, the fullness of joy in his presence.

For **Jesus**, the resurrection is above all his total rehabilitation after having been condemned in a shameful way. It is the luminous 'Yes' of God as opposed to the dark 'no' of human beings. For this very reason, it is the irrefutable testimony that Jesus is the ultimate, final prophet of God. By suffering abandonment and putting himself in God's hands, Jesus ran a risk that could only end well. For this he is truly blessed and his blessings are true. Sin and death, which Jesus took into his own flesh, were thus dethroned and vanquished once and for all. Jesus experienced the resurrection as:

- **transformation** into a spiritual body and a life-giving spirit (1Co 15:44–45).

- **re-creation** as a new man, new father of humanity, and firstborn from among the dead (Rm 5:7; 1Co 15:20ff).

- total **incarnation**, for the fullness of divinity dwells in him bodily (Col 2:9).

- **gift** of the Spirit that makes him in turn a Giver of the Spirit (Jn 20:22).

- **newness** and 'rebirth' in his divine sonship (Rm 1:3–4).

- **receiving** the Name that is above every name (Ph 2:9).

From the moment of his resurrection, Jesus can identify himself totally with the persecuted and the little ones. He is also enabled to take on a sacramental presence though the species of bread and wine to be eaten and drunk by believers. In a word, the risen Lord is the *Fullness of him who fills all in all* (Ep 1:23).

The **apostles**, for their part, experienced the resurrection as the transformation of Jesus the Nazarean into Jesus Christ the Lord, and as their own transformation from mere disciples to witnesses of the Risen Lord. They thus understood that God was already in the Crucified One, whose face, because of the resurrection, will show forth the divine glory. The Gospels say nothing about apparitions of the Risen Lord to his **Mother**. Perhaps this is so that her happiness will find completion in believing without seeing (Jn 20:29), and so that she can be even more pleasing to God (Heb 11:6). In any case, as a mother, the resurrection of her Son affected her to her very depths. From that very moment, she began to experience her glorious assumption in the image of the firstborn from among the dead.

If the Risen Lord sustains and enlivens our faith, his resurrection fully explains **our life in him**. Indeed, the resurrection is at the very origin of the Church and of our faith. Through baptism in his Passover and by receiving his Spirit, we have been transformed into the Body of the Risen Christ. The resurrection is the reason for our hope and the pledge of our future resurrection, assuring us that our work and our efforts for the Kingdom are not in vain. It allows us to recite the Our Father with faith, asking for the hallowing of his Name and the coming of his Kingdom, that is, the resurrection at the end of time. Moreover, what is to prevent us from thinking that women have been given a special privilege and title as the first witnesses of the Risen Lord? Be that as it may, both they and we are well aware that to believe in the *Kyrios* means to follow the crucified Lord, but with the power and grace of the Risen Lord. Thanks to the Risen Lord, we live without fearing death and die without losing life.

Brothers and Sisters, at the beginning of this letter I invited you to contemplate the twentieth century, and to discover the Risen Lord at the heart of it. Time is inhabited by him who is Lord of history. Therefore, our **hope** does not perish and each moment of this life is a seed of eternity. Everything that still has to happen until the end of the world will be an unfolding and an explanation of what happened on the day of the resurrection. On that day, the body of the crucified Lord was transformed by the power of the Spirit and in turn became a source of that same Spirit for all of humanity.

Sunday is the day on which the Risen Lord becomes present from among the dead. For this same reason, Sunday is the day that reveals the meaning of time; springing from the resurrection, it traverses human time, the months, years, and centuries, as a spear, steering them toward the second coming of Christ. Sunday prefigures the final day, the day of the *Parousia*, already anticipated in the resurrection. Amen, *Marana tha*, come, Lord Jesus! Yes, come quickly!

Letters to Superiors in the Various Regions

THE SERVICE OF AUTHORITY

Letter to the Superiors of the
Spanish Region, August 20, 1993

Dear Brother and Sister:

I do not know if I should ask pardon for addressing you with the simplicity of a brother. Were I to do otherwise, I believe that the request for pardon would be obligatory. This initial simplicity is a prelude to what follows: a simple sharing about our service of authority.

As you can see I have not forgotten the request you made during the last meeting of the Regional Conference. Quite the contrary, I have meditated and prayed about this ever since. Today I share with you the fruits I have been able to harvest.

But first, I want to tell you that it has not been easy for me. The obstacles to overcome have been multiple. Nevertheless, for this *apologia*, it is enough to mention the following.

Our father Saint Benedict in his Rule for monks has given us two directories on the abbot, in his words can be found all that needs to be known. What could I add? Comment? Commentaries abound, and then some!

Two of my predecessors, Dom Hermann Joseph and Dom Gabriel, have treated the subject exhaustively and with competence. Why repeat what has already been said? To recall it to your memory? I am certain that your memory is better than mine.

Besides, supposing that I start to write, how am I to order the material? According to the threefold office of Christ: royal, prophetic, and priestly? Analogous to the functions of the Spirit relative to the Church: animation, communion, and motivation? According to the fourfold service of the superior in relation to the person, the community, the Order and the Church? According to the five aspects mentioned in our Constitutions: father, teacher, shepherd, physician, and administrator? By merely detailing a series of concrete obligations proper to superiors?

Still more, how to include in one brief text all that is proper to a superior or superioress? How to include the community within the limits imposed by a letter?

Only one way did I find to weave my way through so many problems: to count upon and take for granted your understanding and kindness.

At last, be it as it may, or even as it may have been, I finally decided to consult my heart and let come what may. This is what came, a series of 'sentences', which I have arranged under five headings for better understanding.

FATHER AND MOTHER

The first one who must believe that he holds the place of Christ is you yourself; this will help you act like Him.

You are not Christ but you hold His place; you do not replace Christ, rather you represent Him, especially in what you do.

He who hears you, hears him. Do not believe that he does what you want and say; rather, you must seek what he wants and make it known.

Your authority is a service to life, and this life requires your service more than your presidency.

The life you give and the life you serve is not your own but that of Another; in order to give and to serve this Life you must die to your own.

In order to serve life you must preserve and promote it, motivate and orientate it. This service is both paternal and maternal. If you are not father and mother conjointly, you will be neither the one nor the other.

The greater your personal maturity, the more able you are to bring others to maturity.

If you want to call forth life, always bear in mind the basic necessities of meaning (purpose and end), group-belonging, and identity proper to every human being.

To animate and give life, you must make yourself present, but not omnipresent; the degree of your co-living is proportionate to the degree of your moral authority.

Your authority is service; for this reason, the greater and better your service, the greater and better your authority.

Your authority receives life and legitimacy from above, but it is underwritten from below by the quality of your service.

The credibility of your authority depends on: your capacity to listen, your contact with the reality of others, coherence between your words and your deeds, your centering on the essential and important, your promptness in taking charge of situations within your competence.

The higher you are, the more you should scan the horizon of the future.

The four plagues in the ambient of monastic authority are: the paternalism that abuses authority by confusing it with power; the fraternalism that denies the diversity and hierarchy of services; the maternalism that needs to protect and shelter; and the infantilism of the person who depends on others for gratification and assurance.

The authority that takes jesting seriously, and the serious in jest, is stupid.

Authoritarianism is the first sign of authority in crisis.

To make your authority felt is to make obedience resentful.

May your authority never result in silencing but rather in making people think.

Many years of service can cause you to seek to be served. Do not permit it.

To keep oneself in authority is to empty it of content and to obliterate service.

Blessed are you if you contemplate the Lord until you are radiant; the Lord will make his face shine in yours for the glory of all.

Exemplary Teacher

To be a teacher you must first of all and always be a disciple of the Word of the one Teacher.

If you want to be accepted as a teacher, cease not to be a witness, not to perfection but to conversion.

If you live what you teach, fear not to repeat yourself in what you say; it will never be the same.

Your teaching must be formative and with a view to transformation; if you only inform, you do not form.

As teacher, you must be capable of articulating and communicating to others the essential values and ends proper to our life.

The objectives of your talks should be: to captivate—to attract the attention and favor of your audience; to enlighten—with the light of doctrine; to motivate—by arousing the affections; to convince— for decision-making.

You communicate well when you take these principles into account: clarity—you are comprehensible; method—you proceed systematically; organization—you shape a harmonious whole; and vivacity— you illustrate with lively examples.

If you do not want your audience to sleep, be brief; if you want to please, be natural; if you want to bore, try to be encyclopedic.

Do not try to be funny, but if you want to communicate and communicate yourself, be enjoyable and enjoy yourself.

The secret key in the art of formation is to know how to motivate, that is: to awaken, to sustain, and to direct interest.

Didactic motivation is the more efficacious the more it is natural, simple, and spontaneous; there is nothing more motivating than certain ways of being and of expressing oneself.

Do not aspire to a monopoly of teaching, unless you want to keep others in ignorance.

Blessed are you if you put a grain of salt in what you say; everyone will find a pinch of sugar in what they feel.

DISCREET SHEPHERD AND SHEPHERDESS

You are truly shepherd when you relate to each person as unique and unrepeatable.

If you listen with the ear and the heart you will be able to know what others are telling you and also what they feel.

Listen to the one who is speaking; it is the simplest form of allowing that person to be and to exist.

The capacity to identify and differentiate oneself, to connect and disconnect oneself is basic to any form of shepherding.

The other will listen to you when you draw near, but not when he feels you are pursuing him.

All of us react to others according to our previous relations to them.

Communication is more an emotional than a cerebral process; hence the importance of beginning by welcoming, continuing and ending by welcoming.

Ask the Lord for prudence; this will allow you to weave your way through the shoals of excess due to precipitation and lack of consideration, and of defect due to inconstancy and negligence.

You seek and find the common good when you try to integrate that which is proper to each one in a superior harmony that integrates without annihilating.

If you shepherd in such a way that the weak may become strong, yet without neglecting the strong for fear of feeling yourself weak, you are a good shepherd.

Life grows slowly; never despair.

Blessed are you if you live everything as grace; you will be graced and agreeable to everyone.

Merciful Doctor

If the miseries of your neighbor arouse your impatience and not your mercy, it is a sign that you have not yet accepted your own.

The great majority of present problems were born in the past. If you are over-permissive in order not to avoid getting into problems, you pile up problems.

The best correction you can offer is a good direction—that which is straight has been well directed.

A small dose of preventive medicine can save you many plagues and incurable diseases.

Do not forget: a sense of humor is moisture that spreads and refreshes when you are tense and hot; laughter is also therapeutic and healing.

Patience can do almost everything provided it be a persevering peace and a power-charged passivity.

Blessed are you if you can distinguish a speck of dust from a mountain; you will avoid for yourself and others a goodly amount of vain worries.

Prudent Administrator

Imitate your Lord in everything: persons first and then things; first, what each one is, and afterward what he does.

The personal responsibility of your collaborators is enriched by the specification of their responsibilities.

Your programs derive their strength from the antecedent participation and consequent responsibility of your collaborators and community.

Programs are most important, but even more so are the persons for whom they are intended and those who carry them out.

Long term objectives will permit you to draw up programs that can motivate and enlighten six-year terms.

Evaluation and 'feed-back' are efficacious means to improve what you have planned, what you have said, and what you have done.

Teamwork affords a real possibility to increase your capacity for presence.

Respect the intermediate instances of authority and these will respect you.

The basic principles that must govern a good organization are the following:

- solidarity: the soldier that creates a bond and reciprocal responsibility between each one of the officials and among the different departments.

- subsidiarity: protection of the autonomy of decision and action of the various officials; what a subordinate superior may do and what is incumbent upon him, should not be done by a major superior.

- participation: a just and proportionate 'input' of each official in the departments that are not his direct responsibility. ('Invasion' is the degeneration of participation, and to shut oneself up in one's castle is its opposite.)

- intervention: the possibility of an operative presence or of advice on the part of a higher authority in order to settle conflicts or solve problems. ('Interventionism' is the degradation of intervention.)

- appeal: the recourse of a subordinate with regard to another who is immediately superior in order to receive advice or assistance. (The 'vaulter' who leaps over instances is the degeneration of appeal.)

If the organization you have set up functions well, it will also function well in your absence.

Wisdom that stems from experience will allow you to be a good administrator and avoid these possible obstacles: servile dependence on experts; absolute confidence in organizations; and waiting for science to confirm what common sense makes evident to you.

It is advisable that the technical and the specialized be entrusted to specialists and handled technically.

'Presidentialism' in an organization is the filling of vacancies with vacancies.

Blessed are you if you reflect before you act and laugh before you reflect; you will avoid doing many stupid things.

★ ★ ★

Once more, just as I did on another occasion, I want to leave this letter unfinished. Life itself, yours and mine, will assume the responsibility to finish it.

But before concluding, I want to testify to my faith in these words of the *Magisterium* of the Church:

> *Mary is present in the birth and education of every religious vocation. She is intimately associated to all its growth in the Holy Spirit. The mission she has fulfilled relative to Jesus, she fulfills for the benefit of his body that is the Church and for every Christian, especially for those who consecrate themselves to follow Jesus Christ more closely. For this reason, a Marian ambient, supported by an authentic theology will assure to the formation of the Religious, authenticity, solidity and joy, without which their mission in the world cannot be fully accomplished* (CIVCSVA, *Potissimum Institutioni* 110).

The Holy Spirit is the principal agent of our growth in Christ and Mary-Mother is his intimate and immediate collaborator. We superiors can do nothing without them and we can do everything with them.

Now I want to hand over the microphone to a great abbot of our Order, Bernard of Clairvaux.

> *The most living and efficacious sermon is the example of deeds: it easily renders persuasive what is said since it shows that what was counseled can be done. Thus, you may be certain, for the peace of your conscience, that in this two-fold precept of word and example reside all the obligations of your charge. And if you are wise, add a third: diligence in prayer in order to fulfill that triple evangelical responsibility to feed the sheep. Understand that the sacrament of that*

trinity will not be distorted by you if you nourish them with word, example, and the fruit of holy prayer. There remain then these three: word, example, and prayer; but the greatest of these is prayer, for as I have said, the word needs to count on the authentification of deeds, that which confers grace and efficacy on the word and the work is prayer (Letter 201:3).

That is to say, by way of conclusion, if we do not have time to pray, we resign in order to have it. Let us not confuse the urgent with the important. First things first!

ATTITUDES TOWARD AGING

Letter to the Superiors of the
Canadian Region, February 8, 1998

Dear Brothers and Sisters,

One need only take a glance at your region to see that *aging* is a circumstance affecting nearly all your communities. The same can be said of monasteries in Ireland and Holland. I recently had opportunity to articulate my own thoughts on the subject of aging to the superiors of the Region of the Isles at their Regional Meeting. With a few modifications and additions, I now pass on to you what I presented on that occasion.

Obviously, it is a reality that eventually affects us all. Time passes on for every human being and, in time, every human being passes on. It must be said, however, that this reality of aging is more in evidence in the First World, mainly on account of its higher quality of life. World statistics indicate that in developed countries the average life-expectancy is seventy-five for men and eighty for women. Only in one country, Japan, does the average life-expectancy reach eighty for men or even eighty-five in the case of women.

The large number of elderly persons in the western countries of the North Atlantic has entailed a series of social consequences that cannot be underestimated. The most notable of these is the loss of *social status* on the part of older men and women: to be old is not valued. Added to this is the *poor social integration* of so many older people, due especially to the increasingly rapid changes in lifestyle all around them. Nor can we ignore the *disorientation* experienced by so many of them with regard to their own roles in a world that prefers practical skill (how to do something) to wisdom (what to do and why). Lastly, many older people feel humiliated and depressed by the slogans of a certain kind of culture.

- The elderly are no longer a model in our modern consumer society.

- The elderly weigh down the efficiency and productivity of scientific-technological society.

- The elderly are of no use for the economical progress and growth of the people.

- The elderly prevent the productive group of society from having a higher quality of life.

Obviously, this 'bad news' has nothing to do with the 'good news' of the gospel concerning mature age. It seems to me that the most important thing is to face this reality with the *right attitude;* otherwise, it will be absolutely impossible to *think creatively* so as to find the practical solutions that are necessary. The experience of many monasteries and of many monks and nuns of the Order teaches us:

- for the older members of the community:

  - not to dramatize the situation. Old age is a natural part of this life: the end of a cycle. Older persons remind us of this.

– not to think of them as a problem. Our older members are not problems, but persons. Nor is age a problem; or if it is, it comes at the age of forty.

– to be grateful for the presence of older members and for the many years of self-giving.

– to follow them. The older members are the Order's 'front lines', who open the way toward the Kingdom. This represents a responsibility for the older members. Their lives are an example to imitate. The younger members are the 'rear guard'.

– to remember. The older members are the historical links uniting the Order of today with its past. They are therefore witnesses of its identity and continuity. In other words, they are witnesses of tradition, of what is permanent at the heart of what is changing. They are the Order's living memory.

– to keep in mind. The older members remind us of our own roots. They put us in contact with the living sources of our life, with the point at which we began to follow the Lord.

• during old age:

– do not forget the meaning of the word, 'old': it comes from the same root as 'altitude' and 'all', and points to a fullness of being. The Latin equivalent is '*vetus*': veteran, experienced: the one who has experienced something and therefore knows how to do it well.

– younger persons expect to receive from their elders:
  • distance from the stress and strain of ordinary life.
  • renewed enthusiasm for their ideals.
  • availability and an understanding of life's deeper meaning; we all like to look for consolation under the shadow of an old oak tree.

- within every person's heart there is the seed of a philosopher. It is during old age that this seed germinates, flowers, and bears fruit. Older persons are those who have clarified the meaning of life through what they themselves have experienced.

- the true older person no longer wants to know things, but to taste them, is no longer driven to act, but lets things happen, is able to accept powerlessness.

- old age can be lived as a pilgrimage toward the final goal: the Father. The downward curve of the body can intersect with the upward curve of the spirit as it progresses and ascends.

- live out what some venerable older members of the Order have said so wisely.

- I am getting old and learning new things every day.
- Learning to live takes a whole lifetime.
- Today is the first day of the rest of my life.
- To lengthen my days I try not to make them short, and to make them pass faster, I try not to count them.
- My days are very long, but the years fly by.
- My ship depends on the wind, not on the oars.
- I live on the threshold of death and am full of curiosity.
- I try to be what I am: an old-timer!
- Mere youthfulness is not youth!
- I ask of God to die young, and the longer he holds off, the better.
- I prefer having all the normal aches and pains of old age to being in good shape and being abnormal.

In any case, we all know that years are very relative. There are young old people and old young people. An old-timer in the Third World can be young in the First World; I myself was relatively old in my own country at the age of forty. I then became a child seven years later when I was elected Abbot General and began to live in Europe!

Similarly, youth is not univocal, but analogous. It is possible to distinguish at least three different experiences of youth:

- first, *physical* youth: until the age of thirty-five. Its end is signaled by the growth of one's midriff.

- second, *existential* youth: until the age of forty. After that, the person wants to try again.

- third, *spiritual* youth: when a decrease of one's life is accepted in wisdom.

Based on all of this, we might say that youth is not so much a period in life as a state of mind, a quality of the imagination, an intensity of affection, a choice of the will, a victory of courage over timidity, and of the taste for adventure over the pleasure of comfort.

We are young as long as we retain the capacity to wonder and to ask as children do: 'What now?' We are young according to the measure of our faith and old according to the measure of our doubts. We are young to the degree that we are open to the other, to life, to the good, to the beautiful, to the great, to the infinite.

Aging is not the result of having lived many years, but rather we become old when our ideals start to limp. If age makes the feet drag, the lack of ideals makes the soul drag. To give up looking at the future with hope and optimism reduces us to dust even before we die.

If we pass from an existential anthropology to a theological one, we can state without hesitation that:

- we have been created in the image and likeness of a God who is beyond all ages and who fulfills them all. He is the youngest and the oldest, since he is limitless love and infinite wisdom. Is not youth a love of life, and old age a wisdom of life?

- God is young because he is Love. Love does not become old, since it is stronger than death. In their love, young persons imitate God and reflect his image.

- an older person imitates God by becoming old, provided that the person acquires wisdom of life, which only the years can give.

Everything I have said here is only meant to help us face the reality of old age with the right attitude. As I said at the beginning, such an attitude makes creativity possible when decisions have to be made.

It seems to me, however, that something more should be said concerning *pastoral care* in old age. I will state it here in the form of short, practical principles.

- Attention should be given to the person at hand: not an old person but this older person.

- There should be service given, but above all, affection: love means appreciating.

- An appropriate activity has to be provided; feeling useful is a form of feeling alive.

- Ways to prolong someone's life are worth little if there are no reasons to live.

- Besides adding years to a person's life, we must try to add life to a person's years.

Age is a gift for which we should be thankful, as Pope John Paul II has reminded us, a gift for the old person him or herself, and a gift for society and the Church. Life is always a gift. Better yet, for faithful followers of Christ, we can speak of a special charism granted to older persons in view of using their talents and energies in an appropriate way for their own happiness and for the benefit of others (Catechesis of 7 September, 1994).

That is all I have to say. May the Lord give us the grace to start from our youth the difficult art of 'geriagogy', the art of growing old. There is no other way to avoid being a burden on other people because of our selfish demands during the time of old age. Let us therefore begin even now to prepare our hearts, praying in the words of this wise nun who has gone before us on the way of following the Lord:

Lord, you know better than I myself that I am growing old and will someday be old. Keep me from the fatal habit of thinking that I must say something on every subject and on every occasion. Release me from craving to straighten out everybody's affairs. Make me thoughtful, but not moody; helpful, but not bossy. With my vast store of wisdom, it seems a pity not to use it all, but you know, Lord, that I want a few friends at the end.

Keep my mind free from the recital of endless details; give me wings to get to the point. Seal my lips on my aches and pains. They are increasing, and love of rehearsing them is becoming sweeter as the years go by. I dare not ask for grace enough to enjoy the tales of others' pains, but help me to endure them with patience.

I dare not ask for improved memory, but for a growing humility and a lessening cocksureness when my memory seems to clash with the memories of others. Teach me the glorious lesson that occasionally I may be mistaken.

Keep me reasonably sweet; I do not want to be a saint—some of them are so hard to live with—but a sour old person is one of the crowning works of the devil. Give me the ability to see good things in unexpected places, and talents in unexpected people. And, give me, O Lord, the grace to tell them so. Amen.

Synods of Bishops

MONASTIC LIFE AND SOLITUDE, AND ENCLOSURE

Bishops' Synod on Consecrated Life,
October 15, 1994

T HE MONK IS A CHRISTIAN WHO CONSECRATES his entire life to the search for and the encounter with God. This is something that the monk has in common with all other Christians. He is not the only one to seek God and he does not claim to do it better than others. However, the monk knows that he is called to make this search an absolute in his life. Because of this, he seeks God truly, frequently, and constantly; neither does he seek anything else but God, nor anything more than God and does not then go from God to something else.

Since the search for God is the sense and ultimate aim of his existence, his life is a life of great simplicity (*simplicitas*). This simplicity (*simplicitas*), that is, the fact of having only one preoccupation and one goal, is the first and most profound meaning of the word *monachos*.

The reason for this search for God (*quaerere Deum*) is evidently the contemplative encounter with God. The entire life of the monk is a path to this end. And the monastic path is characterized by a certain number of means: silent and continual prayer, liturgical prayer, *lectio divina* and the various forms of self denial that lead to the conversion and purification of the heart, and all of this in a climate of solitude and silence. All these means are nothing more than *means*. They are characteristic of monastic life and necessary for it; they are not the essential element. The essential element is the goal; that is, the continual search for the encounter with God, which is always a gift.

In its concrete realization, monastic life has a great variety of forms. One can speak of monastic life as a fundamental human archetype that we find in all the great religious traditions of humanity. One could also recall the variety of forms that christian monasticism has taken in the traditions of the East and the West. Nevertheless, I am going to limit myself to the reality within which I am situated: the contemporary western tradition, in line with the cenobitic benedictine tradition. I am aware that this tradition also has a plurality of concrete forms of life.

I would now like to draw your attention to various themes such as: the lay character of monastic life and the possibility of lay monks assuming the service of abbatial authority, the full reciprocity between monks and nuns belonging to a same spiritual tradition, and the role of monks and nuns in interreligious dialogue. However, for lack of time, I will speak only about one particular aspect of the cenobitic monastic life—solitude and enclosure.

Monastic solitude is a tool for the realization of the search for God (*quaerere Deum*). It is above all a solitude of spirit and a poverty of heart. It also implies a distancing from the preoccupations and activities of the world. In the Middle Ages, this began to be called *fuga mundi*. Perhaps it would be more in line with the great primitive tradition to speak of *fuga ad Deum*? The 'world' from which the monk wants to flee is above all the world that he carries in his own heart: concupiscence of the flesh, covetousness of the eyes, and the arrogant possession of riches. Thus, the monk, separate from all, becomes close to all and brings all to their common origin: God. Solitude of heart and the concentration of all one's strength in the search for God require an interior solitude fortified and manifested by exterior solitude.

All that is the same for the monks as for the nuns. They all have received a same vocation; the fact of being a priest or not is something accidental to the monastic vocation in itself. Now, in the Middle Ages, a type of special enclosure, much more rigid, was established for the nuns. This evolution is easily explained by sociological and cultural reasons; there exists no basic reason why the monastic life of nuns should differ from that of monks on this point.

We often hear about the *problem* of the enclosure. There is certainly no problem with the value or the means that the monastic enclosure is meant to preserve: solitude. Neither can we say that enclosure is a *problem*. The problem, as I see it, rests in the present legislation established twenty-five years ago. This problem comprises several aspects.

- The evolution in the Church since Vatican II in what concerns the condition of women is not reflected in *Venite Seorsum*. One wonders why the Abbess of an autonomous monastery—who, according to the Code of Canon Law, is a major superior, c. 620—does not have the same authority over the enclosure in her monastery as the Abbot has in his. In the present context of respect for the dignity of women, the obligation for enclosed nuns to obtain the consent of a male superior for things as evident as: reasons of health, questions of work, exercise of civil rights, administrative acts, etc. cannot be justified.

- The present legislation, identical for all enclosed nuns, does not respect the particular legitimate traditions and the charism proper to each Order and each spiritual Family. Thus, patrimonies as different as that of Benedictines,

Cistercians, Carmelites, Poor Clares . . . remain under the same canonical norm concerning enclosure. Respect for the diversity of charisms calls for something else.

- The present legislation makes a fruitful presence of the nuns in the life of the Church, very difficult—and in some cases even impossible, for example, in not allowing an active and significant participation of guests and visitors in the liturgy of women's communities. A more appropriate legislation in this regard would allow the traditional monastic hospitality to produce more abundant fruit in the local Church.

- In our day, monastic communities of women are growing rapidly in the Young Churches. The norms on enclosure should take into account these diverse cultural contexts. The inculturation of the Gospel and of monastic life calls for a particular sensitivity in this area.

- A solid human, biblical, theological, and spiritual formation is necessary to live deeply the search for God within a monastic community. Monastic communities of women—in many cases small in personnel—cannot suffice in themselves. To prohibit, in the name of enclosure, joint formation sessions or meetings of women formators or superiors to work in the area of formation, could prevent the realization of the goal that is the purpose of the enclosure, as a means.

With confidence, I ask the Fathers of the Synod to consider what has just been said and to draw up proposals that allow for an up-to-date (*aggiornata*) legislation on the enclosure of nuns. It is only in this way that it can be said in truth that the purity and fervor of the monastic and contemplative life for a large part depend on the observance of the laws of enclosure.

CONTEMPLATION IN THE LIFE OF THE CHURCH

Bishops' Synod on the Americas,
November 22, 1997

I SPEAK FROM MY MONASTIC AND LATIN AMERICAN ROOTS in the name of many monasteries of both monks and nuns throughout the three Americas and the Caribbean area. My intervention deals with the first words of the theme of this present Synod: *Encounter with the Living Jesus Christ*. It is an experience that the **Instrumentum Laboris** describes as an *interpersonal encounter*, specifying that *the proclamation of the mystery of Jesus Christ is oriented toward fostering the personal encounter with him* (6).

The **Instrumentum Laboris** is saying the same thing as the 'Conclusions' of **Santo Domingo**, though with different words. In Santo Domingo, all men and women were invited *to believe in prayer as an expression of convinced, committed faith, of unconquerable hope and of loyal love, which contemplates God in his intimate Trinitarian life and in his saving action in history* (37).

This contemplative prayer always has to be integrated into an apostolic mission to the christian community and to the world, in imitation of the example of Christ. Without contemplation, *prophetic action cannot be understood, since it would not be true and authentic.* Even the Liturgy, which is an encounter with God through signs, *becomes an action lacking depth.* In fact contemplation is something so inherent to the human spirit that when the Church does not offer her rich doctrine and long experience of it, many people—even among Christians—look for satisfaction of their longing for interior life in non-christian practices (47).

That is why the Latin American Bishops declared that *we should be sure all members of God's people assume responsibility for the contemplative dimension of their baptismal consecration and that they learn to pray, following the example of Jesus* (47). In the same way, the New Evangelization requires *forming Christians to see God in their own personhood, in nature, history, work, culture, and all that is secular, so that they can discover the harmony which, in God's plan, is meant to exist between the orders of creation and redemption* (156). Even more urgently, *means have to be taken to give priority in all pastoral plans to the dimension of contemplation and holiness, so that the Church can be a presence of God for contemporary man, who has such a thirst for him* (144). For this purpose, *the shepherds of God's people should provide adequate means for promoting among the laity an authentic experience of God* (99).

We can ask ourselves, 'Where have all these desires, declarations, announcements and proclamations led in practice?' We are more aware today than yesterday that if the Church is not contemplative, it will not be evangelical either. We know by experience that you cannot trust a messenger who has not had a personal encounter with the one who gives him the message. Nor can there be any civilization of love without a loving faith anticipating what we hope for. If our seminarians today are not formed in personal and liturgical prayer, we will not have praying and contemplative priests tomorrow. Moreover, if the Church does not quench the thirst of the millions who are searching for God, who will?

The time has arrived for pastoral commitments and action. As means for promoting personal encounter with the Living Christ, I propose the following concrete steps.

- All necessary means should be taken to make the eucharistic celebration be for everyone a special place for a life-giving, personal, and social encounter with the Living Christ. This means, above all, that he who presides at the celebration be deeply convinced that he holds in his hands the *Sacrosanctum Mysterium* and, secondly, that the celebration be an eloquent expression of inculturated Liturgy.

- All the faithful should be instructed in traditional *lectio divina* by an adequate teaching method, so that God may speak to us as we read, then we respond in prayer, taste him in contemplation, follow him in action, and imitate him.

- *Authentic Catholic expressions of piety* (processions, pilgrimages, sacramentals, devotions, especially Marian devotions) should be fostered. These expressions lead to that deeper devotion that is a prompt and fervent will to give oneself to all that is involved in the service of God.

- Young people, at the time of receiving the sacrament of Confirmation, should be initiated into *discernment of spirits* that, according to the most ancient tradition, consists in feeling what is moving in one's heart, judging whether this movement is oriented toward good or toward evil, and choosing the behavior that those motions of the heart call for. This is how young people will enter into communion with God's Spirit through embracing his will.

- Certain forms of *christian contemplative prayer*, which are both traditional and contemporary, should be made known. An example of this is 'centering prayer,' which is based on the ancient Eastern tradition of 'hesychastic prayer' and the Western tradition of 'The Cloud of Unknowing'. These

forms of prayer will allow many Christians to find in their
own tradition what they are looking for in other ones and
to learn by their own experience what contemplation is,
namely, a manifestation of the grace received in Baptism.

- Parish groups of *spontaneous shared prayer* should be created
  and accompanied, so that they may praise the Lord and
  intercede for their brothers and sisters. These groups celebrate
  the work of salvation with a spirit that is generous, joyful,
  selfless, and festive. That is why they strengthen the bonds of
  christian brotherhood in the unity of the Spirit.

- Our native Americans should be helped and guided to *feel in
  harmony* with God, the Creator of all that exists, in the sacred
  place that for them is the earth, since it is a substantial part of
  their religious experience.

- Our pastors need to be both disciples and teachers of the
  art of contemplating the *signs of the times*, so as to discern
  in them the signs of God and cooperate in his work. This
  is an art that is learned on one's knees, in front of the wide
  stage of the world, and elbow to elbow with the crowds. It is
  not enough to throw light on reality. We have to detect its
  hidden causes and draw out the conclusions for social and
  pastoral action.

As monks and nuns of America, we wish to express our desire to
contribute through our own charism to the New Evangelization.
We commit ourselves to create from within our monasteries spaces
of silence, prayer, and contemplation in which to meet God in
Christ—spaces with plenty of time for selflessness and celebration
of God, spaces where the heart expands to welcome all those who
search and thirst for the living God.

We want to do this in communion with all other Christians who are
deepening their baptismal consecration and their desire for contemplation. They are doing this in increasing numbers but less evidently

than us, in *apostolic movements* and *new forms of contemplative life and spirituality.*

May a contemplative encounter with the living Christ be the source and root of conversion, communion, and solidarity. May these in turn be the criteria for judging the authenticity of any personal encounter with Jesus Christ.

SANCTITY AND MARTYRDOM

Bishops' Synod on the Americas,
December 2, 1997

AMONG THOSE WHO WERE INSTRUMENTAL in the early evangelization of America were numerous men and women of holy life. By living out the good news of Jesus, these distinguished figures have been the most authentic and trustworthy witnesses of Jesus Christ. Nor was there lacking among these many saints—be they canonized or hidden—martyrs of faith, hope, and love.

Moreover, it is of great importance for our America that we not forget the martyrs of our own century (TMA 37). In the midst of such a 'cloud of witnesses' (Heb 12: 1), we have to discern which of these followers of Christ stand out for having sealed their faith by shedding their own blood. Indeed martyrdom has always been considered by the Church as a supreme gift and as the clearest proof of sanctity and charity.

The harsh and glorious reality of martyrdom is very much a part of present-day life in our local churches. There exist among us martyrs who have been recognized and others who remain shrouded in the mystery of God. Bishops, priests and deacons, consecrated persons and lay people have watered our soil with their blood for the cause of Christ and his Gospel. We are a Church of martyrs, a Church that is persecuted in different ways and in different places, marked by the cross and by hope in the resurrection. Our Latin American bishops, gathered at Puebla, have recently stated: *Awareness of the evangelizing mission of the Church has led it . . . to suffer in its members persecution and, at times, death, in witness of its prophetic mission* (Puebla 92). *It is inspiring and heartening to see the spirit of sacrifice and self-denial with which many pastors carry out their ministry in service of the Gospel . . . facing solitude, isolation, misunderstanding, and, at times, persecution and death* (Puebla 668).

The death of some Christians who have opted for inadmissible violence and met their death in armed conflict should not eclipse the luminous testimony of so many others who have lived in fraternal love and died in communion with the Church.

In an America where christian morality is being relativized, where the value of life is on the decrease, where there are multiple offenses against human dignity, where social injustice reigns, where hatred seems to be more powerful than forgiveness, and where, to top it off, we Christians are divided among ourselves, precisely in this America there is need to hear the cry of our martyrs.

- They witness in favor of a culture of life in the face of a menacing conspiracy against life and in the midst of a culture of death.

- They bear witness to their faithfulness to the holy law of God, to the inviolability of personal dignity, to long-awaited social justice, and to the splendor of truth and holiness in the Church, even to the point of willingly accepting a violent death.

- They bear witness to their radical bond with Christ and the Father, sealed by a baptism of blood, which is a strong mortar for the unity of Christians, beyond any kind of division.

- They bear witness to the forgiveness that breaks the cycle of hate and violence. This word of forgiveness, flowing from these witnesses of love, finds its source in the cross of the one True Witness (Rv 3: 14): *Father, forgive them, for they do not know what they are doing* (Lk 23: 33–34).

The martyr's witness is meant primarily for the community of believers, stimulating them to be true to the faith they received, above all to faith in the resurrection. Christ himself is at work in his martyrs in such a way that they testify to the continuity of salvation history and to the Lord's continued presence among his disciples and followers.

We earnestly hope that the memory of these witnesses will remain in the consciousness of our Church in America. They will be for us both a model to imitate and a sure help in our struggle against sin, a struggle in which we have not yet resisted to the point of shedding our blood (cf. Heb 12: 4). To this end, there is need to gather names and evidence for all who have a place in the Martyrology of the twentieth century.

We will thus make present, in a visible way, those members of Christ who have died in him in hope of rising with him. What is more, all those who have undergone the great trial and have washed their robes in the blood of the Lamb will stand above the altar of the eucharistic memorial together with Jesus, the True Witness and Firstborn among the dead (Rv 1: 5), when he becomes a body broken and blood poured out for the life of the world.

Various Writings

PROVOCATIVE REFLECTIONS ON CHARISMATIC ASSOCIATIONS

Reflection Paper on Lay Associate Groups, January 1, 1995

I N VARIOUS PLACES WHERE OUR ORDER EXISTS TODAY, we see persons or groups who want to share our charism in one way or another.

In certain places, this is evident by the presence of rooms or houses set aside for groups (often of young people). There are also groups of benefactors who organize to help some community. Finally, there is no lack of requests for a kind of association in view of some form of oblate program.

These facts, which are relatively new for our Order, coincide with the upsurge of lay people in the life of the Church. In several countries, lay movements have changed the concept and vision of the Church itself.

The recent Code of Canon Law has 'canonized' the desire of lay people to share the life and spirituality of religious institutes. According to Canon 303, each institute can establish a type of association with lay people.

How should we interpret these facts? What is the Lord trying to tell us through this sign of the times that certainly seems like a sign from God.

These questions pertain to the service of the Abbot General, since the Constitutions say that the Abbot General 'is the watchful guardian of the Order's patrimony, ensuring its growth' (CST 82.1).

COMMUNION OF CHARISMS

The theology of the Church as a communion offers a basis for an appropriate link between unity and pluralism in the Church.

In the Church-Communion, states of life are linked together, in such a way that they complement one another. Even if their deep meaning is common to all, each has its original and unmistakable profile. At the same time, they exist within a mutual relationship of service.

The plural unity of the Church is not limited to the different states of life, but is expressed more richly by the pluri-formity of charisms and the communion among them.

Every vocation or form of authentic christian life is a life in the Spirit and, for that reason, a charismatic reality.

In receiving the Holy Spirit, we have all received the 'higher charism' of charity (l Co 12:31). Besides, everyone in the Body of Christ fulfills a service or a function, and it is the Spirit that renders him or her apt for this service or function. Because of this, every Christian is charismatic.

- 'Each one has received from God his or her own gift, one this kind, the next something different' (1 Co 7:7).

- 'The particular manifestation of the Spirit granted to each one is to be used for the general good' (1 Co 12:7).

- 'On each one of us God's favor has been bestowed in whatever way Christ allotted it' (Ep 4:7).

- 'Each one of you has received a special grace, so, like good stewards, responsible for all these varied graces of God, put it at the service of others' (1 P 4:10).

Consequently, Scripture teaches us to consider our capacities, abilities, and professions in all their depth—as gifts to be used for building up the community (cf. Ep 4:12). Vatican Council II, taking up this doctrine of the apostle Paul, tells us that:

> *Whether these charisms be extraordinary or more simple and widespread, they are to be received with thanksgiving and consolation since they are fitting and useful for the needs of the Church. Extraordinary gifts are not to be rashly desired, nor is it from them that the fruits of apostolic works are to be presumptuously expected. Those who have charge over the Church should judge the genuineness and proper use of these gifts. Their office is not to extinguish the Spirit, but to test everything and retain what is good (Lumen Gentium 12; cf. Ad Gentes 28, Apostolicam Actuositatem 3).*

John Paul II in the post-synodal exhortation *Christifideles laici* (n§ 24) takes up and amplifies this teaching from the Council:

> *The Holy Spirit, in entrusting the different ministries to the Church-Communion, enriches it with other gifts and particular impulses, called charisms. These can take the most diverse forms, either as expressions*

*of the absolute freedom of the Spirit who grants them, or as responses
to the multiple exigencies of Church history. . . . Extraordinary or
simple and humble, charisms are graces of the Holy Spirit which
have, directly or indirectly, an ecclesial usefulness, for the edification
of the Church, for the good of human persons and for the needs of
the world. Also, in our day, we can see the expansion of various
charisms among the lay faithful, men and women. They are given to
a determined person, but they can be shared by others so that they
are maintained through time as a living and precious heritage which
engenders a particular spiritual affinity among many persons.*

When we were baptized and confirmed, we were consecrated by
the Holy Spirit, for a mission in the Church through the charisms
that the same Spirit granted us. This charismatic aptitude for mission
takes different forms:

- a *personal* and non-transferable charismatic gift: the case of
  individual gifts such as that of religious founders.

- a *double* charismatic gift: the case of gifts shared in marriage.

- a *collective* charismatic gift: the case of institutes of consecrated
  life, of spiritual movements in the Church and other types of
  christian associations.

The 'collective' or shared charism implies a specific mode of being,
a specific mission and spirituality, a style of life and structure at
the service of ecclesial communion and mission. Participation in
a collective charism facilitates the formation of the members of a
determined group, produces a better cohesion of this same group,
forms a more solid identity, gives the sense of belonging to a spiritual
family, is a source of creativity and strength for responding eagerly
to the signs of the times.

Collective charisms, as gifts of the Spirit, are a dynamic impulse that
continually develop in harmony with the Body of Christ which is
in constant growth. They are entrusted to human groups to be lived

and interpreted, to be made fruitful and witnessed to in the service of ecclesial communion in the different cultural contexts of today's world.

Some of these collective charisms are 'shared', as a gift of the Spirit, by persons belonging to different states of life. From this comes their embodiment in forms of secular, priestly, and religious life.

Every institute of consecrated life, priestly association, missionary regrouping, movement in the Church . . . has at its foundation a collective charism, which is an experience of the Father, by a free gift of the Spirit, to build up and serve the Body of Christ (cf. Paul VI, *Evangelica Testificatio* 11–12; SCRIS, *Mutuae Relationes* 12). The signs that characterize a true charism of a new foundation are the following:

- contribution of something new to the spiritual life of the Church.

- particular effectiveness which can even become an occasion of conflict.

- constant verification of fidelity to the Lord and docility to the Spirit.

- prudent attention to the signs of the times and diverse circumstances.

- a sense of belonging to the Church.

- personal submission to the hierarchy.

- daring in one's initiatives, constancy in commitment and humility in trials and contradiction.

- no authentic charism and innovation without interior suffering and the cross (cf. SCRIS, *Mutuae Relationes* 12).

This collective charism, as a 'founding' charism or charism of the founders, is called 'to be constantly lived, conserved, deepened and developed in harmony with the Body of Christ which is in constant growth' (cf. SCRIS, *Mutuae Relationes* 11).

Collective charisms, besides being shared, can be lived and considered as charisms 'open' to new forms of presence and expression in different historical circumstances.

Finally, it should be understood that it is not the founder who communicates the charism to those who associate themselves with him or her. Only the Holy Spirit is the author of charisms in the Church and it is the Spirit alone who communicates them. The group around the founder is born when a certain number of persons become aware of their own vocational grace upon meeting the founder. They join him or her in order to fulfill their particular call. It can be said that the founder mediates the charism through the spiritual harmony that is established between the founder and the others.

All the charisms, as numerous and varied as they are, are united in the single mission of the group. The different charisms find their identity in their mutual relationship within the center of communion and mission of the group.

THE CISTERCIAN CHARISM

The cistercian charism 'has its origin in that monastic tradition of evangelical life that found expression in the *Rule for Monasteries* of Saint Benedict of Nursia' (CST l). The founders of Cîteaux gave this tradition a 'particular form', certain aspects of which were strongly defended by the monasteries of the Strict Observance (CST l).

Our Constitutions, above all in the first part on the Patrimony, are a good presentation of our charism. However, it should be recognized that they do not exhaust the life and the manifestation of this same charism. In order to have a more complete picture, it would be necessary to consult and take into consideration the other members of the cistercian family.

COLLECTIVE CHARISM: CAN IT BE SHARED AND OPEN?

From what we have already seen above, it is clear that the cistercian charism is a collective one. However, can we also consider it as a charism that is open to being shared by others? What does cistercian history teach in this regard? Can our charism be shared with lay persons in the world? Can it open itself to secular forms, that is to say, to a structure that is not monastic in the juridical sense of the word?

An Open Charism

Do the nine hundred years since the foundation of Cîteaux allow us to say that the cistercian charism is an open charism? That is to say, has the cistercian charism known different forms in the course of history?

The Nuns

The founders of Cîteaux did not want a feminine branch. They felt that the form of life they wanted to live was not made for women. But the apparition of feminine groups of nuns and their insistent request for incorporation, association, and recognition, led the nascent Order to open itself to this possibility. It is thus that the feminine expression of the Order appeared, which in certain cases like that of the cistercian nuns of Montreuil did not have much that was feminine about it. Hermann of Tournai speaks to us about these nuns with a certain astonishment:

> *They rush with all their strength toward the Kingdom of God, impatient to vanquish not only the world but also their sex. They have embraced violently, freely, and spontaneously, the Order of Cîteaux which many strong young men do not dare to do. Renouncing linen clothing and furs, they earn their living by working assiduously with their hands in silence; not only spinning and knitting—works proper to women—but also cultivating the fields, cutting wood with hatchet and sickle, tearing up brambles and weeds, imitating the entire life of the monks of Clairvaux, showing by their life the truth of this word of the Lord: 'Everything is possible to those who believe' (De Miraculis Sanctae Mariae Laudunensis, PL 156 col. 1001–1002).*

The Lay Brothers

No one has ever doubted that the lay brothers have shared the cistercian charism since the beginning. However, the lay brothers were not monks and very often they did not live within the monastery. There is no doubt that the presence of the lay brothers was an enrichment of our charism and in no way an impoverishment of it. Thus with the lay brothers there appeared very early in our history a new form of our charism. The same can be said about the 'family brothers' who were present in our monasteries from the beginning.

The text of the *Exordium Parvum* on the lay brothers is well known: 'They thus decided, with the permission of their bishop, to receive lay brothers, who would keep their beards and be treated like themselves during their life and at their death, with the exception of not having the status of monks' (*Exordium Parvum* 15:10). In one of the Statutes of the first General Chapters, we read:

> *The work of the granges ought to be done by the lay brothers and day laborers. With the permission of the bishops, we receive lay brothers,*

as family brothers and as coadjutors, under our care in the same way
as the monks, and we consider them as brothers and sharers of our
goods, both spiritual and material, just like the monks (Collection of
1134; Canivez l:14; cf. Chapter 20 at the end of the *Summa*
Carta Caritatis).

The Military Orders

In a certain manner, with the advent of the military Orders, another
cistercian face appeared. The 'spirit' that animated the Knights of
the Temple was not foreign to the charism of Cîteaux: if Cîteaux
had given the 'New Monastery', the Templars were thus, according
to Saint Bernard, the 'New Combatants Militia', that is, a new form
of monasticism and a new form of knighthood.

This is even more true of the Order of Calatrava. In 1164, Abbot
Gilbert of Cîteaux and the co-abbots meeting in General Chapter,
in response to Don Garcia, head of Calatrava, wrote thus:

As for what you have humbly asked, i.e., to have a share in the
communion of goods of our Order, we willingly consent, not just as
though you were family brothers, but as real brothers.

The Chapter of 1164 left in the hands of the Abbot of Scala Dei,
with the counsel of his filiations in Spain, the task of determining
the 'form of life' that should be observed in the Order of Calatrava
(*Bullarium Ordinis Militiae de Calatrava*, Madrid, A. Marín, 1761,
pp. 3–4). Later in 1187, Calatrava will be fully incorporated into
Cîteaux as a filiation of Morimond.

In practice, the knights of Calatrava were never cistercian monks in
the strict sense. One could say that they constituted a third class of
persons, together with the monks and the lay brothers. It should be
noted that Pope Eugene IV, in 1440, substituted the vow of chastity
for the vow of conjugal chastity in particular cases.

The Cistercian Family

There exist at present, three great branches on the cistercian tree. Using another image, we could speak of the cistercian family composed of the Order of Cîteaux (oc), the Cistercian Order of the Strict Observance (ocso), and the autonomous Congregation of Saint Bernard, associated to the ocso. To these three groups, we could also add the Order of Bernardine Nuns of Esquermes and the Bernardines of Oudenaarde. Can we doubt the cistercian identity of certain of these communities just because they are engaged in teaching or in other forms of the apostolate compatible with monastic life?

In conclusion, our long history shows us that the cistercian charism was open to different forms along the way. Our charism has thus been an open charism and, in a certain sense, a shared charism. It is also true that the various forms that our charism has known have been and are still monastic forms, with the exception of the military Orders and the lay brothers, from a canonical point of view.

A Shared Charism

Is it possible to conceive of the cistercian charism as a charism shared with lay persons in the world, thus making room for a secular cistercian form?

Let us say, first of all, that our charism, like all charisms, is a gift of the Spirit to build up the Church as the Body of Christ. No one possesses the cistercian charism as private property. Our charism basically belongs to the Church. The Spirit can share it with whomever he wants, in whatever measure and in whatever form.

We Cistercians have given a historical monastic form to this particular gift of the Spirit. This monastic form is an integral part of the original charism from the beginning. However, that does not prevent the charism from being shared with the lay brothers, the family brothers, and the knights of the military Orders, as we have seen.

Can the fact that lay people of today feel drawn by the cistercian charism and recognize themselves in it, be understood as a sign that the Spirit wants to share it with them, so that the cistercian charism receive a secular form at this moment of our history?

If the answer to this question is affirmative, a whole series of questions arises: Is there place for mutual recognition and complementarity? Can we speak of mutual charismatic association? Is it true that identity exists only in relationship? What do we have to share that is of value? What are the principal dangers that all this entails?

TENTATIVE ANSWERS

It is not for me alone to answer the questions raised here. The answers must be found in a common search, in the light of the Holy Spirit, and in an atmosphere of discernment of what the Lord of History is saying today to his Church.

Nevertheless, in order to encourage this search, while remaining open to different and even contrary opinions, allow me to give a preview here of several elements contained in any reply.

A Charism Shared with Lay People?

The monastic nature of our Order (CST 2) does not prevent several elements of its spirituality (CST 3) from being shared with lay people in the world. In fact, the *Rule* of Saint Benedict was followed for centuries by oblates who lived outside of the monasteries. Various monasteries of the Order of Cîteaux belonging to different congregations have lay oblates living in the world.

Separation from the world (CST 29), a particular characteristic of our monastic life, should not make us forget that, as members of the Church, our monastic life has 'an authentic secular dimension' that sinks its roots in the mystery of the Word Incarnate. It is certain that all the members of the Church participate in its secular dimension, but in different ways. The 'secular character' of the lay faithful is different and complementary to the secular dimension of monks and nuns (*Christifideles laici* 15).

Our monastic zeal for 'the growth of the Kingdom of God and the salvation of the whole human race' (CST 31) also includes 'the restoration of the entire temporal order' (*Christifideles laici* 15). Our hidden apostolic fruitfulness (CST 3:4) finds a profound harmony with and is completed by the vocation of the faithful laity 'called by God to work as it were from within for the sanctification of the world, as a leaven, by the exercise of their particular tasks' (*Christifideles laici* 15).

Our mission to announce the Gospel by our contemplative presence (CST 68.1) is not exclusive and does not exclude others. On the contrary, it allows for the complementarity of the contemplative presence of lay people immersed in the heart of the world. The particular mission of our charism is not exhausted by our own way of living it. The involvement of the laity in our charism and mission will make its reality and usefulness more evident.

In practice, the mystery of the Church–communion implies an exchange of spiritual gifts at the service of the new evangelization.

Consequently, responding to the question about sharing our charism, I believe that the fact that lay people today feel attracted to the cistercian charism and recognize themselves in it, can be understood as a sign that the Spirit also desires to share it with them, so that the charism receives an added secular form at this moment of our history.

Mutual Recognition?

In the course of history, lay persons associated in different ways to religious institutes kept a certain relationship of dependence on them. This has changed recently. In numerous cases, the request of lay people to participate in the charism of an institute has come from the fact that they feel actually in possession of the charism. It would seem that the experience of Peter in the house of Cornelius is repeating itself, though on another level: 'Could anyone refuse the water of baptism to these people, now that they have received the Holy Spirit? . . . I realized then that God was giving them the identical gift he gave to us . . . and who was I to stand in God's way' (Ac 10:47; 11:17)?

Something similar is happening among us. In our case, when the Order is recognized as historically in possession of the cistercian charism and is questioned about its presence, we must make a discernment on the similarity and authenticity of the charism received by our lay interlocutors.

This also implies an openness on our part to allow ourselves to be discerned concerning the fidelity of our lives to our Constitutions. This discernment also concerns our response to contemporary challenges and the signs of the times.

In the two ways just indicated, it seems to me that we can speak of a mutual charismatic recognition—being recognized, we recognize others in order to be recognized again.

A Charismatic Association?

Since the seventh century, monasticism has been influenced by a certain style of lay life growing up around it, which led to the 'monastic family', in a broad sense. One can say the same about the

Canons Regular and the Mendicants. We know that around the
Mendicants were born the second orders (that is, the consecrated
life for women), the institution of penitents, and the third orders
for the laity.

More recently, various kinds of groups have appeared of religious
Congregations and Societies of Apostolic life who are nourished by
the spirit and who participate in their mission. These groups have
received a wide variety of names: collaborators, partners, associates,
affiliates, colleagues, and so on.

Today, in the context of renewal of the laity and new lay movements,
one finds the phenomenon of lay people who, individually or in
groups, search for a kind of link with institutes of consecrated life.
It seems to me that it is correct and acceptable to give the name
of *charismatic association* to this phenomenon. The theology of the
Church as a living communion, in which all vocational charisms
are of the same origin and have the same end, is the adequate frame
of reference which justifies this name.

Perhaps in a few years, it will be out of style to speak of charismatic associations. The Spirit breathes where he wills, but his work
is always a work of communion. Will we see the day when we
will speak of 'charismatic communion' to refer to the communion
between monks/nuns and lay people in the same charism?

Is Identity in Relationship?

In the light of all the above, it is clear that today it is neither valid
nor appropriate to define vocational identity from a static and closed
perspective. Identity in the different ways of life within the People
of God emerges from the dialectic process of Church life. The distinction of each charism is established in a context of convergence-
divergence, communion-separation.

Consequently, I do not hesitate to affirm the following: our cistercian identity is a reality that allows us to identify ourselves by what distinguishes us within a dynamic of relationships and not of juxtapositions and exclusions.

A clearly defined identity will keep monks from playing at being seculars and these latter from playing at being monks. It will respect the vocations and ways of life proper to each.

What can we share?

The question is a valid one. In general, it seems to me that a start in answering this question should keep in mind the following components of our charism:

- **the following of Jesus:** those aspects of the mystery of Jesus, the Christ, which are given to us as the foundation and the model to follow according to our charism.

- **insertion into the Church:** a specific way of life, of identification with the Church and of being at the service of the local Churches.

- **a concrete spirituality and mission**: which when shared permit the formation of a single religious family.

To arrive at this triple and fundamental objective, we should help the lay people drawn by our charism to do a secular re-reading of this charism. An initial confrontation with our Constitutions can help in this regard.

The cistercian spiritual masters teach everyone to find counsels and directives for the spiritual life in the *Rule* of Saint Benedict. The benedictine *Rule* offers a rich doctrine on humility, obedience, silence, and the fear and love of God. Our Fathers also developed many aspects of life in the Spirit that are hardly found in Saint Benedict, for example: the doctrine of the image and likeness of God, the necessity of self-knowledge to come to the knowledge of God, the journey of the soul toward God, the doctrine on love of the brothers and sisters and of God, the mystical experience, and so on.

Bernard of Clairvaux wrote 'with the aim of building up' (*SC* 27.1). We can ask ourselves: build up what and whom? The answer seems to me to be this: to build up the christian and cistercian life, in the cloister and outside the cloister.

We thus have much to offer and to share. We also have as much to receive: the experience of our charism as lived by the laity is called to enrich the monastic experience of this same charism. Also, as *Christifideles Laici* 61 says so well: 'In their turn, the faithful laity themselves can and should help priests and religious in their spiritual and pastoral path'.

What are the Dangers?

In the face of danger there are only two possibilities: to flee or to confront. The first is already a defeat, the second can be an opportunity for victory. I am aware that the success of charismatic associations is a gift that is difficult to obtain. It seems to me that the three principal problems to solve are:

- **in the order of connection with the Order:** how to establish and organize an adequate link and equality.

- **in the order of identities**: how to safeguard the indispensable differences and autonomies.

- **in the order of formation:** how to establish formation programs without falling into an apostolic activity foreign to our life.

Indeed, it is not easy to establish connections that unite without merging. Quite the contrary, they should unite by differentiating, as true love does. Neither is it easy to form people effectively without a serious formation program.

In spite of the risks, I think it is important to be open to the possible creation of charismatic associations with seculars or with lay people consecrated as individuals or as groups. In the last analysis, it is a question of discerning all this and retaining what is good.

In order to discern, we need to have criteria. For what concerns the local monastic community, I suggest the following criteria:

- **a clear monastic identity**, assimilated and lived, with a certain ability to communicate this identity.

- **intensity of life in the Spirit** that can stimulate and encourage lay people to live the cistercian charism without damaging their own secular vocation.

- **the capacity to help discover and guide new ways** of bringing to life the cistercian charism in the heart of society.

THE SPIRITUALITY OF THE POSTSYNODAL EXHORTATION
Vita Consecrata:

Orientations for a Reading from within the Latin-American
Context Conference at the Semi-Annual Meeting of the
Union of Superiors General, Arricia, May 24, 1996

I HAVE BEEN ASKED FOR A CONTRIBUTION that will be of
help toward a global presentation of the APOSTOLIC EX-
HORTATION ON CONSECRATED LIFE (= VC) in re-
lation to the sensibility and challenges of consecrated life in
Latin America; more particularly, how to present in Latin America today the essential lines of the spirituality of consecrated life
according to the Postsynodal Exhortation.

To this end, I will begin by presenting twelve keys to the reading
that can contribute to an intelligent and attentive reading of the
Exhortation. Afterwards I will point out some of the characteristics
and themes that seem to me important to underscore in order to
bring them to the attention of the reader. Thirdly, I will address

the theme of spirituality and attempt in this way to demonstrate its pertinence with the spiritual sensibility of the Continent of Hope. I will conclude with some evaluative suggestions and others to stimulate study and the living of the life.

Reading Key

A reading key is a guide and a medium of interpretation, that is, an orientation for the reading of a text and its correct interpretation. A true reading key consists of a reality that underlies in some way the whole text, and which illumines it in its entirety and in its parts.

I do not think that these reading keys are Latin American, unless they are considered as such from the simple fact of having been presented by a Latin American.

I consider, however, that they may facilitate an intelligible and intelligent reading of the Exhortation; and even more since these 'keys' are used simultaneously to unlock its mysteries and exult in its treasure. Here, therefore, are the twelve reading keys:

- ecclesial context: continuing from the two preceding Synods, on the Laity and the Priesthood; the states of life in their unity and in their reciprocal complementarity.

- feminine and masculine sensibility: the author (authors!) of the document is a man who directs himself above all to consecrated persons the majority of whom are women.

- pluralism of forms and contexts: consecrated life is present in the Universal Church, on the five continents and in very different cultures; no form is exhaustive and each and all manifest it.

- in response to a lack and a nostalgia: our western society of today needs witnesses to spirituality (Chapter 1: '*Confessio Trinitatis*'), solidarity (Chapter II: '*Signum fraternitatis*'), and service (Chapter III: '*Servitium caritatis*').

- Tabor or the Icon of the Transfiguration: to go up the mountain in order to participate in the glory of Christ and to descend to the valley in order to participate in his service and his cross.

- the connecting thread of the evangelical counsels: from the theological and trinitarian dimension to the social impact as an evangelical counterculture.

- two leading theological themes: charisma and charisms of the Spirit, the following and imitation of Christ.

- two omnipresent categories: consecration and mission.

- the centrality of Christ: Everything is explained by our conformation to Christ and our identification with him. This is the central nucleus of the spirituality of those consecrated.

- open door: In order to continue the reflection so as to intensify the gift of the consecrated life in its triple dimension of consecration, communion, and mission.

- the Life in first place: The life of the following of Christ in the Spirit is not easily reduced to definitions and distinctions; to rationalize it is to impoverish and suffocate it.

- creative fidelity: The renewal promoted by Vatican II is an ongoing process; supported by the historical recollections of the past we are to build future history.

Some Characteristics

There are many peculiarities, characteristics, or notable aspects of the Apostolic Exhortation. I confine myself to highlighting the following among other possibilities.

- tone: positive, stimulating, admiring, and full of gratitude for the gift of consecrated life.

- referring to all the Synodal Propositions: in an organic presentation of them all.

- scope of those addressed: not only the consecrated but also pastors, clergy, laity, and all who wish to know of the wonderful works of the Lord.

- typology of the consecrated life: from monastic life to the newer and present-day forms, progressing from the order of virgins, hermits and widows, institutes totally dedicated to contemplation, apostolic religious life, secular institutes, and societies of apostolic life.

- the founding charism: as font and point of reference obligatory for the life and mission of each consecrated person and of each institute.

- theological and doctrinal clarifications: religious consecration and religious identity, relationship between the states of life.

- themes for study: the discipline of enclosure in monasteries of contemplative life, mixed institutes, new forms of consecrated life.

- influence of eastern and western tradition: divine beauty, response to the mystical intuition of the face of the Trinity; imitation and apostolic following of Christ.

- the socially deformed images of God: the myriad services of consecrated persons ministering to the countless expressions of human suffering.

- the priority of formation: upon it depends the future of consecrated life.

- communion and collaboration with the laity: inviting them to a deeper participation in the spirituality and mission of the Institute.

- the challenge of inculturation: confronted with discernment and daring, dialogue and evangelical incentive.

SPIRITUALITY

It is difficult to delineate the theme of spirituality in the Apostolic Exhortation. The reason is simple: if spirituality is lived theology, then all of the theology of the Exhortation has something to say about spirituality.

At any rate, in order to help in the reading and dissemination of the Exhortation we will say a word on: unity as a basic presupposition, the terminology of our theme, the major texts, the concept, the characteristics, the ways and means of consecrated spirituality, and its validity for Latin America.

Presupposition

There is no doubt that unity or unification of life is one of the fundamental notes of the spirituality of consecrated life and of the consecrated life as such. Division undermines and destroys the life, unification strengthens it and makes it fruitful.

The Exhortation deals with the theme or reality of unity on a triple plane: that of love, that of action and contemplation, and the plane of consecration and mission. Let us look at the most characteristic texts.

- Unity of love

    - 'Such service (especially among the poor and the outcast) is itself a sign of how the consecrated life manifests the organic unity of the commandment of love, in the inseparable link between love of God and of neighbor' (VC 5).

    - 'On the whole, under the ever creative guidance of the Spirit the consecrated life is destined to remain a shining witness to the inseparable unity of love of God and of neighbor. It appears as the living memory of the fruitfulness of God's love even in the human and social realms' (VC 63).

    - The consecrated person 'must be trained in the difficult art of interior harmony, of the interaction between love of God and love of one's brothers and sisters; they must likewise learn that prayer is the soul of the apostolate, but also that the apostolate animates and inspires prayer' (VC 67).

    - 'The specific contribution of consecrated persons, both men and women, to evangelization is first of all the witness of a life given totally to God and to their brothers and sisters in imitation of the Savior, who out of love for humanity made himself a servant . . . Those who love God, the Father of all, cannot fail to love their fellow human beings, whom they recognize as brothers and sisters' (VC 76–77).

    - 'Because of this pre-eminence, nothing can come before personal love of Christ and of the poor in whom he lives' (VC 84).

- Unity between action and contemplation

- 'In every age consecrated men and women must continue
to be images of Christ the Lord, fostering through
prayer a profound communion of mind with him (cf. Ph
2:5–11), so that their whole lives may be penetrated by an
apostolic spirit and their apostolic work with contemplation
(cf. Proposition 7; VC 9)'.

- From this perspective (orientation toward the Father) 'the
charism of each institute will lead the consecrated person to
belong wholly to God, to speak with God or about God,
as is said of Saint Dominic, so that he or she can taste the
goodness of the Lord (cf. Ps 34:8) in every situation' (VC 36).

- 'Institutes involved in one or other form of the apostolate
must therefore foster a solid spirituality of action, seeing God
in all things and all things in God. In fact, 'it is necessary
to know that just as a well-ordered life tends to pass from
the active to the contemplative, so the soul generally returns
with profit from the contemplative life to the active life
in order more perfectly to sustain the active life with the
flame ignited in contemplation. Thus, the active life ought
to lead to contemplation and sometimes, from what we
see interiorly, contemplation should more effectively call
us back to action' (Saint Gregory the Great, *Homilies on
Ezekiel,* Book II,II, 11). Jesus himself gave us the perfect
example of how we can link communion with the Father
to an intensely active life. Without a constant search for this
unity, the danger of an interior breakdown, of confusion and
discouragement, lurks always near. Today as yesterday the
close union between contemplation and action will allow the
most difficult missions to be undertaken' (VC 74).

- 'If, on the one hand, the consecrated life contemplates the
sublime mystery of the Word in the bosom of the Father
(cf. Jn 1:1), on the other hand it follows the same Word
who became flesh (cf. Jn 1:14), lowering himself, humbling
himself in order to serve others. . . . The fact that consecrated

persons fix their gaze on the Lord's countenance does not diminish their commitment on behalf of humanity; on the contrary, it strengthens this commitment, enabling it to have an impact on history, in order to free history from all that disfigures it' (VC 75).

- 'Saint Vincent de Paul loved to say that when one is obliged to leave prayer to attend to a poor person in need, that prayer is not really interrupted because "one leaves God to serve God"' (VC 82).

• Unity between consecration and mission

- 'Those whom God calls to follow him are also consecrated and sent into the world to imitate his example and to continue his mission. Fundamentally, this is true of every disciple. In a special way, however, it is true of those who, in the manner that characterizes the consecrated life, are called to follow Christ 'more closely' and to make him the 'all' of their lives. . . . This is the challenge, this is the primary task of the consecrated life! The more consecrated persons allow themselves to be conformed to Christ, the more Christ is made present and active in the world for the salvation of all. . . . . religious will be all the more committed to the apostolate the more personal their dedication to the Lord Jesus' (VC 72).

We can now ask ourselves, where in practical daily life should the accent be placed in order to facilitate union? The Postsynodal Exhortation answers: 'Consecrated persons, because of their specific vocation, are called to manifest the unity between self-evangelization and witness, between interior renewal and apostolic fervor, between being and acting, showing that dynamism arises always from the first element of each of these pairs'(cf. 1994 Synod of Bishops) (VC 81).

Terminology

In addition to the term 'spirituality', the Exhortation utilizes a triple vocabulary. This variety of terms shows the richness of the reality alluded to and the difficulty of grasping it within one concept. It also shows the current differences of thought that converge in the Postsynodal text.

In the concrete, the Exhortation speaks of 'spirituality', 'spiritual life, or life in the Spirit', 'sanctity and sanctification', 'conformation in Christ', and 'cultivation of the inner man'.

- Spirituality:

  - spirituality peculiar to the institutes, particular style of sanctification and apostolate, Ratio and proper spirituality (VC 30, 48, 93).

  - the spirituality of communion (VC 46, 51).

  - the spirituality of the consecrated life in the plan of theological studies of diocesan clergy (VC 50).

  - inviting the laity to participate in the spirituality of the institutes (VC 54).

  - an active spreading of the spirituality beyond the borders of the institute (VC 55).

  - consecrated participants in ecclesial movements, and the conflict that can arise with the spirituality of the proper institute (VC 56).

  - the spirituality of new forms of evangelical life (VC 62).

  - the Ratio Institutionis should present the path to follow

in order to assimilate fully the spirituality of the respective institute (VC 68).

– the apostolic, ascetical, and mystical dimension of consecration (VC 71).

– the spirituality of apostolic action (VC 74).

– the need to nourish oneself at the fount of a solid and profound spirituality (VC 93).

– The institutes and communities as schools of authentic evangelical spirituality (VC 93, cf. 94).

– The Word of God as primary source of all christian spirituality (VC 94).

– The Eucharist as the fount of the spirituality of each institute (VC 95).

• Spiritual life or life in the Spirit:

– the spiritual life as the principal occupation of cloistered nuns (VC 59).

– life in the Spirit as the primary and principal dimension of ongoing formation (VC 71).

– spiritual life is life in Christ and according to the Spirit (VC 93).

– the spiritual life ought to occupy first place in the program of each institute in order for them to become schools of authentic evangelical spirituality (VC 93).

– the Word of God is a clear and perennial fount of spiritual life (VC 94).

- Sanctity and sanctification:

  – the evangelical counsels as privileged means toward holiness (VC 35).

  – identity proper to each institute and its particular style of holiness (VC 48).

  – to tend toward holiness is the program of all consecrated life in the perspective of renewal (VC 93).

  – striving toward holiness through educational work (VC 96).

- Conformation with Christ:

  – cohesive and conformative identification with Christ of all of one's existence (VC 16).

  – identification with Christ, assuming all his sentiments and his way of life; explicit desire for a total conformation with him (VC 18).

  – the Spirit configures the consecrated with Christ even to the cross (VC 19).

  – a living memorial to the mode of living and being of Jesus (VC 22,29,32).

  – identifying with Christ means taking up Mary's way of life.

  – a fuller configuration from the time of baptism (VC 30),

  – proper to the consecrated is the special conformation with Christ virgin, poor, and obedient (VC 31).

  – transfigured existence is the fruit of contemplating and bearing witness to the transfigured face of Christ (VC 35).

– in each founding charism there predominates a profound desire to be conformed to Christ to give witness to some aspect of his mystery (VC 36).

– the guarantee of all renewal depends on conformation with Christ (VC 37).

– the goal of formation and of consecrated life consists in conformation with the Lord Jesus and with his total sacrifice (VC 65).

– the more the consecrated soul is conformed with Christ the more is Christ made present in the world for the salvation of men (VC 72).

– *do not forget that you, in a very special way, can and must say that you not only belong to Christ but that 'you have become Christ!'* (Saint Augustine, on Saint John's Gospel, XXI,8. VC 109).

• Cultivation of the inner man:

– not closed within himself and open to history (VC 103).

In many of the texts just quoted, the terms are utilized in a double sense, that is, general and particular, for example: the spirituality of consecrated life in general and the spirituality of an institute in particular. The term 'charism' is also used in this double sense: general and particular. Still more, often the Exhortation speaks of the charism in a sense close to or equivalent to that of the spirituality.

Major texts

In this section, I will present those texts or blocks of texts most bearing on the theme concerning us:

- diverse forms of Consecrated Life (VC 6–12).

- guidance by the Spirit of sanctity (VC 35–40; cf. 33).

- life and spiritual orientation of the cloistered (VC 59).

- the rich spirituality of religious brothers (VC 60).

- the primacy of life in the Spirit (VC 71).

- the spirituality of apostolic action (VC 74).

- definitive commitment to the spiritual life (VC 93–95).

Obviously, each one of these major texts deserves a special commentary, but this would be to take us beyond our present purpose.

The concept

In the paragraph on commitment to the spiritual life in response to the challenges of the present-day world, we find a very rich descriptive definition of the spirituality of the consecrated life. The paragraph in question says as follows:

We may say that the spiritual life, understood as life in Christ or life according to the Spirit, presents itself as a path of increasing faithfulness on which the consecrated person is guided by the Spirit and configured by him to Christ, in full communion of love and service in the Church. All these elements, which take shape in the different forms of the consecrated life, give rise to a specific spirituality, that is, a concrete program of relations with God and one's surroundings marked by specific spiritual emphasis and choices of apostolate, which accentuate and represent one or other aspect of the one mystery of Christ. When the Church approves a form of consecrated life or an institute, she confirms that in its spiritual and apostolic charism are

> *found all the objective requisites for achieving personal and communal*
> *perfection according to the Gospel* (VC 93).

It is not difficult to see that the text utilizes a varied terminology; it speaks of life in Christ, life according to the Spirit, spirituality, spiritual and apostolic charism, and a plan of evangelical perfection. It also refers to consecrated life in general and the varied forms of consecrated life, to the individual person, and to communities of persons. The christological, pneumatological, and ecclesial emphasis is evident, to say the least.

Characteristics

The preceding descriptive definition can be augmented by a list of indications or characteristics which shape and define the spirituality of the consecrated life. It is in this way that the aforesaid spirituality receives a unique and characteristic identity in the heart of the ecclesial communion. These characteristics are:

- eschatology: 26–27.

- espousal: 34, 59.

- ecclesiality: 3, 29–33, 46, 47–50.

- gratitude (spousal): 104–105.

- paschal dimension: 23–24.

- trinitarian dimension: 14–22 ,41, 111.

- communitarian dimension: 21, 41–42, 45.

- creative fidelity: 36–37.

- prophecy and martyrdom: 84–86, cf. 87–92.

- mariology: 18, 28, 34, 95, 112.

It would be interesting to discern the 'feminine' and 'masculine' aspects of the ten characteristics listed. In some cases, they are evident, in others not as much.

Means

Spirituality runs the risk of becoming merely 'spiritualistic' and empty talk if it does not offer concrete means that lead to operative options. We speak thus of:

- prayer, *ascesis*, and spiritual combat: 38, cf.71.

- ascetical study related to the search for God: 98.

- *lectio divina*, Eucharist, Liturgy of the Hours, the Sacrament of Reconciliation, spiritual direction, holy rosary: 94–95.

- humble and austere lifestyle: 82, 90, cf.75.

- discernment, personal and of the signs of the times: 68, 73, 79, 81, 84, 94.

- the Evangelical Counsels: 16, 18, 20–22, 30–31, 35, 87–92, 93.

- mission and service: 72–76.

As we can see, the Evangelical Counsels have pride of place; in matters of the consecrated life it could not be otherwise. It is important to emphasize the place of discernment as a means of searching for and discovering the will of God, as much in personal life as within the framework of history.

Validity for Latin America

Let us listen now to the voice of the Latin American Magisterium and to other representative voices in relation to the spirituality of the consecrated life. I will try in this section to show briefly the validity for Latin America of the spirituality presented by the Postsynodal Exhortation.

- Medellin (1968) recommended to religious: 'Develop and deepen a theology and a spirituality of the apostolic life, as it is necessary to acquire a mentality that values supernaturally the penitential elements that envelop the apostolate and enhance the exercise of the theological and moral virtues that go with it' (XII:11,a).

  – The Exhortation with its constant preoccupation with the 'unity of love, of contemplation and apostolic action, consecration and mission' establishes the basis for this spirituality. The discernment of the signs of the times, as presented in the Exhortation, seems to us to be in like manner a privileged means toward a spirituality of the apostolic life.

- Puebla (1979) based its theology-spirituality of the consecrated life on the 'call to the radical following of Christ, identifying oneself with Him according to the Beatitudes' (742).

  – While the following (of Christ) is the basic premise (although not developed) of the Apostolic Exhortation, the reality of the Beatitudes, however, just barely appears.

- The four basic tendencies of the consecrated life in Latin America according to Puebla are: experience of God, fraternal community, preferential option for the poor, insertion in the life of the local church (726–738).

  – These four representative tendencies are amply evident in the Exhortation. The first of them, the experience of God (internalizing and deepening of the faith-life, integrating prayer and life), occupies quite a central place under the names of 'spirituality, life in the Spirit, life in Christ, sanctity, and sanctification' as we have already seen.

- In his 'Apostolic Letter to the Religious of Latin America' of June 29, 1990, the pope indicates as primordial 'an authentic experience of God, which is like a new name for contemplation' and urged them to 'evangelize out of a profound experience of God' (25).

  – The Exhortation presents this experience of God in terms of conformation with Christ and transfiguration on Tabor.

- In Santo Domingo (1992) 'the call to sanctity' occupies a central place (Word, Liturgy, Eucharist, *Religiosidad popular*, Contemplation) directed to all the Church and the 'renewed spirituality demanded by the new evangelization' (31–53). Consecrated persons are not exempt from this call, on the contrary, one of the pastoral lines says rightly: 'foster the vocation to holiness among Religious' (92).

  – This call to holiness, as we have seen, is amply echoed by the Apostolic Exhortation.

- Curiously, in the 'Document of Santo Domingo' the theme of the 'following' is applied to the whole church, to secular institutes, and above all to young people; with respect to them a pastoral program is proposed: 'Let there burst forth a spirituality of the following of Jesus that will further the bonding between faith and life' (116). But little or next to nothing is said in relation to the consecrated life.

- In its Global Plan for 1991–1994 CLAR invites us to 'deepen and consolidate the spirituality that is born from the preferential option for the poor, so that it may be the source of the dynamism and the inspiration of the new evangelization'. It would be a case of a spirituality eminently christocentric, incarnated, prophetic, and contemplative, based and breathed in through the reading and praying over of the Word of God with the poor and out of the painful lived reality of our people. It means a spirituality 'that springs from a new experience of Christ present in the poor, who invites us to follow him and to collaborate with him in the building of his Kingdom, in affective and effective solidarity with the most needy' (*Linea inspirada* III).

  – Once again, there is no doubt that numerous elements are found in the Exhortation that can contribute in one way or the other to this spirituality, although the accent on the reality faced by the people be missing. Interesting in this respect is what is said on the predilection for the poor and the promotion of justice (VC 82).

  (The other inspirational lines were: to take up the new evangelization with greater creativity; to continue living the preferential option for the poor as the fundamental inspiration of the ecclesial life and mission of religious life; renewed effort toward the inculturation of the Gospel; greater ecclesial communion; and evangelization beyond set boundaries.)

- It is also fitting to mention the eighth challenge enumerated by a group of theologians and members of CLAR on the occasion of the International Congress on Religious Life Today (Rome, November 1993): 'To live the experience of God, source and summit of consecration, with joy in the love and following of the poor Jesus, sharing in the faith, the hope, and the poverty of the people. The Word of God gives strength for this spiritual journey; it occupies a central place in prayer, in the search for and execution of the will of God, in union with the people'.

– In the light of this text, we can deplore the lack of a more specific treatment of the theological virtues in relation to the following of Jesus in the Postsynodal Exhortation.

• In its Global Plan for 1994–1998 CLAR invites us to 'deepen and consolidate the spirituality that is born in the experience of Christ the Evangelizer and is nourished by inculturated evangelization and the preferential option for the poor so that it may be a fount of dynamism and inspiration for religious life in Latin America and enable it to be shared with the laity'.

– Again, in the Exhortation we can find numerous elements that can contribute to the spirituality inculturated and shared with the laity.

(The other inspirational lines are: Option for the poor; inculturation of the Gospel; Ecclesial communion; Woman and the feminine.)

Conclusions

To conclude I would like first to establish a strict relationship between spirituality and renewal of consecrated life; second, to add some suggestions in order to continue the reflections and bring them to every day life; and third, I would like to offer an appraisal of the Postsynodal document.

• Renewal

– 'While it is true that the renewal of the consecrated life depends primarily on formation, it is equally certain that this training is in turn linked to the ability to establish a method characterized by spiritual and pedagogical wisdom, which will gradually lead those wishing to consecrate themselves to put on the mind of Christ the Lord' (VC 68).

– 'To tend toward holiness: This is in summary the program of every consecrated life, particularly in the perspective of its renewal on the threshold of the third millennium. The starting point of such a program lies in leaving everything behind for the sake of Christ, preferring him above all things in order to share fully in his Paschal Mystery' (VC 93; cf. 39,112).

• Addition

– It would be interesting to compare the major texts of the Apostolic Exhortation on spirituality, especially nos. 35–40, with:

- *Laborem Exercens* 24–27 (Elements of the spirituality of work).
- *Familiaris Consortio* 55–64 (The family, a community of dialogue with God and in the service of man).
- *Christifidelis Laici* 16–17 (Called to holiness) and 59–60 (Unity of life, spiritual formation).
- *Pastores Dabo Vobis* 19–33 (Spiritual life of the priest) and 45–50 (Spiritual formation).

– From an objective point of view and having as a goal the communication to others of the riches contained in the Exhortation we could:

- Define each of the sections or major and minor parts.
- Determine the specific content of each.
- Pay close attention to the sources.
- Single out parallel passages.

- Make comparisons with other Magisterial texts.
- Point out innovations.
- Follow out and enlarge upon a specific theme.

– From a subjective perspective, the following questions could help us to arrive at an existential deepening of our understanding of the Exhortation:

- Illumination: What does the text say?
  What in it, do I not understand?
  What lights does it offer me?

- Affection: What sentiments does the text arouse in me?
  What sentiments do I project on it?
  What parts leave me unmoved?

- Adhesion: To what does the text invite me?
  What stands in my way?
  What means does it offer me?

- Action: I live out what I have read!
  I evaluate my life by the light of the Apostolic Exhortation.

- Evaluation

– There is no doubt that spirituality or life in Christ according to the Spirit occupies a most important place in the Exhortation. This fact ought to move us to gratitude and to action. Without spirituality, the consecrated life would cease to be a life!

– The reiterated emphasis placed on the unity and unification of the life is of capital importance. The divorce between the love of God and love of neighbor, between contemplation and action, and between consecration and mission has been the bane of spirituality down through the ages.

– Perhaps some would have preferred a more 'systematic' treatment of spirituality, such as that offered by the Exhortation *Pastores Dabo Vobis*. But I do not know if this effort at systematization would be appreciated by the great feminine majority to whom the document is addressed.

– The theme of following Jesus according to the evangelical counsels could have found its traditional and ever relevant complement in the evangelical Beatitudes.

– The theology and spirituality of the cloister can be enriched by the biblical and traditional theme of the 'desert'. In this way it would also be a source of inspiration for so many who seek God in institutes integrally dedicated to contemplation. (The addition of the word 'grave' in exclaustrations for 'just reasons' would deserve a complete commentary on its own, but this would take us beyond our present purpose.)

– Interesting and welcome to apostolic spirituality is the presentation of discernment of the signs of the times as an indication of the working of God in human history.

– The invitation to foster and sustain the effort of all Christians toward perfection through spiritual initiatives and a sharing of particular spirituality is a magnificent challenge and a stimulus toward cooperation with the Lord in one's own sanctification.

In short and, finally, in conclusion, if we live all that the Postsynodal Exhortation on the spirituality of consecrated life says to us we would hardly have time to lament over what is lacking to it. Let us take advantage of the present moment. Let us begin. The Kingdom of God is to be made a reality!

TOWARD A THEOLOGY OF OUR MONASTIC CONTEMPLATIVE LIFE

Reflection Paper for the Secretaries of
Regional Formation, August 20, 1997

T HE NINTH CENTENARY OF THE FOUNDING OF
CÎTEAUX is an invitation to reflect, pray, and renew.
It is truly a unique moment, a passage through our
midst of the Lord who invites us to a new life in his
life-giving Spirit. There are already many initiatives taking place
to commemorate the event and to activate the founding charism
received by our first fathers.

In this context of celebration, I would like to speak with you about
a desire I have carried in my heart for several years. In other circumstances I have spoken of the need to develop a 'monastic anthropology for cenobites' that is open to the reality of cultural pluralism.
Some attempts have already been made in this regard and other
efforts are in the making. Let me just say that I give my full support
and encouragement to whatever can be done in this field. However,
this is not the theme that I wish to speak about.

I have also been asking myself whether the time is not ripe to begin to develop a 'Theology of Cistercian Life.' Some works on this subject already exist. They were written by individual authors, but there is still much to be done. There is need to work together to produce something that would be open to differences of gender, to transcultural realities, and to the multicultural world in which we live.

The Postsynodal Exhortation, *Vita Consecrata*, and all the preparatory documents for the Synod of 1994 on Religious Life offer a frame of reference that is both new and in continuity with the teachings of Vatican II. Consequently, we cannot ignore the long road traveled since the Council. It has been a journey often accompanied by timely words from the Church's Magisterium. Here are its successive stages:

- spiritual renewal and institutional *aggiornamento*: *Perfectae caritatis* (1965).

- rediscovering the person: *Ecclesiae sanctae* (1966) and *Renovationis causam* (1969).

- emphasis on community life and evangelization: *Evangelica testificatio* (1971).

- reformulating the sense of Church communion, contemplation and mission to the world: *Mutual Relations* (1978), *Religious and Human Development* (1980), *Contemplative Dimension of Religious Life* (1980).

- new institutionalization: *Essential Elements* (1983), *Code of Canon Law* (1983), *Redemptionis Donum* (1984).

- emphasis on formation: *Potissimum institutioni* (1990).

- pre-synodal stage of crisis, retrogression, repetition, exhaustion, deeper reflection, new beginnings and new forms emphasizing the religious community: *Lineamenta* (1993), *Instrumentum Laboris* (1994), *Fraternal Life in Community* (1994) and the Pope's *Wednesday Catechisms* (1994–1995).

Nor can we ignore the larger context of life in the Church and the world: the shift of Christianity toward the South and East; the global program of a new evangelization; the deep social, economical, and cultural changes typical of a new era.

To help kindle your enthusiasm, I wish to share with you some of the guiding principles and features that this theology would have.

PRINCIPLES

To draw up a 'Theology of our Cistercian Life' (= TCL), we have to take into account the following elements.

- Our new Constitutions give us a valuable beginning for a theology of consecrated life and, in particular, of our cistercian monastic life.

- The TCL must be for our monks and nuns, not they for a theology. It is therefore a means, not an end. What may be appropriate today may not be so tomorrow.

- The TCL should make our monastic identity explicit, guide our form of life and our mission, as well as our place in the Church and the world. That is to say, it should clarify the meaning, purpose, and goal of our existence, and motivate our lives.

- The TCL should be, at one and the same time, essentialist and existentialist. It will be essentialist in so far as it presents our life as an all-embracing project of absolute search for

God, as fraternal communion, conversion, and prayer for
the Church and the world, and as the following of Jesus
and availability to the Spirit. It will be existential by being a
concrete, historical project to be lived and thus give a form
to one's existence.

• In the last analysis, our cistercian life itself is the criterion for
discerning the quality and authenticity of a TCL.

FEATURES

It is not easy to sum up in a few words the features that should identify a TCL. Moreover, such an undertaking strikes me as somewhat
dangerous, though not rash. So let us run the risk.

• The TCL should start from the **contemplative experience**
of monks and nuns. It is a question of reflecting from the faith
on a life of faith that is centered on God and lived by persons
who are 'consecrated' to God by the action of God himself.
Such reflection should have the same characteristics as faith
itself has, namely, it should be theological, christological,
ecclesial, sacramental, communitarian, contemplative,
missionary, testimonial, historical, and eschatological. At
heart, a TCL is a spiritual theology able to overcome the gap
between doctrinal reflection and concrete life by having life
precede reflection.

• Like all good theology, it must stress a **unifying theme**
that brings together all the different aspects of the subject.
This unifying theme has differed throughout the history of
consecrated life. At this moment, the principal themes that
direct our vision and channel our energies are the following:

  - **consecration:** understood as the divine action causing a
  total gift of self into the hands of God.

- **manifestation** of God: a reflection of the life of the Trinity and of the great things God has done in the transfigured life of those consecrated to him.

- **representation** of Jesus' own way of life: the Church and the world need some people who incarnate in a selective and exclusive way the memory of its original, most Jesus-like features.

- **following** of Jesus: loyalty and conformity to the person of Jesus is nourished and manifested in a life of evangelical simplicity.

- **charism**: by putting the person of the Holy Spirit at the center of consecrated life, the religious is seen as a Christian characterized by spontaneity, fortitude, daring, freedom, originality, and flexibility.

- **prophet**: witnessing to community life, correcting errors by offering alternate models and bringing to birth by new life and new words.

- **reminding us** of Jesus: whether by recollection and celebration or by subversion and conversion.

- **parable** of God's kingdom: spoken by the Holy Spirit and able to become an instrument of cultural change or a countercultural sign.

It is important, after beginning with one of these themes, to integrate the other ones and bring them down to daily life.

- A TCL orders or **systematizes** in a particular way the common, essential elements of all consecrated life. This includes vocation, consecration, evangelical counsels, community, formation, prayer, asceticism, mission, and the like.

- A TCL must define a monk and a nun by what they are in **relation**—not in opposition—to other human beings, other Christians, other Catholics. Only in terms of a Church, which is Communion, can we understand personal vocations oriented as complementary services for the common mission of the Church to the world. What is different and original has to be understood as something complementary. Monks and nuns have to be able to tell the laity, 'With you we are Christians and for your sake we are monks and nuns'.

- More than a state, monastic existence is a **process**. It was born as an act of life and can only be understood correctly as a concrete expression of life. That is why the TCL cannot ignore the history of consecrated life in the Church and has as its task to describe a form of life for persons totally committed to searching for God in such a way that he may become the life of their lives. Thus, our TCL can very well be a type of narrative theology.

- Something else that cannot be ignored is the fact that cistercian life has had different expressions or **incarnations** throughout its history. Therefore a TCL must take into account the different accents and currents within our one spiritual family and be marked by an authentically 'ecumenical' cistercian spirit.

- Nor can it be overlooked that the cistercian grace, from its very first years, has been lived by both men and women. This fact will color our theological reflection with a quality of reciprocal **complementarity** between the genders.

- A correct TCL has to refer to the evangelical **mission** and service that are part of all forms of consecrated life. Our mission is explained from our identity, but the latter can also be understood in terms of mission. In fact, mission is identity in its most vital and dynamic aspects. The mission of our monastic life to the Church and the world can be understood in several ways: for example, as witness, transcendence, prophecy, service, intercession or representation.

- The **identity** of our monastic life must reside in its particular form and not just in a certain degree or intensity, as in the phrases, 'more completely', 'closer to', or 'more fully'. The TCL has to pinpoint the different original form by which the monk and the nun incarnate realities that are common to all Christians, such as the following of Jesus, consecration to the Lord, service and witness, personal and communal prayer, ascetical discipline, evangelization, and mission.

- **Cultures** are, to a great extent, at the origin of different forms of consecrated life. These forms are inevitably marked by a cultural stamp. So there should not be a divorce between monastic life and culture. That is why the TCL should study their mutual interrelationship and should speak about a monastic life that is inculturated, and about a culture marked by monastic life.

- An authentic TCL has to be useful for renewing, encouraging and establishing our lives on solid principles. If it does not provide this vital service, it is a sign that it did not proceed from lived experience.

I leave you here with this concern of mine, which I hope will become the concern of some or many of you. Let us continue to pray, so that these desires may be crystallized in some concrete project by the work of the same Spirit whom I believe inspired them, for the good of many brothers and sisters of the Order, and also for the good of the Church and the world.

MYSTICISM: KEY TO THE RE-EVANGELIZATION OF THE CANONICAL CONTEMPLATIVE LIFE

Association of British Contemplatives, Contemplative Challenge 2000, York, June 21–25, 1999

INTRODUCTION

The 'adapted renewal' of consecrated life proposed by the Second Vatican Council (*Perfectae Caritatis* 2) implied a simultaneous:

- *renewal*, that is, a rediscovery of the original, essential, permanent values.

- *adaptation*, or discovery of up-to-date ways to express and live these values.

- *process*, since renewal is not limited to a single action, but rather to the creation of attitudes that will then be expressed in concrete acts.

Looking back over these recent years, we can easily see all the positive good that has been achieved: the primacy of the Gospel, the return to the heritage of each Institute, adaptation to the here and now—this particular place at this particular period of time—with consequent reforming of structures and institutions. All of this has helped us clarify what the charism of consecrated life is, and what the charisms within it are. Thus, we have been able to write our new Constitutions.

The limitations of what has been achieved are also evident, despite the variety of circumstances and situations. Here are some of these limitations in the renewal process.

- There is an abundance of new words without the corresponding new ideas; in other words, a change of vocabulary but no change of vision.

- There is still need to pass from declarations to programs and from programs to daily life.

- There are still confusions to be clarified, such as between poverty and economy, personalism and individualism, generosity and activism, liberty and independence, unity and uniformity, fidelity and habit, authenticity and spontaneity, dialogue and debate, asceticism and gymnastics, charism and hobby, transformation and change, perseverance and survival.

We need not be surprised at this. True renewal is a permanent necessity. Thirty-five years after the Council, we still hear the Church Magisterium saying:

> *Institutes of Consecrated Life are thus invited courageously to propose anew the enterprising initiative, creativity, and holiness of their founders and foundresses in response to the signs of the times emerging in today's world. This invitation is first of all a call to perseverance on the path of holiness in the midst of the material and spiritual difficulties of daily life. But it is also a call to pursue competence in personal work*

*and to develop a dynamic fidelity to their mission, adapting forms, if
need be, to new situations and different needs, in complete openness to
God's inspiration and to the Church's discernment. But all must be
fully convinced that the quest for ever greater conformity to the Lord
is the guarantee of any renewal that seeks to remain faithful to an
Institute's original inspiration (Vita Consecrata 37).*

So it is not strange that reference is made today to '**refounding**' institutes of consecrated life. In this context, *refounding* is the expression
of creative fidelity facing the challenge of '*re-locating*' the charisms
and the new '*network of presences*'. *Refounding* means, in our particular case, returning radically to the foundations of contemplative life
so as to live our charism meaningfully in a new, different cultural
context.

It is in this context that I wish to speak about a '**new evangelization**'
of the canonical contemplative life, so that it can be '*good news*', that
is, a gospel for the man and woman of today. To do this, we have to
emphasize christian faith as *life*—as a total, integrating experience.
More exactly, we have to accentuate the **mystical dimension** of
our lived christian experience and center it on the experience of
Christ himself.

I have heard that in some areas of the Anglo-Saxon world *mysticism*
is referred to ironically as 'Mist-I-cism':

- **MIST**: as beginning in **mist,** a fog or the clouds.

- **I**: as the center in a process of self-centered navel-gazing.

- **CISM**: that is, ending in **schism,** separation from the
  community or opposition to institutional religion.

To avoid misunderstandings, let us say from the start that religious
experience is either integral and integrating or it is nothing. **Christian experience** is *par excellence* a structured experience: it takes up
all aspects of the person and integrates them hierarchically. It is an

experience of relationship with God, which implies that the whole human being is involved, spirit-soul-body, in a relationship that pulls the person toward the fullness of the divine Being. We can say synthetically that the christian experience is an integral human event, determined by the relationship between a believer and divine revelation, this revelation being Christ himself; all of which is even more valid when it is a question of the christian mystical experience.

It is true that the word, 'mystical', does not appear in **Sacred Scripture**, but it is possible to clarify what is meant by the word by looking at Scripture. The Bible is no stranger to the reality that the term 'mystical' expresses. Scripture speaks to us in a wide variety of ways about the relationship between God and humans, and about how the latter share in the life and mystery of God.

The first and most basic fact can be stated as follows. Long before we took an interest in God, God was already concerned about us (Is 40:27; 49:14–16). God is the first to break silence by his creating word (Gn 1). He is at the door and knocks (Rv 3:20). Paul quotes the prophet Isaiah and has the Lord say, '*I let myself be found by the one who was not looking for me*' (Rm 10:20).

'Mystical' teaching according to the Bible states that the human being is known/loved by God before he or she knows/loves God (Ga 4:9). Scripture constantly affirms the primacy of divine revelation over human searching and of grace over merit; the kingdom of God grows like a seed in the earth, even while the farmer is sleeping (Mk 4:26–29). To put it briefly, divine *eudokia* (*good will*) always comes before human good will (Lk 2:14).

This God, who always walks ahead of us and then comes to meet us, reveals himself above all:

- in **Salvation History**: as witnessed to in the early creed of Israel (Dt 26:6–9; Ps 136; Jos 24:1–13) and by christian faith in the Incarnation, which sees God's supreme Revelation and perfect Temple in the **flesh** of Christ (Jn 1:14; 2:19–22; 1 Co 6:19).

- in the **cosmic temple** of creation (Ps 19; 104) or in the **Temple of Mount Sion** (1 K 8).

- through his efficacious **Word** that makes the arid earth of human existence fertile (Is 55:10–11).

The second fundamental teaching of Scripture on mysticism is this: *Immanû-'el*, or 'God with us', demands a free, loving dialogue from his created children. God gives himself so that his creature can receive him. Christ knocks at the door and speaks; the believer must open to him and reply. Scripture uses some basic categories to present this reality of giving and receiving, knocking and answering.

- **Agape**. It is clear that God takes the initiative (I Jn 4:10,19; Eph 2:4). The human person answers in two ways: vertically toward God and horizontally toward neighbor (Dt 6:5; Mt 22:37; Jn 15:12). It is precisely the horizontal dimension that serves as a gauge to verify the authenticity of the mystical experience, which, at its height, lets the human person love as God loves (1 Co 13; Mt 5:48). This category of *agape* brings with it a rich set of symbols.

  - **The Father** cares for and educates his children lovingly by means of purifying trials (Dt 8:5; Hos 11:1–4).

  - **The Mother** expresses her love in the intensity and tenderness of a relationship of total trust (Is 49:15; Ps 131; cf. Lk 15).

  - **Nuptial love** is portrayed by the prophets starting with Hosea (1–3; Is 54; 62:1–5; Jr 2:2; Ez 16) and reaches its height in the Song of Songs.

- **Communion**. Here it is a question of the *abiding and remaining* presented by John the Evangelist in the discourses of the Last Supper (Jn 13:17) and in his First Letter (1:7; 3:16; 4:7, 11, 16, 20–21). This category is also present in the symbols of:

  - the **Vine** and the branches (Jn 15).

  - the **Bread** of life (Jn 6).

- **Life**. This is the broadest category of giving and receiving, because it lets God be all in all (1 Co 15:28). It is a category that is expressed, in its turn, in different ways:

  - **by a New Covenant**, which implies a pouring out of the divine Spirit and a change of hearts (Jr 31:31–34; Ez 36:24–27).

  - **by belonging**, as the Psalmist says, *I am yours, Lord* (Ps 119:94). Saint Paul says it even better: *For me to live is Christ . . . It is no longer I who live, but Christ lives in me . . . Our Life is hidden with Christ in God* (Ph 1:21; Ga 2:20; Col 3:3).

  - **by eternity.** Mystical life never ends, because it is divine life itself (Ps 16:2, 10–11; 73:23–28). The Christian who has shared in the Passover of Christ will live forever with the Lord (Ga 6:17; 1 Th 4:17), since nothing now can separate him from that love, which is the love of his God (Rm 8:35–39).

For the time being, this is sufficient for introducing christian mysticism. However, I would like to add that christian mysticism is distinguished from other forms of mysticism by the following qualities or **characteristics**.

- It is grace, a **gift from God** and not a fruit of human effort. Therefore, it presupposes a humility in the person receiving it, so that he or she does not search for special religious experiences, but only for union with God ('agreement of wills').

- It refers to the **christian mystery** and to a particular way of living it. It is uniform with the mystery and never supercedes it.

- It passes through the **humanity of Christ**, or at least opens the Christian in the direction where Christ's humanity can be found, which implies a Passover quality of death and life, passion and resurrection, cross and glory.

- There is **no separation** between spirit and matter. These two dimensions have been united by the mysteries of the Incarnation and the Resurrection. The whole person has been redeemed and purified by the Passover of Christ.

- It implies a **social and ecclesial dimension**. A mysterious flow of grace is generated in mystical union, which is poured out over the Church and over all humanity.

- It is born, nourished, and reaches its fulfillment in the exercise of **christian love**.

In other words, christian mysticism is inseparable from Christianity as an organized institution, liturgical celebration, Gospel ethic, or theological reflection.

Let us now look at the present cultural situation in the North Atlantic countries. Most sociologists agree in stating that we are living at a moment of cultural transition. Rather than speaking about an age of change, they speak about a change of age.

Like all transitional periods, ours is one of crisis. We are living at a critical moment, such as the christian West did in the fourteenth and fifteenth centuries. At that time, the period of the 'Renaissance' was simultaneously the end of the Middle Ages and the dawn of the Modern Age. So, we are living in a critical hour that is open to a new birth but that, at this moment, is marked by crises of:

- **life**: there is a change from seeing life as absolute and sacred, to thinking of it as a 'purely biological phenomenon'.

- **identity**: there is a change from a closed, complete conception of identity, to thinking of it as an open process.

- **sexuality**: there is a change from a genital and biological approach, to one that is open to choice by the person, by the culture or scientifically.

- **ideology**: there is a shift from ideology as 'the organization of life's meaning' to a de-ideology that 'feels good'.

- **meaning**: there is a shift from signs that have lost their meaning to signs that are truly or supposedly meaningful.

- **time**: there is a change from helping someone to 'use time well' to teaching that person to 'waste time well'.

- **paradigms**: there are changes from large 'frames of reference' to partial frames of reference.

- **humanity**: there is a shift from a human nature that is masculine, cerebral, and rational to a humanity that is feminine, heart-centered, and affectionate.

From the viewpoint of **religion**, we are also experiencing an important transitional crisis. Simplifying it to the extreme, we can say that, if religion was something pathological in modern culture, in the new 'postmodern' context, religion is therapeutic. In postmodern values and language, we find a new appearance of the divine, but accompanied by a deinstitutionalizing of religion. What are the causes of this phenomenon? There are many different answers:

- the recovery of our traditional mystical heritage.

- the impact on Western culture of its meeting with Eastern cultures.

- saturation with the dictatorship of reason.

- the need for mystery to counteract science's pretense of explaining everything.

- the need for self-denial and self-giving to counteract the monopoly of efficiency, consumerism, waste and violence against nature, mother earth and the environment.

- amazement at, and fear of, human power, which can transform nature by genetic engineering and atomic science, but cannot control the ongoing consequences of this transformation.

Everything seems to show that the western culture of the North Atlantic, marked as it is by the postmodern shift, is **thirsting for mystery,** wearied of ideologies, moralisms, dogmatics, and ritualism. Such a cultural context lets us reevaluate genuine religious experience and the mystical dimension of christian life. In so doing, we need to avoid falling into a type of mystical fideism that tends toward a heresy of feeling that all are already one without conversion. That is also why we *are in duty bound to offer a generous welcome and spiritual support to all those who, moved by a thirst for God and a desire to live the demands of faith, turn* to us (*Vita Consecrata*, 103).

To conclude, I take for granted that each and every one of us is ready to obey literally and lovingly the *Code of Canon Law,* at least the canon that says, *Contemplation of divine things and assiduous union with God in prayer is to be the first and foremost duty of all religious* (can.663). Therefore it is not necessary to speak about the need for daily Eucharist, adoration of the Blessed Sacrament, *lectio divina*, personal prayer, celebration of the Liturgy of the Hours, praying the rosary, and a yearly spiritual retreat. I presuppose all that, and without these basic exercises, it is better not to speak, but to keep silent.

MYSTERY—MYSTICISM—THE MYSTIC

Mystery

The word **mystery** is not synonymous with *enigma* or *problem*. A mystery is incomprehensible, but not unintelligible. If it were unintelligible, it would be *absurd*. Mystery refers to the deepest dimension of reality. It points to the ultimate nucleus that gives meaning to all that exists. That is why a human being is a mystery and has been created for mystery. Human understanding and love are able to embrace mystery, although many times sin encourages reason to think that mystery can be eliminated.

In **paganism**, the mysteries were, strictly speaking, 'sacred rites revealed only to those initiated in them'. In the Alexandrian eremitism of the second and third centuries, the term begins to indicate a religious philosophy.

In a purely christian context, **Saint Paul** uses the word 'mystery' in its meaning of a religious teaching. He is influenced by jewish wisdom literature and jewish apocalyptic, which was untouched by any greek influence. For Paul, the mystery is:

- the divine plan, hidden at first, then manifest, to establish a relationship between God and the human race in Christ.

- in Christ, communion of men and women with God is achieved through sonship. Christ the Mediator is the same *Christ in you, the hope for glory* (Col 1:27), who joins the Church to himself as his own body (Col 1:24). In other words, it is a divine plan or project of sonship and brotherhood: *those he foreknew he also predestined to be conformed to the image of his Son, so that he might be the firstborn among many brothers* (Rm 8:29).

- revealed and fulfilled in the Church, is known and lived by Christians in different ways. Among these ways, the outstanding one is the inner experience given by the Holy Spirit. In this sense, Paul speaks of *full knowledge and wisdom* (Ph 1:9–10; Ep 1:15–19; Col 1:3–5, 9–12; 2:2–3; 3:9–14; 2 Co 2:6–10), which is basically a normal experience of the Spirit who interiorly transforms the believing Christian by causing Christ to dwell in that person's heart and rooting him in love (Eph 3:16–7).

Christian mysticism must always be understood as referring to this mystery.

The **Fathers** of the Church embrace the Pauline concept of mystery in different ways. We can say very synthetically that the mystery is the divine plan of salvation in Christ by the Spirit. It is a plan that is hidden, then revealed, with the characteristics of being:

- **eternal**, since God conceived it from endless ages and forever.

- **free**, since the mystery springs from the totally free decision of the divine will.

- **intelligent**, because it is the fruit of a wisdom that is infinite and divine.

- **loving**; since love is the content of the mystery and also its final end.

- **historical**, because it became visible and continues to be so in particular times and places.

- **personal**, because the mystery is addressed to each human being in his or her uniqueness.

- **communitarian**, including everyone in a fraternal relationship of love that takes place in the Church.

- **present**, because the mystery refers to the 'nowness' of each one of us.

- **liturgical**, since it is meant to be celebrated with active participation and through efficacious symbols.

- **irrevocable**, for God neither repents of, nor withdraws his committed word.

- **transcendent**, since the mystery always goes beyond our capacity to understand it.

- **in Christ**, implying that the mystery of man is clarified in the mystery of the Incarnate Word (*Gaudium et Spes* 22).

We can now ask ourselves the following question: In what does the christian mystery basically consist? We answer that, strictly speaking, there are only **three** absolutely original Mysteries:

- the mystery of the Most Holy **Trinity**.

- the mystery of the redemptive **Incarnation** of the eternal Son of God.

- the mystery of the gratuitous **deification** of human beings.

All the other truths of faith are mystery in so far as they are related to these original mysteries. Therefore, mystical experience refers to these three basic mysteries and only secondarily, by derivation, to other mysteries. All of them find their synthesis and fulfillment in Christ.

Mysticism and the Mystic

Mysticism is a **human reality** that is not limited to any particular religion. It is the apex of the encounter between the absolute Being and the human being. There have been mystics in all times and places. Since the human person has been created in God's image, it is not absurd to say that the depth of the human soul is capable, under certain circumstances, of experiencing something of the divine presence, even when human reason may not understand what is happening.

That is why Vatican II affirms that: *An outstanding cause of human dignity lies in the human person's call to communion with God. From his conception and birth man is already invited to converse with God, for the person would not exist were he or she not created by God's love and constantly preserved by it* (*Gaudium et Spes* 19). Consequently, the desire for mystical experience is something intrinsic to human nature. Every human being comes from the same Creator, so that the deepest element of human nature is always the same, namely, to have been made in the image of God and to have an inner thrust toward the perfection of his likeness.

Before the advent of Christianity, the word 'mystic' was used in **greek culture** to denote a 'secret' that was ritual, not doctrinal. When the term passed into Christianity, it acquired a doctrinal and experiential connotation, so that to understand the word we have to understand the meaning of mystery, which is what we have just seen.

Now the purpose of the christian mystery is to be **revealed and embraced** through knowledge and love. The degrees of its reception will depend on the light and fire communicated by the Spirit and on human dispositions. Revelation and faith together constitute the mystery of the meeting of God and man in Christ Jesus.

> *In his goodness and wisdom God chose to reveal Himself and to make known to us the hidden purpose of his will by which through Christ, who is the Word made flesh, humankind might in the Holy Spirit have access to the Father and come to share in the divine nature (Dei Verbum 2).*

Growth in the reception of the mystery goes from the simple act of believing up to the mysterious **experience** that is called 'mystical'. We all, however, are called to grow. Saint Paul offers up his labors for the Christians of Colossae, so *that your hearts may be encouraged as you are brought together in love, to have all the richness of fully assured understanding and perfect knowledge of the mystery of God, Christ, in whom are hidden all the treasures of wisdom and knowledge* (Col 2:2ff.).

It is in this context that we can remember Jesus' question to his disciples, with the dialogue that followed: *'Who do you say that I am?' Simon Peter said in reply, 'You are the Messiah, the Son of the living God'. Jesus said to him in reply, 'Blessed are you, Simon son of Jonah. For flesh and blood has not revealed this to you, but my heavenly Father'* (Mt 16:15–17).

The patristic texts referring to *mystikós* refer to four interlocking realities:

- the **mystical–biblical** dimension, that is, the allegorical meaning of Scripture, the key meaning of which, in fact its only meaning, is Christ.

- the **mystical–liturgical** dimension, especially the celebration of the Eucharist in which the reality of the mystery is the content of both the Scripture readings and the Sacrament.

- the **mystical-spiritual** dimension, referring to a direct and almost experiential knowledge of God through deep communion with him.

- the **mystical-transformative** dimension, by which the mystery contemplated in Scripture and celebrated in the Liturgy is fulfilled in Christians by accomplishing their divine transformation.

The preceding clarifications help us understand what and who **mystics** are. Simply put, they are all those who enter into the Mystery and let themselves be transformed by it, that is, by God. In this sense, every baptized person is a mystic, but that does not mean that every baptized person has a conscious mystical experience. Generally, the mystical experience of the baptized is latent and formless on the level of consciousness and affectivity.

More particularly, mystics are those persons who have experienced the revelation of the mystery, thanks to a mysterious divine touch of knowledge, love, light, and fire.

Our experience of the mystery, that is, our awareness and living out of its presence and communication, is always combined with an ascetic life. The experience transforms us ethically, since it makes us one with God in mutual love and agreement of wills.

Christian mystics find their inspiration and their original source in the mystic *par excellence,* Jesus of Nazareth. Jesus' consciousness of himself as Son reached a peak moment on the day of his baptism, but there were other key moments: Tabor, Gethsemane, and Golgotha. Above all, Jesus mystically reaches the height and the depth of the mystery in his experience of the resurrection. The Last Supper discourses (Jn 17) show the johannine understanding of Jesus' awareness that he is different from God his Father, yet not different;

they are one and they are not one. This experience of unity in diversity and of diversity in unity is only possible through love, because love simultaneously unites and differentiates. The mystical experience of Jesus is first Trinitarian, but at the same time Messianic. His experience is one of intimacy with the Triune God, who is Love, and therefore also with God's saving, loving will.

However, Jesus is not only the model of mystical life for all Christians. He is also the *image of the invisible God* (Col 1:15; 2:9), *the refulgence of his glory, the very imprint of his being* (Hb 1:3). This is what makes him the only way to have access to the Father (Jn 14.2; Ep 2:18) and the one on whose face we contemplate the divine face (2 Co 4:6). Christ, therefore, in his humanity, especially in the mysteries of his death and resurrection, is the foundation of christian mysticism. Saint John invites us all to push on toward union with Christ and to *remain in him* (Jn 6:56; 15:4–16), since the essence of eternal life consists in *knowing the Father and the one whom he sent* (Jn 17:3).

Mystical Experience

The word, 'experience', has not always had good press relations in the Latin christian world, but it has always enjoyed a favorable press in the Eastern christian Churches. Many western Christians and theologians seem to have forgotten the traditional thomistic teaching about 'knowledge *by inclination* or connaturality' (*Summa Theologiae*, II,II,45,2,c). To avoid misunderstandings, I want to begin by explaining what meaning I do **not** give to the term, experience:

- an **emotional** meaning, which would exclude the use of freedom or of one's conscience.

- an **experimental** meaning, which would presume to take possession of the object so as to verify it.

- an **immediate** meaning, which would end up affirming total oneness with the Absolute.

Therefore, when I speak of experience I do not refer to the above three uses of the word, but rather I mean:

- a **knowledge,** which is the fruit of remaining in what has been accepted.

- a **happening** that is fully human and authenticated in a relationship.

Applying the above to **christian mystical experience**, we would have to say that the latter is a unifying event of life determined by its openness to the God revealing himself to us in Christ; or it is a knowledge based on faith, which embraces divine revelation in Christ. This can be enriched by the words of Saint Thomas: *this understanding or connaturality with divine things flows from the charity that unites us to God.* It is thus a *wisdom* and a *gift* of the Holy Spirit that permits the lover and the beloved to *dwell in* each other mutually (*Summa Theologiae*, II,II,45,2,c; cf. I,1,6,ad 3; I,II,28,2).

Christian mystical experience is therefore a mode of faith, a particular way of living the faith. It is at the service of the faith, is discerned by the faith and witnesses to the faith. It exists only within the faith of the Church, that is to say, it is connected to the sacramental celebration of the faith and to the reading of the Word of God in faith and in the Church.

It only remains to add or clarify **five important features** of christian mystical experience. First of all, it is not something separate from Christianity as a religion, but is a particular, concrete aspect of Christianity. In the second place, this experience should be thought of, above all, as a process or way of life more than as an isolated experience of God. Thirdly, this experiential process of communion with God is transformative and deifying. In the fourth place, instead of speaking of mystical experience, it would be better to speak of experiencing the Mystery. Finally, it would be even better to speak of experiencing the risen, active, living Christ.

The Experiences of Jesus

Let us look for a moment at the experiences Jesus had during his baptism, in Gethsemane and on Golgotha, with a brief reference to his resurrection. There is nothing more Christian than Christ's own experience of the mystery!

Baptism

Our concern now is to go beyond the Gospel narratives to understand the historical event. So, we focus our attention on **the facts**. In the first place, we affirm that the baptism of Jesus is an historical fact that caused not a little scandal: Is Jesus less than John (cf. Mt 3:14ff.)? Jesus is among his people. At a sign or word from the Baptist, he is immersed in the Jordan.

- *He was baptized in the Jordan by John* (Mk 1:9).

- *After all the people had been baptized and Jesus also had been baptized.* (Lk 3:21; cf. Jn 1:26: *There is one among you*).

All the evangelists describe the descent of the Spirit even though the details vary and can be considered as personal contributions of each evangelist. The meaning of the event is that this is the inauguration of the prophetic ministry of Jesus, who is God's final, eschatological messenger (cf. Mt 5:17), which is why God's Spirit is upon him.

Likewise, all the accounts agree that there was a solemn divine proclamation from heaven, although once again the details differ.

The proclamation interprets the descent of the Spirit as the fulfill-ment of Isaiah 42:1, *Behold my servant whom I uphold, my chosen one, in whom my soul is well pleased. I have poured out my Spirit on him and he will bring forth justice to the nations.*

- Mark 1:9–11; Matthew 3:13–17, and Luke 3:21–22: *You are (this is) my beloved Son; in whom I am well pleased.*

- John 1:32–34: *I have seen and testified that he is the Son of God.*

According to the synoptic Gospels, what happened at the Baptism can also be understood as something that Jesus **experienced** (as against John 1:32–34, where it is John the Baptist who sees and testifies):

- *On coming out of the water he saw . . .* (Mk 1:10).

- *As Jesus was praying, heaven was opened . . .* (Lk 3:21).

But what **meaning** did this experience have for Jesus? When he was baptized, Jesus had a double experience: he experienced his sonship in relation to God the Father and he experienced the strength of the Spirit. This is how he had a special understanding of his identity and his mission, which he immediately put into action.

Nothing rules out the possibility that the idea contained in Isaiah 42:2 was previously present in Jesus' mind, but it meant something very special to him at his baptism in relation to his **mission**:

> *He will not cry out or lift up his voice, or make it heard in the street; a bruised reed he will not break, and a dimly burning wick he will not quench . . . I, the Lord, have called you in righteousness, I have taken you by the hand and kept you; I have given you as a covenant to the people, a light to the nations, to open the eyes that are blind, to bring out the prisoners from the dungeon, from the prison those who sit in darkness* (Is 42:2–3, 6–7).

Jesus seems to have attributed considerable **importance** to the hour of his Baptism. He once referred to his baptismal experience in a controversy with the authorities in order to show the source of his authority, as if he were to say, 'My authority is based on what happened when I was baptized by John in the Jordan' (Mk 11:27–33).

On the day of his Baptism, Jesus received an extremely important revelation about himself and about God; God reveals himself to him as a father reveals himself to his son, namely, fully, as *Abba*. It is not strange that he would later say:

> *All things have been handed over to me by my Father. No one knows the Son except the Father, and no one knows the Father except the Son and anyone to whom the Son wishes to reveal him* (Mt 11:27).

The linguistic and stylistic elements of Matthew's text, which I have just quoted, point to the linguistic world of a Semite, not to a johannine or greek world. *'Have been handed over to me'* (*paredóze*, in the aorist) indicates a unique past event: the Baptism! (Note that John 5:19–20 is in the present tense: *The Father loves his Son and shows him everything that he himself does.*) The Father granted Jesus the revelation of a **mystery**: the mystery of being the Son of God the Father, and the mystery of God's will to save humanity through the work of his Messiah. Jesus must **communicate** this to others, which in fact he does.

- To the disciples is revealed the mystery of the Kingdom (Mk 4:11).

- Jesus reveals these things to the childlike (Mt 11:25).

- The disciples see and hear what the former prophets and righteous people did not know (Mt 13:16).

- Jesus brings the final revelation (Mt 5:17).

To sum up, in his baptismal experience, Jesus discovers anew his identity of Son, together with the continual presence of the Father in his life, the power of the Spirit dwelling in him, his mission to save through suffering, and the message of the Kingdom. In other words, he receives a mystery to be revealed and a mission to be accomplished out of his own deepest identity.

Gethsemane

Beyond the narrative of the evangelists, it is easy to discern the nucleus of Jesus' **experience**, namely, his relationship with his disciples and with God the Father. Jesus is alone. The disciples have arrived at the heights of misunderstanding (cf. Mk 4:13) and are separated from the Master. However, is Jesus really alone, or is he with his Father?

Despite the **silence**, the relationship of Jesus with his Father is experienced through heart-rending **symbols** and in the prayerful **gift** of self.

The **chalice** is the visible expression of the invisible will of the Father. It is equivalent to the *hour*. That is, it expresses the mysterious plan of God for humanity, what has been irrevocably decided by God and therefore will come to pass. It means the handing over of Jesus into the hands of sinners, the expiating death of the Just One, the Servant, who is raised up above the earth to draw all things to himself. It is the glorification of Jesus and of the Father.

Jesus **prays** and asks for the possibility to have the chalice pass, without drinking from it. But finally, from the depths of his being, he embraces it: *Your will be done! Shall I not drink the chalice that the Father gave me* (Jn 18:11)? The inspired author of the Letter to the Hebrews (Hb 5:7) tells us that Jesus offers himself to the one who was able to save him from death:

- with *prayers*, i.e., insistent petitions based on one's own poverty and need; and *supplications,* emphasizing even more the insistence of the prayers.

- *with loud cries and tears* to be saved from death, like the just man in Psalm 21:3,25.

In the presence of the chalice, Jesus *kneels down* and *falls prostrate* (Matthew and Luke, as a sign of acceptance). Mark's version is more dramatic and says that Jesus *fell to the ground,* that is, he was humanly a broken man. In other words, the immediate presence of the chalice causes terror and horror. The pathetic experience of Jesus, presented by the evangelists with tragic overtones, tells us about:

- *sadness* (Matthew and Mark), the opposite of joy, caused by the lack of a good (the absence of the Father?). It is not an ordinary state of sadness, but a *killing* sadness, *even to death*: a deep sadness, as in Psalm 41:5–6, *Why are you cast down, my soul, why groan within me?*

- *distress* (Matthew and Mark), interior resistance and agitation as a result of a deep upheaval.

- *horror* (Mark), an inner tearing apart, helplessness, terrifying surprise, shivering fright.

- *agony* (Luke), anguish with a sweat of blood, anticipation of a battle, need of help from an angel.

- *trouble* (John), as he had experienced it in the presence of Mary of Bethany weeping over the death of her brother, Lazarus (Jn 11:33), or like the experience of the disciples when they heard of Judas's treachery, Peter's denials, or Jesus' departure (Jn 14:1).

Jesus **prays** his fear, discouragement, surrender, and agreement. The Father is **silent**, with his hand still outstretched and the chalice still offered. The Father is there, yet not there. Jesus accepts the chalice offered him, in naked faith and with God remaining silent. He **knows** that there is only one way to establish the Kingdom of sons and brothers, only one way to reveal fully the mysterious plan of God and to make it become active in power; namely, he must offer himself up to death by handing his life over into the hands of sinners.

Instinctively Jesus longs to stay alive, even though in his will he wants to be faithful to the Father: *He learned obedience from what he suffered* (Hb 5:8). He had become identified with the mission he had received. He had embodied the Kingdom and had shown admirably what it was. And now he is going to die without establishing the Kingdom on this earth! The chalice seems to contradict the very existence of the Kingdom. The work of his entire life seems to be crumbling. A single road is open to him—give himself up blindly to death.

The **rejection** by his enemies is now crowned by that of his friends: Judas betrays him, the disciples go to sleep, deny him, and will soon prove their cowardice by running away. Despite it all, Jesus **accepts** his destiny, which is the will of the Father. He drinks the cup. In the midst of his total loneliness, he remains **united** to God and continues to call him, *Abba, my Father* (Mk 14:36). He keeps **faithful** to his original experience and deepest mystery. He sinks into the jaws of death, into the bottomless abyss of God's mysterious plan.

Golgotha

The **last** words of a person, like a prologue to the silence of death, are often significant and sum up all the life that went before them. They are often also a personal **experience** and a last message directed to posterity. That is why we are so interested in the last words of Jesus on the Cross before he gives up his spirit.

The evangelists differ in this respect, but only apparently so. The underlying fact and basic message is the same for them all.

- Mark mentions two cries, the second one being wordless: '*Eloi, Eloi, lema sabachthani? My God, my God, why have you forsaken me?*' . . . *He gave a loud cry and breathed his last* (Mk 15:34,37).

- Matthew also mentions two cries, with the second one wordless: '*Eli, Eli, lema sabachthani? . . . Jesus cried out again in a loud voice, and gave up his spirit* (Mt 27:46, 50).

- Luke has one cry with words: *Jesus cried out in a loud voice, 'Father, into your hands I commend my spirit'; and when he had said this he breathed his last* (Lk 23:46).

- John has no cry, just a word: *He said, 'It is finished'. And bowing his head, he handed over the spirit* (Jn 19:30).

The obvious fact is that Jesus died crucified and giving a **loud cry**, which is unusual for someone who is crucified and therefore dying from asphyxia. This explains the surprise of the centurion (Mk 15:39: *When he saw how he breathed his last he said, 'Truly this man was the Son of God!'*).

But what did Jesus cry out when he breathed his last? Those who were there believed that they heard Jesus call out for Elias (cf. Mt and Mk: *Eliyahu* abbreviated to *Eliya*). Yet how did they pass from *Eloi* (Mark) or *Eli* (Matthew) to *Eliya ta' (Elias, come)*? Perhaps what Jesus said, and what led to the confusion, was, *Eli atta (You are my God).*

This cry, '*You are my God (Eliatta)*', is found seven times in Scripture. Not counting Isaiah 44:17 and Psalm 144, the other four occurrences are significant:

- Psalm 22:11, the final words of the lament of the abandoned just man. Note that Psalm 22:19, about dividing his garments, is found in Mark, Matthew, and John. And Psalm 22:2, *My God, my God*, is found in Matthew and Mark.

- Psalm 31:15 is a prayer in trial inspired by Jeremiah. Note that the words, *Into your hands I commend my spirit*, from Psalm 31:6, are found in Luke.

- Psalm 63:2 is a prayer about *thirsting for God*. Note the reference in John to thirst, as in Psalm 22:16 and 69:22.

- Psalm 118:28, *You are my God, I thank you*, is the conclusion of the *Hallel* (Ps 113–118) sung after Easter, which is referred to in Mark 14:26.

All these reflections lead to an understanding of Jesus' experience on the cross as follows: Jesus dies reciting Psalm 22 in Hebrew. In verse eleven of this psalm, there is the phrase, *You are my God (Eli atta)*. To someone who speaks Aramaic this could sound like *Elliya ta (Eliah, come)*. By dying with the words, *Eli atta (You are my God)*, on his lips, Jesus shows his radical, even violent, trust in God. He continues in the same attitude of union with his Father that he proclaimed at Gethsemane. Despite all that has happened, he dies confessing that God is his God, that is, his Father. Jesus dies like the persecuted righteous man of the Psalms (Ps 22; 31; 63), thirsting for God in the loneliness of the desert, pronouncing the final words of the *Hallel*, which celebrate the ultimate victory of God over the enemies of the Covenant.

Jesus on the cross was in a desperate situation, but he was not desperate. He was not abandoned by God, but God gave him over to abandonment at the hands of his enemies. Faith was never lacking, but only its light and brightness.

Resurrection

At Gethsemane Jesus had prayed, *Not what I want, but what you want.* On Golgotha, in the convulsions of death, he cried out, *You are my God.* And so it was. God was his God, his Father, and so he freed him from death by resurrection, but only after passing through death. What can we say about the experience of Jesus at the moment of the **Resurrection**? Let us contemplate the mystery, as sons and daughters in the Son.

- Through the pain of abandonment (Mt 15:44) and by commending himself into the hands of the Father (Lk 23:46), Jesus engaged in an adventure that could only turn out well. This is why he is blessed and why his Beatitudes are true (Lk 6:20–23; Mt 5:1–12). Condemned by men, he was reaffirmed by God. The Creator's 'Yes' rang gloriously in his ears, silencing the accursed 'No' of creatures (Ac 2:22ff.)! After being made sin for us, he experienced in his own flesh the victory over sin and death (Rm 8:3; 2 Co 5:21).

- His mortal body was transformed into a spiritual body, a life-giving spirit (1 Co 15;44–45). He experienced himself as recreated into a new man, a new Adam, the firstborn among those who have been brought to life (Rm 8:27; 1 Co 15:20ff). He felt like the Giver of the Spirit (Jn 20:22). He was born again in his divine sonship (Rm 1:3–4). He received the Name which is above every other name (Ph 2:9). He experienced the perfection of his Incarnation, as the fullness of the deity began to dwell in him bodily (Col 2:9).

- He multiplied his saving presence, since he is the fullness of the one who fills all things in every way (Ep 1:23). Thus, he can be identified with the little ones and with those who are persecuted (Mt 25:31–46; Ac 9:5), and can be hidden in the eucharistic mystery under the appearance of bread and wine (Mt 26:26–27).

The mystical experience of Jesus is the **model** and the **foundation** of the christian mystical experience. In Jesus Christ, the experience of God and of the 'mystery of God' become one. They harmonize historically with each other at the highest level, since Jesus is the *Mystery of God!* (Rm 16:25–27; Col 1:26). Our mystical experience is an experience of the Mystery: *to live in Christ, to die and to rise with him* (Ga 2:20; Ph 3:10).

Our Experience

All the truths of faith are mystery insofar as they are related to the mysteries that we have called the 'original' ones: Trinity, Incarnation, and Deification. Consequently, mystical experience refers to these three basic mysteries and secondarily to the others, all of them being summed up and fulfilled in Christ.

In the religious context of the world and the Church today, we are more familiar with the christian mystical tradition that emphasizes the subject who experiences. This displacement from what is objective—Biblical revelation and liturgical celebration—to what is subjective began in the twelfth century with the strong emphasis put by the Cistercians on personal experience, even though they never neglected the outer dimension of objective mystery. The subjective tendency reaches its height in the sixteenth century with the spanish mysticism flowing from the Carmelites. Actually, both aspects—the subjective and the objective—are always together. The christian mystic experiences the Mystery, while at the same time experiencing him or herself as transformed by it.

From this perspective we can define mystical experience—without enclosing it in finite limits—as a 'delicious wisdom': a personal, freely chosen, affective, and transforming penetration into the Mystery by knowledge and love, fruit of a special divine action. We can distinguish the following constitutive **elements**:

- divine enabling action.

- new light of knowledge and new fire of love.

- active passivity.

- immediacy that is mediated.

- intuition of the Presence.

- reciprocal union and communication.

- revelation of different aspects of the Mystery.

What is perhaps the most constitutive and individuating element of mystical experience is a sudden awakening of our attention to a Presence. Since an act of faith does not terminate in its formulation but in the reality that the formulation tries to express, we can say that mystical experience is a unified attention to the reality formulated by our faith.

The history of christian mysticism lets us identify various **types** of mystical experience. It is obviously impossible to establish an exhaustive typology of them, since mystics are not a special type of person. It is rather that each person is a special type of mystic! Besides, the mystery of Christ is unfathomable, both in its content and in the ways it can be approached. Even though our words are inadequate, we can speak of a mysticism of essence and a mysticism of betrothal, a mysticism of light and a mysticism of darkness, a mysticism of interiority and a mysticism of conformity, a contemplative mysticism and an apostolic mysticism, a cosmic mysticism and an historical mysticism, a mysticism of absence and a daily mysticism.

From another point of view, it is helpful, for clarity's sake, to look at a tripartite typology that is well rooted in tradition.

- There is **substantial** mystical experience, consisting of infused contemplation, loving knowledge, warm light, a living flame, rays of darkness, resonant silence, midnight sun, midday moon, and so forth. This experience has a dual emphasis or two different qualities, which are not opposed and usually are complementary.

- The emphasis can be put on **knowledge**: the affirmative or *cataphatic* way described by Origen in his *Homilies*, by Pseudo-Dionysius in his treatise *On the Divine Names*, by Saint Bonaventure in *The Journey of the Soul to God*, by Saint Ignatius of Loyola in the *Spiritual Exercises*.

- The emphasis can be put on **love**: the negative or *apophatic* way described by Gregory of Nyssa in his *Life of Moses*, by Pseudo-Dionysius in his *Mystical Theology*, by the author of *The Cloud of Unknowing*, by Meister Eckhart in his '*ontological apophaticism*', or by Saint John of the Cross in the *Dark Night*.

- There is **accidental** mystical experience, made up of a variety of phenomenon such as ecstasies, raptures, visions, locutions, revelations, touches, and so forth.

- And there is **ordinary** mystical experience, characterized by alternations of presences and absences, consolations and desolations, light and darkness, emptiness and fullness, thirst and relief, etc.

Unfortunately, when there is mention of mysticism or mystical experience we usually think or talk about **accidental** experiences, not of what is essential or really important. This has caused many misunderstandings and a fear of such phenomena that has, in turn, produced a rejection of both mysticism in general and of many authentic mystics. In saying this, I do not want to discredit the many mystics who experience these phenomena. I only want to clarify that the substantial, constitutive core of mysticism is not there. On the other hand, it would be an impoverishment not to recognize all that these observable occurrences can teach us about human nature in its relation to the Absolute.

I also want to say that substantial and ordinary mystical experience is part of the normal development of the life of grace and of growth in the theological virtues. In this sense, we are all mystics. Mystics are not special people. They experience the same realities as any other

Christian, but they do so in a different way. God's grace works in them as it does in other persons, but mystics know that grace is working and they have varying degrees of evidence.

It is obvious that mystical experiences can occur in an infinite variety of intensities and **degrees**. The capacity to 'experience' varies according to persons and circumstances. The love of God, which is self-communicating, is given according to the form and measure of the person who accepts it. God's wise and loving providence adjusts the intensity of his self-gift according to our greater good and his mysterious ways of salvation.

Now I would like to examine more closely two basic, traditional experiences that are easily recognizable in the context of our contemplative life: the experience of *desire* and that of the *Eucharist*. We place ourselves under the teaching of the female Doctors of the Church. We will consult some significant texts taken from the writings of Catherine of Siena, Teresa of Avila and Thérèse of Lisieux. I am especially interested in the witness of the last of these three Doctors. It is good to remember that the writings of the mystics are not understood when they are read by mere human reason. We have to let these texts echo in our hearts and bear fruit in our own search for God.

Desiderium

In the West, the theme of spiritual desire is intimately linked to the person of Saint Augustine of Hippo. The augustinian tradition entered into medieval cloisters through the Liturgy, *lectio divina*, the *Rule* of Saint Benedict, and the influence of Saint Gregory the Great. Saint Bernard of Clairvaux drank deeply and was nourished from this diffused Augustinianism present in the monasticism of his time. In this tradition, the desire for God is marked by the following principal characteristics.

- Experiencing **absence** is the basis for experiencing desire.

- **Alternation** of presence and absence arouses desire.

- The moral quality of desire depends on its **object**.

- Desire is by nature **affective** and resides more in the will than in the intellect.

- The desire for God is a command from **being** itself, not simply a matter of free choice.

- This divine desire is only fulfilled in eternal life, in **eschatology**.

We, who are still far from the heavenly homeland, love by desiring the end of our pilgrimage. Experiencing this absence spurs us on in the search for God. This search, in its turn, implies an asceticism of renouncing other satisfying objects that are more accessible but less worthy and that occupy the place of God.

The most important feature of Saint Augustine's conception of desire is its **ontological** nature: the desire for God is constitutive of human nature. There exists an innate capacity for God in all human beings. There is a pre-elective orientation toward God. This is the meaning of the fact that human beings have been created in the image of God: *You made us for yourself and our heart is restless until it rests in you* (Augustine, *Confessions* I,1). Or, as Saint Bernard of Clairvaux will say when he talks about the human being: *How privileged a creature, that it be capable of eternal blessedness and of the great God's glory! (Egregia criatura, capax aeternae beatitudinis et gloriae magni Dei—Conv* 15; *SC* 27:10).

This ontological desire is at the root of every desire. It is the innate desire of the part for the whole, of the creature for the Creator and of the image for its exemplar. The mutual, complementary attraction of man for woman is the most powerful reality showing this innate desire existentially. The other side of this desire is the frightening void of the contingent being when it is separated from the whole.

Thus understood, desire is a fundamental dynamic of the soul. It is the source and root of love, the psychic longing where the desire for God can flourish. When desire comes into consciousness and is converted by the will searching for God, it becomes the loving desire of God.

The search for God through desire found its justification and verbal expression in the inspired book of the **Song of Songs**. When the soul has nothing belonging to itself but everything in common with God, it is called *bride*. This is she who says, *Let him kiss me with the kiss of his mouth*. It is a *soul thirsting for God*. The *bride* shows herself to be worthy of this kiss by her *intense desire* for her Spouse (Bernard, *SC* 7:2; 32:3).

As you know, devotion to the humanity of Christ has developed remarkably since the twelfth century. It found a favorable environment in the context of spiritual desire and spiritual betrothal. Here was also born, in the lived experiences of nuns, a mystical, affective and feminine current of spirituality that embodied the spiritual teachings of the cistercian Fathers from the preceding century. This spirituality flows especially from the doctrine of Bernard of Clairvaux and William of Saint-Thierry on the **soul as spouse**, thirsting and longing in burning desire for love. This flowering of feminine spirituality, which coincided with the new place and new vision of women and which began in that century, helps us to understand many women mystics, such as:

- Saint Hildegard of Bingen (+1179), Benedictine

- María of Oignies (+1213), Beguine

- Saint Lutgard of Aywières (+1246), Benedictine

- Saint Claire of Assisi (+1253), Foundress of the Poor Clares

- Hedwig of Antwerp (+ c.1260), Beguine

- Beatriz of Nazareth (+1268), Cistercian

- Mechtilde of Magdeburg (+1288), Benedictine

- Saint Margaret of Cortona (+1297), a married Franciscan Tertiary

- Saint Matilda of Hackeborn (+1299), Benedictine

- Saint Gertrude of Helfta (+1301), Benedictine

- Blessed Angela of Foligno (+1309), a married Franciscan Tertiary

- Saint Bridget of Sweden (+1373), married Foundress of the Bridgittines

- **Saint Catherine of Siena** (+1380), consecrated Dominican Tertiary

- Blessed Julian of Norwich (+1420), recluse

- **Saint Teresa of Avila** (+1582), Discalced Carmelite

- Saint Catherine de Ricci (+1590), Dominican

- Saint Rose of Lima (+1617), Dominican Tertiary

- Saint Mariana of Quito (+1645), lay virgin

- Saint Margaret Mary Alacoque (+1690), Visitandine

- Saint Veronica Giuliani (+1727), Capuchin Poor Clare

- **Saint Thérèse of Lisieux** (+ 1897), Discalced Carmelite

• Saint Gemma Galgani (+1902), Passionist associate

• Saint Elizabeth of the Trinity (+1906), Discalced Carmelite

• Saint Teresa of the Andes (+1920), Discalced Carmelite

The list could continue, but I have wanted to limit it to persons who have been officially beatified or canonized. It is interesting to see that this nuptial mysticism of conformity to Christ brings its followers to the mystery of the Trinity, the Redemption, the Eucharist, and the Church. These mystics 'know' that they are daughters of God the Father, dwelt in by the Spirit, at the service of the Church and the world. It is not surprising, therefore, that they express their experiences sometimes in erotic language and at other times in words of a daughter or a mother. Some of their writings also witness to the God with whom 'we are united and know as someone unknown' (Thomas Aquinas, *Summa Theologiae*, I,12,13 ad 1). We will not go into the revelations, visions, and other accidental phenomena of the lives of the mystics I have just mentioned—even though all of that is interesting—either as ways of approaching the Mystery or from the viewpoint of religious anthropology and depth psychology. What we ourselves are interested in is the *intensio cordis*, the *desiderium*, which moved them so deeply and steered them so constantly toward their Lord and *Sponsus*, Jesus Christ.

Catherine of Siena

Saint **Catherine of Siena** is usually portrayed as a woman of desires. At the beginning of her great work, *The Dialogues*, she presents herself as *stirred up by a devouring desire for the honor of God and the salvation of souls'*(c.1), and adds that *this was an immense and continual desire* that became a *frenzied desire* during the eucharistic celebration (c.2). Desire is the only thing infinite that the human creature possesses and the infinite God desires to be served infinitely. Thus, desire expands the human heart, making space available for God and for everyone (c.92). It would be interesting to read, in this same work, all her teaching on tears (cc.87–96), where she treats of their types, value, and fruit. The infinite variety of life-giving tears depends on *the will's desire to weep for the love of God* (c.91).

Blessed Raymond of Capua, Catherine's biographer, has preserved for us the Saint's prayer when, as still a child, she consecrated her virginity to God:

> *Oh most blessed and holy Virgin! You were the first among all women to consecrate your virginity to God by a perpetual vow, and he granted you the grace to be the Mother of his only begotten Son. I ask your indescribable mercy not to take my merits or my failings into account, but to grant me this great grace. Give me as Bride to the one I desire with all the love of my soul: your most Holy Son, our one Lord Jesus Christ. I promise both him and you that I will not accept any other husband, and with all my strength will preserve my purity intact for him (Life, I,III:1).*

Raymond himself also tells us about Catherine's passing from this life to the next: *Seeing that the hour of her passing was near, she said, 'Domine, in manus tuas commendo spiritum meum'. Having said this, and as she had desired for so long, that holy soul was freed from the flesh and united forever, undividedly, to her Spouse, whom she had loved so ineffably.* (*Life*, III,IV:8).

Teresa of Avila

Saint **Teresa of Avila** tells us that the first fruits of her devotion to prayer were '*a desire for solitude . . . , to receive Communion, to go to Confession much more often, and to desire him*' (*Life*, 6:4). These desires sometimes became burning 'exclamations': '*Woe to me; woe to me, Lord! How long this exile is! And how difficult it is live with this desire for my God! . . . Let my desires please you, my God, who deserve all my submission, and do not look at my unworthiness*' (*Exclamations*,

15). Hoping to lessen her suffering, Teresa wonders if '*perhaps I will desire not to desire You*' (*Exclamations*, 6), and she herself replies by singing:

> *My God, how sad*
> *Life is without You!*
> *I long to see You*
> *I want to die.*
>
> . . . .
>
> *My tortured soul*
> *Moans and faints:*
> *Who can bear being*
> *Away from her Beloved?*
> *Stop it now! Stop!*
> *End this pain and grief!*
> *I long to see you*
> *And want to die.*
>
> . . . .
>
> *In vain does my soul*
> *Search for you, my Master!*
> *Always invisible,*
> *You never satisfy it*
> *But just make it burn*
> *Until it cries out:*
> *I long to see you*
> *And want to die.*
>
> —*Poems*: Woes from Exile

Saint Teresa also tells us that *sometimes I have such immense desires to receive Communion that I do not know how they can get any stronger.* It happened that, one rainy day when she could not leave to go to church: *I was so beside myself with that desire that, even if they had threatened to cut off my breasts, I think I would have gone, no matter how much rain was coming down.* When she arrived at the church, she entered into a deep rapture, thanks to which: *I understood, without seeing anything, that everything I could possibly desire was all here* (*Life*, 39:22).

This experiences of an immense desire for communion with and in the Lord taught Teresa how to discern the authenticity of such desires. She had to face her clearest case of wrong desires when she was at the monastery of Medina del Campo. The story is well told in her book on *Foundations* (6:9.23). The conclusion that Teresa draws is the following: *Believe me that the love of God—I do not say 'is', but 'can seem to us to be'—a desire arousing the passions so strongly that it leads to a sin against him or takes away the peace of the soul which is full of love. The result is that she does not listen to reason.* [In this case] *it is clear that we are seeking ourselves and that the devil will not rest until he puts us to the test at the moment when he thinks he can most hurt us.* (*Foundations*, 6:21)

Thérèse of Lisieux

It is interesting to note that the words, 'desire' and 'to desire', appear three hundred ninety-five times in the written works of Saint **Thérèse of Lisieux.** This is especially significant when we realize that the writings of Thérèse are not all that extensive. She herself tells us that the content of her autobiography, *Story of a Soul*, consists of '*How it pleased Jesus to satisfy my desire and how he alone has always been my unspeakable sweetness*' (*Autobiographical Manuscripts*, A,36). Desire accompanied her during her whole religious life and never left her, even after her death. During her postulancy, she wrote to Sister Agnes of Jesus, '*My only desire is always to fulfill the will of Jesus*' (*Letter 74* of Jan.6, 1889). Six years later she has the same desire when she makes her offering as a victim of merciful Love: *I desire to fulfill perfectly your will . . . I desire to be holy* (*Prayer 6* of June 9, 1895). And at the end of her life she writes to one of her spiritual brothers, Father Roulland: *I count on not being inactive in Heaven. My desire is to keep working for the Church and for souls* (*Letter 254* of July 14, 1897).

One day before the beginning of Lent 1895, Thérèse writes a poem for herself. It is one of the few writings that were not a response to a request from someone else. The poem bursts forth from Thérèse's heart during the three days of permanent exposition of the Blessed Sacrament prior to Ash Wednesday. It is the Forty Hours Adoration in reparation for the excesses of Mardi Gras before the beginning of Lent. In this poem, Thérèse tells what she wants to do for the rest of her life. The words, '*Living on Love*', appear seventeen times!

Dying of Love is a truly sweet martyrdom,
And that is the one I wish to suffer.
O Cherubim! Tune your lyre,
For I sense my exile is about to end!
Flame of Love, consume me unceasingly.
Life of an instant, your burden is so heavy to me!
Divine Jesus, make my dream come true:
  To die of Love!

Dying of Love is what I hope for,
When I shall see my bonds broken,
My God will be my Great Reward.
I don't desire to possess other goods.
I want to be set on fire with his Love.
I want to see Him, to unite myself to Him forever.
That is my Heaven . . . that is my destiny:
  Living on Love!!!
  —Poem 17, Living on Love, February 26, 1895

That same year, on June 9, Feast of the Most Holy Trinity, Thérèse writes her '*Act of Self-offering as a Victim of Holocaust to the Merciful Love of the Good God*'. To appreciate the importance of this text, it should be born in mind that the previous day, June 8, there had been read in the refectory the death notice of a Carmelite sister of Lucon, Sister Marie of Jesus, who had offered herself as a 'victim to divine Justice' and had died crying out in her anguish, '*I carry the weight of the rigors of divine Justice: Divine Justice!*' The offering of Thérèse lies at the other end of the spectrum. She says openly, '*Immense are the desires that I feel within my heart, and it is with confidence that I call upon Thee to come and take possession of my soul'*. It ends as follows:

> *That I may live in one act of perfect Love, I offer myself as a victim of holocaust to thy merciful Love, imploring thee to consume me without ceasing, and to let the tide of infinite tenderness pent up in thee, overflow into my soul, so that I may become a very Martyr of thy Love, O my God! May this martyrdom, having first prepared me to appear before thee, break life's thread at last, and may my soul take its flight, undeterred, into the eternal embrace of Thy Merciful Love. I desire, O my Well-Beloved, to renew this oblation an infinite number of times at every heartbeat, till the shadows retire (Sg 4:6) and I can tell thee my Love Eternally Face to Face! (Prayer 6, July 9, 1895)*

Thérèse's blood sister, Celine, had already been in the monastery for a year. She had taken the name of Sister Geneviève. For the feast of Saint Celine, October 21, 1895, she asks Thérèse to write a poem reminding Jesus of all that she had given up in order to follow him. Thérèse writes the poem, but in a completely contrary sense, describing all that Jesus has done for us. At this moment of her life, Thérèse is full of light and her faith is brilliantly clear and fiery. Two strophes of this poem, the twenty-sixth and the thirtieth, are of particular interest to us as reflecting the heart of Thérèse.

> *Remember, Jesus, Word of Life,*
> *How you loved me and even died for me.*
> *I also want to love you to folly.*
> *I also want to live and die for You.*
> *You know, O my God!, all that I desire*
> *Is to make you loved and to one day be a martyr.*
> *I want to die of love.*
> *Lord, my desire,*
> *Remember.*

> *My only Love, grant my prayer.*
> *Ah! give me a thousand hearts to love you.*

But that is still too little, Jesus, Beauty Supreme.
Give me your divine Heart Itself to love you.
   Lord, my burning desire,
    At each moment,
     Remember.
        —*Poem 24* of Oct. 21, 1895

On May 31, 1896, Thérèse composed a song for a sister in the noviciate. Reading between the lines, we can see her inner solitude and the *thirst for love* that burns inside her: the ardent desire that God, who is Love, consume her entirely. The song ends as follows:

I thirst for Love, fulfill my hope.
Lord, make your Divine Fire grow within me.
I thirst for Love, so great is my suffering.
Ah! I would like to fly away to you, my God!

Your Love is my only martyrdom.
The more I feel it burning within me,
The more my soul desires you.
Jesus, make me die
Of Love for You!!!
        —*Poem 31*, May 30, 1896

On her last card of farewell to Abbé Bellière (August 25, 1897), her spiritual brother, one month before she died, Thérèse writes: *I am unable to fear a God who has become so small for my sake . . . I love him!*

I realize that human desire in itself is **ambiguous**. Existentially, our ontological desire is lived out in a complex mesh of distortions and trickeries: narcissism, leading us to think of ourselves as sublime because we do not accept our limitations; megalomania and fantasies of supreme power compensating for our lack of self-esteem; and illusions of all sorts. The Spirit has the difficult task of putting our desire back into place, redirecting it, purifying and transforming it, all of which he does through alternations of presences and absences, darkness and light, deserts and oases.

While cooperating with this theological purification of our psychological mechanisms, we also have to be very aware of the social context in which we live. That is why we need to ask ourselves about the influence of the **consumer** society in arousing our desires and attractions. Possessing things and using them are the driving forces of life in this society, which is characterized by a polytheistic presence of many small, seductive objects and values. Consumerism, with its lust for such objects, produces personalities that are increasingly narcissistic.

- A narcissistic **man** is obsessed by himself and his self-image. For him, to live is to feel, and the stronger these feelings, the better. The extreme type of the 'narcissistic man' is the uncommitted navel-gazer who could not care less about anything, except himself.

- The narcissistic **woman** takes pleasure in herself in order later to please others. She cultivates her 'womanhood' in order to sell it to a man and thus both she and he are consumed.

Advertising and consumer reports put us in front of a make-believe world and separate us from the real world, as can be seen in the contrast between TV advertisements and the misery of many who look at them. Or else the media present the real world as something to be consumed at a distance merely out of curiosity, as in news reports about disasters on the other side of the globe or the love affairs of socially significant people.

The search for God by desire for him, and by conformity to Christ as a spouse, requires a demanding asceticism of our desires—their re-ordering. We have at least to ask ourselves, 'Are our basic desires, such as for activity, affirmation, fulfillment, harmony and complementarity, ordered to our social desires for solidarity, participation, broad-mindedness, and the like? And are these latter desires ordered to spiritual ones, such as for freedom, equality, hope, love, immortality, and the Absolute?'

Eucharist

We have to understand in a completely realistic way the words of
Jesus as he instituted the Eucharist: *Take and eat; this is my body* (Mt
26:26). The subject of the sentence, '*this*' (bread), is identified with
the predicate, '*my body*' (the person of Jesus). If we believe that
Jesus was and is the Only Son of God, the conclusion is that the
consecrated bread and wine is Christ really present. The Eucharist
is, above all, the sacrament of presence, since it is the sacrament of
christian passover and salvation, who is Christ himself in person.

At each eucharistic celebration, Jesus speaks to us: *Behold, I stand
at the door and knock. If anyone hears my voice and opens the door, then
I will enter his house and dine with him, and he with me* (Rv 3:20).
Our Eucharist celebrations make these apparitions of the Risen
Christ present. They let him fulfill his promise: *I will come to you*
(Jn 14:18–22). The Eucharist is the sacrament of the coming of the
Lord in person. Our desire for this visit is the motivation for our
daily celebration of the Eucharist. With the Spirit and the Bride
we cry: *Maranatha!, Come, Lord Jesus!* (Rv 22:20). In the Eucharist,
Christ loves his Church and gives himself up for her (Ep 5:25). The total
self-gift of the Bride, the Church, responds to this self-gift of the
Lord, the Spouse.

The eucharistic celebration reaches its apex in the Lord's words,
Take and eat; take and drink. To take is to hold. However, it is not
only to hold, but also to be held. The Eucharistic celebration is
communion in a mutual self-gift and in reciprocal possession. This
is how Jesus' words are fulfilled: *You are in me and I in you* (Jn 14:20).

Eucharistic communion is the royal door for entering into the mystery, for becoming mystically transformed. The Eucharistic mystery
is the best place for mystical experience. Christ is devouring fire, so
it is normal that our hearts burn in the darkness of faith when his
Bread is broken, shared, and eaten.

Catherine of Siena

Blessed Raymond, Saint Catherine's biographer, tells us repeatedly about her love and desire for the Eucharist. Catherine's delight at receiving Holy Communion was so great that her heart skipped for joy inside her, *making such a loud noise that her companions around her heard it clearly . . . It was not surprising that a human heart given to supernatural realities should beat supernaturally. This is what the Prophet sang about when he said: My heart and my flesh ring out their joy to God, the living God* (Ps 83:3—*Life*, II,VI:3; cf. II,II:1).

It was clear for Catherine that in eucharistic communion, *the soul is in God and God in the soul, just as a fish is in the sea and the sea in the fish* (*Dialogues*, c.2). God's providence for the human creature appears with total clarity in the Eucharist, which is *nourishment satisfying everyone who hungers for this bread, but not the person who is not hungry, because it is a food that wants to be eaten with the mouth of holy desire and enjoyed with love* (*Dialogue*, c.135).

On February 14, 1379, after receiving Holy Communion, Catherine breaks forth with this exuberant prayer.

> *Oh Eternal Trinity, you who are crazy with love! What did you get out of our redemption? Not a thing, since you do not need us and are our God. Then who received the benefits? They were for man alone. What unthinkable Charity! Just as you gave yourself to us as perfect God and perfect man, so you remained as perfect food so that we would not faint from weariness as pilgrims in this life, but would be strengthened by you, our heavenly Food. Oh selfish man, what has God left for you? He has left really everything: God and man wrapped in the color of bread. Oh Fire of love, was it not enough to have created us after your image and likeness, then to have re-created us to grace in the blood of your Son, without giving yourself entirely to us in food, you, essential divinity? Who obliged you to do it? No one except your own charity, you who are crazy with love.* (*Exclamation, prayer*).

The eucharistic experience of the Doctor of Siena is at the basis of all her teaching. She knows what she is talking about when she speaks of:

- the infinite dignity of the Sacrament of the Body and Blood of Christ (*Dialogues*, c.110).

- the practice of spiritual communion, that is, *receiving communion by holy desire* (*Dialogue*, c.66).

- the fruits produced by the Eucharist in the soul of the worthy recipient: *The strength of this sacrament remains in the soul, that is, she retains the warmth of divine charity and the mercy of the Holy Spirit. There remains in her the light of the wisdom of my only begotten Son. The eye of her understanding is enlightened by this wisdom so that she can know and see the teaching of my Truth and my Wisdom* (*Dialogue*, c.112).

Teresa of Avila

Saint Teresa was amazed to see *so great a majesty disguised in so small a thing as the Host* and all the graces that she received through the Eucharist (*Life*, 28:8; 38:19–21; *Matters of Conscience*, 12; 43; 39). We have already seen the desires aroused in Teresa by the Eucharist. Moreover, she will never forget the wonderful mercy of spiritual marriage that took place on November 18, 1572 when Friar John of the Cross gave her only half a Host, knowing that she liked the large ones (*Matters of Conscience*, 25).

In her commentary on the Our Father, she writes at length about the '*daily bread*' which we ask for today. This provides her with a splendid opportunity to speak about eucharistic communion. It is worthwhile listening:

> So, dear Sisters, anyone who wants it should ask for this bread. We, too, should ask him, for he always listens, and we should entreat the

Father to give us the grace to prepare ourselves to receive so great a gift and such heavenly a nourishment. Since our bodily eyes do not enjoy seeing him—since he is hidden—may he reveal himself to the eyes of the soul and let himself be known . . . Stay with him willingly, since this is a very profitable hour for the soul. Jesus makes good use of it, so keep him company . . . When you have just received the Lord and have him in person before you, close your bodily eyes and open those of the soul to look at his heart, as he looks at yours. For I tell you—as I have said before and will again many time—that if you form this habit of being with him (and not just for a day or two, but whenever you receive communion) and have this type of relationship, you will often rejoice in his bounty. His goodness is not so well disguised that he does not let you know him in many ways, according to your desire to see him. And if you really desire him, he will reveal himself completely to you (Way of Perfection, 61:1–10; cf. 62:1–2).

Thérèse of Lisieux

We consult now the little Doctor of the Carmel of Lisieux. Thérèse prepared herself with great fervor for the day of her First Communion, which took place on May 8, 1884, in the chapel of the benedictine nuns of Lisieux. She speaks of it as the *first kiss Jesus gave to (her) soul*. She continues by saying that on that day *it was not just a look but also a fusion. There were no longer two of us. Thérèse had disappeared, like the drop of water that is lost in the heart of the ocean.* Thus was fulfilled what Jesus had promised when he said: *Whoever eats my flesh and drinks my blood remains in me and I in him* (Jn 6:56). Thérèse says that in her succeeding Communions: *I felt flooded with such great consolations that I look on them as one of the greatest graces of my life* (Autobiographical Manuscripts, A, 35–36).

Obviously not everything was consolation. Transforming grace itself can be, and often is, painfully dry, especially at the time of prayer after the Eucharist: *I cannot say that I have received consolations during my thanksgivings. It is perhaps the moment in which I have received the fewest . . . This seems natural, since I have given myself to Jesus not as someone who wants to receive the visit for the sake of her own consolation, but on the contrary, for the pleasure of him who gives himself to me.* Thérèse prepared herself during this very special time and trusted in the help of Our Lady, but *all that does not keep distractions and sleepiness from coming to visit me. Yet, as I leave thanksgiving and see how badly I have made it, I make the resolution to stay in thanksgiving all the rest of the day . . .* (*Autobiographical Manuscripts, A, 79–80).*

In several of her poems Thérèse shows us the joy of being able to share through Communion the very life of Jesus and thus to rest in his arms:

O Bread of the exiled! Holy and divine Host,
It is no longer I who live, but I live on your life.
　　　—Poem 24:29, September 21, 1895

I am your cherished bride,
My Beloved, come live in me.
Come, your beauty enthralls me
Transform me into Yourself!
　　　—Poem 25:7, Fall, 1895

Oh! what a happy moment when in your tenderness
You come, my Beloved, to transform me into yourself.
　　　—Poem 32:3, June 7, 1896

But his love has chosen us.
He is our Spouse, our Friend.
We are all like hosts
Which Jesus will change to Himself.
　　　—Poem 40:6, November 1896

Only abandonment thrusts me
Into your arms, O Jesus.

That is what makes me live
From the life of your friends.
         —*Poem 52:7*, May 31, 1897

We would also have to read the four eucharistic poems written by
Thérèse for Sister Saint Vincent de Paul, who spent long periods of
prayer before the Blessed Sacrament (*Poems* 15; 19; 25; 32). Here is
the one (n.32) composed on June 7, 1896, on the Feast of Corpus
Christi. Everything is summed up in its title: *Heaven for Me! (Mon
Ciel à moi!)* We find there a progression of experiences: Jesus looking
on her, full of love; prayer as a heart to heart encounter with him,
which becomes intercession for the Church; union of love in the
Eucharist that transforms us; the likeness of a daughter to her father;
total abandonment on the heart of the Father; the indwelling of the
Trinity in the loving heart of Thérèse. From beginning to end, she
very discreetly evokes her own *trial of faith*, with her reply of a *smile*
to the God who seems distant:

To bear the exile of this valley of tears
I need the glance of my Divine Savior.
This glance full of love has revealed its charms to me.
It has made me sense the happiness of Heaven.
My Jesus smiles at me when I sigh to Him.
Then I no longer feel my trial of faith.
My God's Glance, his ravishing Smile,
    That is Heaven for me!

Heaven for me is to be able to draw down on souls,
On the Church my mother and on all my sisters
Jesus' graces and his Divine flames
That can enkindle and rejoice hearts.
I can obtain everything when mysteriously
I speak heart to heart with my Divine King.
That sweet prayer so near the Sanctuary,
    That is Heaven for me!

Heaven for me is hidden in a little Host
Where Jesus, my Spouse, is veiled for love.
I go to that Divine Furnace to draw out life,
And there my Sweet Savior listens to me night and day.
Oh! what a happy moment when in your tenderness
You come, my Beloved, to transform me into yourself.
That union of love, that ineffable intoxication,
    That is Heaven for me!

Heaven for me is feeling within myself the resemblance
Of the God who created me with his Powerful Breath.
Heaven for me is remaining always in his presence,
Calling him my Father and being his child.
In his Divine arms, I don't fear the storm.
Total abandonment is my only law.
Sleeping on his Heart, right next to his Face,
    That is Heaven for me!

I've found my Heaven in the Blessed Trinity
That dwells in my heart, my prisoner of love.
There, contemplating my God, I fearlessly tell him
That I want to serve him and love him forever.
Heaven for me is smiling at this God whom I adore
When he wants to hide to try my faith.
To suffer while waiting for him to look at me again
    That is Heaven for me!

The Bride of the Song of Songs tells her Spouse that: *your love is better than wine* (Sg 1:1). We should not be surprised, then, that all christian mystical tradition speaks about *sober drunkenness* and *spiced wine* as powerful symbols of the experience of those who feel and know themselves to be *drunk in God*.

Saint John of the Cross does not hesitate to sing: *I drank from my Beloved*, to indicate that in transformation by love *the soul drinks from its God according to its substance and its spiritual faculties* (*Spiritual Canticle*, 26:4–5).

Moreover, this all happens most especially and above all during Holy Communion. An anonymous medieval poet expressed his desire for this in the song: *Sanguis Christi inebria me* (*Make me drunk, O Blood of Christ*).

The doxology that concludes the Eucharistic Canon expresses the climax of the *Mysterium fidei,* the Mystery of Faith. Here the central nucleus of the eucharistic sacrifice is converted into *sacrificium laudis*. When the climax is reached, the Church addresses the Father through the ordained minister, in these words: *Through him, with him, in him, in the unity of the Holy Spirit, all glory and honor is yours, almighty Father, for ever and ever.*

In the Eucharist, all the baptized can draw near to the unfathomable mystery of Christ, to his communion with the Father. In fact, they can not only come near, but also dive into this mystery of trinitarian redemption, deification, presence, and mutual indwelling.

CONCLUSION

There is still something to say, or rather something to repeat. Mystical experience is an **experience of love**. Moreover, since it is not a short-lived experience, but rather a life-long path to follow, we can say that mystical experience can be lived as a **permanent act of falling in love**. This last phrase seems to be self-contradictory since, in human affairs, falling in love is characterized precisely by being transitory and belonging to the start of a loving relationship. However, in a divine relationship things are different, besides being analogous.

God always has the initiative. His Love consists precisely in this: *not that we have loved God, but that he loved us* first (I Jn 4:10); not that we have given ourselves to God in love, but that *the Son of God has loved me and gave himself up for me* (Ga 2:20). Falling in love mystically is a pure grace from the God who is In-Love and who gives himself up so that we can be in-love.

A look at some aspects of the experience of **falling in love humanly** can help us to understand what we mean. I speak from a masculine perspective and hope not to contradict the experience of women. Falling in love is a sudden or gradual upheaval, in which routine gives way to surprise. It is something that comes upon us and therefore we think of it as spontaneous. One's life is at stake and one's heart becomes vulnerable, unconditionally open to someone who is different from you. One's feelings become arranged in a new constellation centered around this particular person.

The person in love experiences himself and starts living authentically. He wants to be totally himself and demands the same from the other person. Being in love implies living austerely. In the presence of the one thing needed, the person forgets his many needs. He lives democratically—he is attracted and attracts, must give and has the right to receive.

As creatures, we are needy beggars. We need infinity. We long for fulfillment. We need to be balanced by another. Falling in love is precisely an experience of transcendence and fulfillment, which presupposes a previous dissatisfaction and lack of fullness. The conversations of those in love are full of, 'everything and forever,' or 'no one can ever separate us.'

Here are five features of this peculiar phenomenon of human love. They are all present as well in someone divinely in love.

- **Attention** is concentrated, lengthy, absorbed, and exclusive. The beloved is everywhere and always present. The rest of the world no longer exists.

- **Attraction** needs the presence of, and communion with, the beloved. Everything leads to her. Life has only one direction: her.

- **Discovery**: the one in love perceives hidden worth and finds latent values. Rather than being blind, he is clairvoyant and discovers what others do not see in her.

- **Ecstasy**: the self departs. It is launched above and beyond its own limitations, which do not disappear but are simply ignored. In communing with the *you* of the beloved, one forgets one's own *I*, since only the *we* is alive.

- **Exaltation**: there is new vivacity on all levels of existence and activity, a general interior empowerment. The one in love feels powerful: with her, he can and will do everything. Now life is wonderful and he, along with her, is the first to stand in wonder.

So it is not surprising that the first great, historical christian mystic, Mary, the wife of Joseph of Nazareth, should sing out: *My soul proclaims the greatness of the Lord and my spirit rejoices in God my savior, for he has looked upon his handmaid's lowliness. . . . The Mighty One has done great things for me.*

Let us look for a moment at the experience of **looking**. It is an experience that reveals hidden mysteries in those who look at each other with love. Women know this better than men. The words, *He has looked upon his handmaid's lowliness* (Lk 1:48), sum up Mary's experience of the Annunciation and point to the Spirit who came upon Mary, overshadowing her with the power of the Most High.

Mary *found favor with God* (Lk 1:30), which is equivalent to saying, 'God has gratuitously looked on you with love and come down to you to fill you with blessings and to protect you from all harm. Recognize and accept this tender look of love that transforms you and makes you totally pleasing in his sight. Give your consent to this infinite love.'

God loves us not because we are lovable but in order to make us lovable, worthy of love. The person re-created in love by the divine look attracts a second look from God. God looks with favor on someone in order to find his favor in him or her, as Saint John of the Cross says:

> *When first our eyes met*
> *My glance pierced your heart,*
> *But your eyes held a glory*
> *Mirrored in mine.*
> *Lost in confusion,*
> *I could only stare*
> *And worship with my eyes*
> *What I saw in you.*
> —*Spiritual Canticle*, 32

God's gaze is always a look of a love that is all-powerfully creative, or re-creative. Mary's experience of being looked on by God can be put this way.

- **God** looks with a look that:

    - chooses, by calling and separating from others.

    - is true, since it reveals himself and reveals her.

    - discerns, by valuing and personalizing.

    - challenges, by empowering and activating.

    - is powerful, to create and re-create.

    - saves, by redeeming and by grace.

    - transforms, causing a before and an after.

- **Mary** lets herself be looked upon.

- By letting herself be looked upon, she:
  - accepts not being unnoticed.
  - lets herself be known and caressed, then is troubled and fears.
  - feels like someone.
  - experiences herself as affirmed, then is flattered and rejoices.

- Once looked upon, she can:
  - look.
  - challenge.
  - affirm.

- As she is looked upon, she recognizes that she is **Poor**:
  - lacking, as a creature.
  - needing the Creator.
  - earthly, from the earth.
  - empty, so as to receive.
  - lowly, to be exalted.
  - grateful, for the riches of God.

- As she is looked upon, she calls herself the **Handmaid**:
  - dependent, nothing without the Lord.
  - relativized, to serve.
  - submissive, with no conditions.
  - freed by the One she serves.
  - free to serve him.
  - grateful, since to serve God is to be loved and to love.

- As she is looked upon, she realizes that she is **Virgin**:
  - a woman, a body-soul composite belonging to the feminine sex.
  - a bodily person capable of pleasure and of rejoicing in the joy of God.
  - a personalized body offered as a sign and seal of total giving and total receiving.

- a desire to be and to remain desired by God.
- an emptiness for him, who is present.
- an aloneness, for a greater solidarity.

- As she is looked upon, she experiences becoming **Mother**:
  - sharer in the fruitfulness of the Spirit.
  - link in the age-old chain of life.
  - desiring to be a mother, but above all loving it.
  - doubly alive.
  - projected from within herself, beyond herself.
  - tenderly strong and strongly moved.

- As she is looked upon, she realizes that she is **Bride**:
  - resting with no regrets, intimately, mutually, and respectfully.
  - entirely and forever!

Mystics who have fallen in love and received God's look like this know that they have no other work in life but the service of love for God and for their neighbors. If we ask them to explain this, they will reply: *Say that I am missing, wandering in love; that once I was straying but now I am found* (cf. John of the Cross, *Spiritual Canticle*, 28–29).

★   ★   ★

The end of our century thirsts for mystery. Many people, including many Christians, hope to quench their thirst in other religious traditions or in esoteric spiritualities. The hour has come to present them the Mystery of Christ and to let ourselves be mystically transformed by him. What are needed are witnesses to the long-distant closeness of the Father and to the revealing work of the Spirit. We are sought by trinitarian Love. The divine Persons are ahead of us in love. What is urgently needed are men and women of prayer, so that there will be many teachers of prayer.

I could have said many other things. Some themes have not even been touched, like mysticism and evangelization, mysticism and martyrdom, mysticism and sexuality, mysticism and discernment, mysticism and ecumenism, mysticism and interreligious dialogue. They remain to be discussed and deserve our interest and reflection. What has been said has been said so that you may believe that Jesus is the Christ, the Son of God, and that through this belief and this love, you may have life in his Name.

Homilies

THE REIGN OF GOD AND
THE SCHOOL OF CHARITY

Homily at the Conclusion of the General Chapters,
September 30, 1993

T HE JOINT MEETING AND THE GENERAL CHAPTERS come to a close today. The Lord Jesus tells us: *Leave, set out on your way, announce that the Kingdom of God is in your midst.*

What is this Kingdom that we must announce when we return to our communities? It is the utopia of a history worthy of the human being created man and woman in the image and likeness of God. It is the utopia of the divine sonship by adoption and universal brotherhood. It is a matter of something utopian, which does not mean impossible, but rather something that can be partly realized if we have faith and if we cooperate with the Lord to the point of offering our own blood.

However, what does this Kingdom mean for us monks and nuns? How do we transpose this Kingdom into the monastic key? What does all this mean for us here and now, at the end of the joint General Chapters, when we are nearly ready to set out on the way back to our houses?

The kingdom is our *schola caritatis*. In this school, Christ alone is the Master, and we are all his disciples. He himself, as Master, teaches us that discipline of mutual love, which is the distinguishing mark of his disciples. He who loves his neighbor is in communion with the will of the Master and loves him; he who does not love his neighbor offends the Master and excommunicates himself from mutual communion with him and in him.

We are not hermits in community, but rather cenobites in the desert. We are not supposed to have many hearts and just one face, but only one heart with a variety of faces and a single vision. Would to God that we might always exclaim along with our fathers: *singula sunt omnium, omnia singulorum* (Each thing belongs to everyone, and everything belongs to each).

Let us share with our brothers and sisters the good and joyful news of the kingdom: brotherhood that blossoms into filiation, that is to say, for us Cistercian monks and nuns, cenobitism that ripens into mysticism.

Throughout these General Chapters, we have worked on the reports of our communities concerning the contemplative dimension of our lives. Has not the moment come to face our cenobitic reality as basis, proof, and manifestation of our contemplation?

MARY PONDERED ALL THESE THINGS IN HER HEART

Homily at the Interreligious Monastic Encounter,
Gethsemani, July 26, 1996

W E CHRISTIANS HONOR MARY, the Mother of Jesus Christ, with the name *Sedes Sapientiae*. Let us ponder a little on the meaning and scope of such a title.

In the Judeo-Christian tradition, wisdom takes on a religious meaning. It is wisdom that instructs us about God's will and God's actions in view of our salvation. This divine plan of salvation comes to its culmination in Jesus Christ. Saint Paul, therefore, speaks of Jesus Christ as the *Wisdom of God* (1 Co 1:24, 30).

If Wisdom consists of God's plan of salvation, formed from all eternity in Christ, it is no wonder that the Mother of Christ has come to mean for Christians the living throne of Wisdom. She in turn is also a disciple or daughter of Wisdom, for hers was a life of attentive listening to Wisdom incarnate (Lk 7:35).

Biblical revelation tells us that those who keep the Word of God and put it into practice form a special bond with Wisdom. Indeed the wise man or wise woman is likewise brother or sister, spouse, son or daughter or friend of Wisdom. Though a concomitance of such relationships is impossible on the human level, it is possible when it comes to relations with God.

According to the wisdom literature of the Old Testament, there is a beauty to Wisdom that seduces and elicits love. The wise man thus desires to take Wisdom for his bride: *Therefore, I determined to take her to live with me. . . . When I enter my house, I shall find rest with her, for companionship with her has no bitterness, and life with her has no pain, but gladness and joy. . . . In kinship with wisdom there is immortality, and in friendship with her, pure delight* (Ws 8:2 ,8, 16–18). It is by fidelity to the law that one obtains Wisdom and she will come to meet the wise as a *mother* who exalts her *children* and who helps those who seek her (Si 15:1–2; 4:11). In other words, since Wisdom comes from God, drawing near to her in intimacy makes it possible to be in close union with God (Ws 6:12–21).

They once said to Jesus, *'Your mother and your brethren are standing outside, desiring to see you'. But he said to them, 'My mother and my brethren are those who hear the word of God and do it'* (Lk 8:19–21). True kinship, that is to say, does not derive from flesh and blood but from listening to the Word of God in a personally committed way. Mary's greatness consisted principally in this: she offered her womb and her heart to the eternal Word and Wisdom of God—her womb and her heart, but above all, her heart: *Blessed rather are those who hear the word of God and keep it* (Lk 11:27–28).

To practice Wisdom is to recall the saving deeds of God throughout history and to keep them in one's heart, following the norms of conduct that derive from them. They are wise who store up the deeds of grace that make known the goodness of the Lord (cf. Dt 4:1–8; Ps 107:43). Israel is a people that listens, remembers, and puts into practice, for in this consists Wisdom: *Instruction in understanding and knowledge I have written in this book, Jesus the son of Sirach, son of*

Eleazar of Jerusalem, who out of his heart poured forth wisdom. Blessed is he who concerns himself with these things, and he who lays them to heart will become wise. For if he does them, he will be strong for all things, for the light of the Lord is his path (Sir 50:27–29).

We find this sapiential attitude in Mary. She perseveres in the remembrance of the actions and words of her Son, the Wisdom of God, not in a static way, however, but actively, that is, looking for the right explanation, doing the exegesis, interpreting (*symbállo*; Lk 2:19, 51). She was able to go beyond the obscurity of faith, recalling and understanding all that her Son said and did.

Mary is *Seat of Wisdom* in a two-fold way, for not only did she carry the Son of God, Wisdom incarnate, in her womb, but she also kept God's word, uncovering its mystery. This vocation and avocation of Mary apply to the whole Church and to each Christian. We are all invited to listen and penetrate, treasure and interpret the meaning of Sacred Scripture. Thus will we become seats of Wisdom, seats of the divine presence: *Those who love me will keep my word, and my Father will love them, and we will come to them and make our home with them* (Jn 14:23).

Our faith seeks to love in order to understand and beget. This is what theology is. The theologian is a believer and a lover who enters into mystery and is transformed by it. Through the experience of *lectio divina* as a contemplative path for seeking and finding God, we become mystics. Mary—mystic, theologian, and woman of wisdom—is offered to us as a help and a model.

For she who conceived God by faith promises you the same if you have faith; if you will faithfully receive the Word from the mouth of the heavenly messenger you too may conceive the God whom the whole world cannot contain, conceive him however in your heart, not in your body. . . . He who created you is created in you, and as if it were too little that you should possess the Father, he wishes also that you should become a mother to himself. 'Whoever', he says, 'does the will of my Father, he is my brother and sister and mother.' O faithful soul, open wide your bosom, expand your affections, admit no constraint in your heart, conceive him whom creation cannot contain. Open to the Word of God an ear that will listen. This is the way to the womb of your heart for the Spirit who brings about conception . . . (Guerric of Igny, *The Second Sermon for the Annunciation*, 4. CF 32, p. 44–45).

AN INVITATION TO CONVERSION

Homily at the Opening of the General Chapters,
October 4, 1996

W E HAVE JUST HEARD SOME GOOD NEWS, a Gospel, but it does not sound like good news. The 'Woe, woe, woe' of our Teacher, Jesus, wakes us up from our daily sleep precisely today, at the beginning of our General Chapters, the beginning of this fourth Mixed General Meeting. The Lord says to us, Woe to you, Cistercian Order of the so-called Strict Observance! Woe to you if you do not listen and accept this invitation to conversion!' (cf. Lk 10:13–16)

A short time before, Luke tells how the Master asserted his will to go to Jerusalem despite the mortal danger that implied, and how different persons tried unsuccessfully to follow him in his journey. Then he named seventy-two disciples whom he sent to announce the Kingdom of God. The episode of sending these disciples finishes with the 'Woe, woe, woe' we have just heard. Nothing can be as disgraceful as not accepting and embracing the Kingdom of God. To convert is to enter into his Kingdom.

The Beatitudes are a gift from God. They are not obligatory: we are free to accept them or not. They are words of grace, but also of obligation and warning. We also need the woes, the 'evil tidings', because we are free. We can reject salvation and destroy ourselves. The curses are not the action of God, but rather the action of 'non-God.'

The 'woes' are located in this context of the evil tidings. They are not irrevocable curses or condemnations, but rather cries of grief, pathetic warnings: in a word, an urgent invitation to conversion. Their crudeness is due in part to the very nature of Gospel life and monastic life: radical, absolute truth. Anyone who feels called to this life will understand these 'woes'. They are an urgent invitation to be faithful to the Lord and to the vocation we have received.

But what is this Kingdom of God to which the Lord invites us to change the direction of our lives? The Kingdom of God is:

- the 'good news' of Jesus, the central message of his preaching and life program.

- the preaching of God's Kingdom is the greatest threat to the world and to the 'established order', that is, disorder, of things, and to our egoistic mediocrity.

- something utopian, which does not mean impossible, but partially achievable if we have faith and work with God even to the shedding of our blood.

- the utopia of a history worthy of human beings created as men and women in the image and likeness of God.

- the utopia of divine filiation by adoption, and of universal brotherhood by redemption.

The Kingdom of God, therefore, is not a geographic or static reality, but a dynamic one, namely, God himself ruling, exercising his sovereignty as the loving Father of his children.

After the great fact of the Master's resurrection, the teaching of the Apostles no longer concentrates on the Kingdom of God, but the God of the Kingdom, or more precisely, on the Risen One who gathers within himself the children of God who were dispersed so as to convert them into brothers and sisters of each other. From now on, conversion to God's Kingdom means conversion to Jesus Christ.

John Paul II, our pope, told us recently that: To *strive after sanctity is, then, the program of every truly consecrated life, especially in the context of renewal at the threshold of the third millennium. It is a program that should begin by leaving everything to follow Christ, putting him before everything else so as to share his Paschal Mystery fully (VC 93; cf. 39, 112).*

Brothers and Sisters, nuns and monks, we are called to conversion, to change more and more into the living and life-giving Person of Jesus Christ. We are invited to anchor our lives and sink deeper roots into his way of living for the Father—his contemplative sonship—and for the brethren or the sisters his school of fraternal life. Our way of life, our *conversatio morum, is* our radical, exaggerated, blessed way of conforming ourselves to the Lord by making him active and present in the Church and the world. Without this anchoring and rooting of our lives in Christ, we cannot really accept being called Christians or his followers according to the Gospel.

Sisters, Brothers, our 'contemplative dimension' and our 'School of Charity' finds its unity in the only Teacher in this school, the only true contemplative: Jesus the Christ, the only Son of God, born of the Virgin Mary by the grace of the Holy Spirit.

RICH BEFORE GOD

Homily at the Conclusion of the General Chapters, October 21, 1996

T HE GOSPEL THAT HAS JUST BEEN PROCLAIMED is telling us here and now: 'Fools, do not store up treasure for yourselves, but make yourselves rich in the sight of God' (Lk 12:13–21).

What meaning does this divine word have for each one of us, for our communities, and for the Order as a whole? What does it mean to make oneself rich in God's eyes?

Immediately following this parable the Lord tells His disciples and tells us: seek the Kingdom of God and he will give you all the rest, because where your treasure is, there will your heart be (Lk 12:31, 34). In the epistle just read, Paul speaks to us of salvation gratuitously given by a God rich in mercy (Ep 2:1–10).

For us Christians and Cistercians, there is only one acceptable wealth—that of the Kingdom given by an immensely rich God.

In the three years to come, our communities and the entire Order will question themselves in relation to this subject: 'The cistercian grace today, conformity to Christ,' that is, the gift God made to Cîteaux so that Cîteaux may present it to the Church and the world.

This divine gift consists of a particular form of life that makes us citizens of God's Kingdom in a way that is both common and different: common as Christians, different as Cistercians.

This gift, once received, is intended to be given. We exist for the Church and for the world and it is this way that we exist for Christ and for God. The more we are of Christ and of God, the more we are for the Church and for the world. This means, in other words, that our cistercian life is supposed to be 'an evident sign of the Kingdom of God' in the heart of diverse cultures (cf. PC 1,2); to be a sacrament is an essential need of our own being. When monks try to be like 'everybody else' we become 'no one'. The Church and the world need Jesus Christ made real and present through our cistercian living.

May the Lord help us at the close of this Mixed General Meeting and in the years to come, to be rich in the sight of God with the riches of the Kingdom bestowed on us by an immensely rich God. These riches received in order to be given, are the mystical espousals and cenobitic unity in conformity with Christ. He is the Spouse of the Church, the cistercian Christ. Amen.

THE MAD UTOPIA OF
MONASTIC LIFE

Homily at the Monastic Studies Week,
Cardeña, January 24, 1998

TODAY'S GOSPEL DEPICTS FOR US THE REACTION OF JESUS' family to his actions: *When his family heard it, they went out to restrain him, for people were saying, 'He has gone out of his mind'.* (Mk 3:20–21) Immediately afterward, the teachers of the law will say that he is possessed by a demon.

Why did they say that Jesus was mad? Was it the healings, the exorcisms, or his authoritative doctrine? No mad man can heal or cast out demons, but mad men are known to make speeches . . . What teaching of Jesus made him deserve to be called mad? It was his teaching on the *Reign of God*.

It is precisely this 'utopian' teaching of Jesus that forms the basis of any intention of christian, and accordingly, monastic renewal.

The *Reign* or *Kingdom of God* is the 'cause' for which Jesus put his entire life and person at stake. The principle characteristics of this *Reign* are the following:

- a plan that is indissolubly bound up with the God of the Kingdom. It is a matter of God and his plan of salvation in history—not a static or place-bound reality but rather a dynamic one, that is, God reigning and exercising his sovereignty. Thus, the praxis of the *Reign* is based on a very concrete image or concept of God (Mt 6:10; Lk 11:2).

- good news for the sociologically poor (those 'looked down upon') and the economically poor (the 'have nots') (Lk 4:18–19; Mt 11:4–5).

- salvation that transcends our history and yet transforms it from within (Mk 4:26–32; Mt 13:33).

- joyful news of salvation rather than judgment or condemnation (Lk 4:18–19 and Mt 3:10).

- a gift for all without any kind of exclusion or boundary (from Bartimeus to Zaccheus) and the only absolute before which all else is either relative or given in addition (Mt 6:33; Lk 12:31).

- a new, contrasting, and alternative reality that calls for a conversion and a choice (Mk 4:15). The preaching of the *Kingdom of God* is the greatest threat to the world or the 'established order (or disorder)' inasmuch as it presents:

  – a social alternative: *But many who are first will be last, and the last will be first* (Mk 10:31). The loose young woman from skid row will enter the *Kingdom* before the righteous monks of the monastery of the Immaculate Conception!

  – a political alternative: *Whoever wishes to be great among you must be your servant* (Mk 10:43). Let him who would be abbot offer to clean the toilets, and may the Abbot General do the general clean-up!

- an ethical alternative: It is what proceeds from the heart that defiles, *but to eat with unwashed hands does not defile* (Mt 15:20). To omit a psalm during the divine office, to enter or go out of the enclosure, to have a full stomach on a fast day . . . These defile no one!

- a religious alternative: to love God and *'to love one's neighbor as oneself'—this is much more important than all whole burnt offerings and sacrifices* (Mk 12:33). You can be sure that if someone, about to receive communion, was to say: 'Stop, wait a minute, I have to be reconciled with Brother Melchisedek'. We would think, 'He is interrupting the celebration'.

- a theological alternative: *Love your enemies and pray for those who persecute you, so that you may be children of your Father in heaven* (Mt 5:44–45). It is precisely to his enemies that the Father shows his greatest kindness, that is to say, to each and every one of us!

To sum up then, for Jesus, the *Reign* or the *Kingdom of God* consisted in a generous offering of salvation and a pressing invitation to conversion. The parables of *the workers in the vineyard* (Mt 21:1–16), of *the pitiless servant* (Mt 25:14–30) and of the *prodigal son* (Lk 15:11–32) are excellent illustrations of this.

Whether or not we want to accept it, we have to be aware that a renewal of monastic life is not possible without this utopian passion, which means:

- to cry out against an unacceptable situation.

- to strive toward a future that we intuit and desire.

- to anticipate ardently the future in the present.

At all times, monastic life has always had and will always have something utopian about it. Would perhaps the names of so many of our monasteries have something to tell us: Bellafuente, Aguahermosa, Puerto de Salvación, Ntra. Sra. Del Paraíso, ValdeDios, Scala Dei, Celda de los Angeles?

In conclusion, if at least some do not consider us mad, we have no way of knowing whether, in fact, we are being conformed to the image of Christ and with him renewing all things. Amen.

POVERTY, MYSTICISM, AND CISTERCIAN COMMUNION

Homily on the Occasion of the Ninth Centenary of the Foundation of the Abbey of Cîteaux and the Birth of the Cistercian Charism, March 21, 1998

THE AUTHOR OF THE *EXORDIUM MAGNUM* MAKES the foundation of Cîteaux take place on March 21, on the Solemnity of Saint Benedict, which that year, 1098, coincided with Palm Sunday. We all know that this date is more of a symbol than a chronological fact. That is precisely why we are interested in it: *The New Monastery is a new flowering of the benedictine charism, a new springtide in the paschal mystery* (*Exordium Magnum* XIII).

The identity of a religious group such as the 'Cistercians' lies in the interpretation given to themselves by the original group of founders and by the present members. This means that the primitive documents and the original experience have something to tell us, just as the contemporary documents and our life today do. The Holy

Spirit, who inspired the original charism, also inspires the way that charism has been lived and enriched in different times and places. Our identity is constituted by both the original charism and the experience we now have of it.

It is in this sense that the readings chosen for our celebration today speak to us about *following the poor Jesus, in order to enter into his mystery and into communion with him and with all other human beings.* We must let this anniversary celebration enlighten our history and make it fruitful, so that the past becomes new life in the Risen Jesus. Let us look at this message and receive its grace by reflecting on the three readings we have just heard.

Sell all you have, then come and follow me

The Gospel speaks to us about a rich man who wants eternal life, but he is not willing to give up his wealth. The result is that he does not follow Jesus and remains in sadness. The text continues, telling us how difficult it is for a rich person to enter the Kingdom of Heaven. At the end of the reading, the Lord promises eternal life to those who have left everything to follow him. However, many who are first will be last, and the last will be first (Mt 19:16–30).

This whole scene reminds us of a very significant passage in the *Exordium of Cîteaux* (I:3–4). It reads as follows:

> *Since possessions and virtues do not coexist for long, a few wise and farsighted men of that holy community [Molesme] chose to commit themselves to heavenly things rather than to be embroiled in human affairs. From then on, because of their love for the virtues, they began constantly to think of the fruitfulness of poverty and how it produces manly qualities.*

Our First Fathers were keenly aware that *you cannot live or serve God without material goods.* Nevertheless, *the less we have, the better* (Saint

Bernard, *Ps.XC* 5:2—*quanto strictius, tanto melius*). The reason is simple: *Temporal goods are licit if they are not loved, and illicit if they are. Whether they are loved or not, however, they are not of great benefit since they soon pervert and seduce the heart of their owner.* (Saint Bernard, *Ep* 462:7).

Purity of heart is not possible without getting rid of all superfluities and living in the simplicity of poverty. It lies in following and imitating the *poor Mother of the poor Christ* (Guerric, *Pur* 4:6).

However, what does this mean for us today, in a world impoverished by its accumulation of wealth, by its bad distribution of it, and by the atrociously bad purposes for which this wealth is used. Without any false messianic pretensions or heroics, both the Gospel and our Fathers invite us to:

- *renounce* material goods in order to obtain the greater, the only good—Jesus.

- *eliminate* private individual ownership that is a terrible vice.

- *work* to earn one's daily bread and to share it with those who have no bread.

- *simplify* our existence in order to enter by the austere way that leads to life.

- *share* goods we have with those who are dispossessed of this world's goods.

- *prefer* those human beings who have been most broken by our inhumanity.

The day that this Gospel poverty is freely embraced, transforms our communities as a whole, and spreads to all our structures and institutions; then we will really be able to proclaim the Good News of the Kingdom, which is *to live in the greatest possible solidarity with*

others, no matter what the cost, and save the life of all by losing your own.
Then we can denounce the anti-Kingdom and its slogans: *Get the*
most profit at the least cost for your own benefit.

If our witness of poverty gives a poor impression, it is because we
call ourselves poor but do not want to become poor. Yet—it is
the Lord who speaks—only the poor and the little ones enter the
Kingdom and its mystery.

He led him into the cloud. Face to face he gave him his commandments.

The wise Ben Sirach meditated on the sacred history of his people.
His wisdom flows from such meditation. History teaches him how
God works on those who belong to him. Knowing God's work
leads to discovering his Being. Moses was a good man who found
grace in the eyes of all, loved by God and by his fellow human
beings. God showed him a part of his glory and let him hear his
voice. He brought him into the cloud of his own mystery and there,
face to face, gave him his commandments (Si 45:1.5).

The figure of Moses has always been rich in symbolic value as a
model of holiness, ascent to God and mystical union with him.
Therefore, it is not strange that, for our cistercian authors, Moses
praying on the mountain should be a symbol of monks and hermits
(Saint Bernard, *3 Sent* 118). Among those who follow the Lord in
his entrance procession into Jerusalem, there are some who are like
Moses: *Those who are in the rear can only see his back, like Moses . . .*
Those who are beside him can look at him from time to time, but hurriedly
and not continuously or perfectly . . . Compared with the others, the latter
see him more face to face, as is also said of Moses . . . But not even Moses
had the full vision in this life (Saint Bernard, *Palm S.* 2:7). It is not
surprising that a Cistercian of the second wave speaks as follows:

> *Joy, love, delight, and sweetness, vision, light, glory: this is what*
> *God asks of us and what he made us for. True order and true religion*

*consist in doing what we were made to do. So let us contemplate the
supreme beauty, let us take delight in what is utter sweetness, let us
fight tooth and nail against whatever is opposed to it. Let us orient
all our activities to this end, our work and our rest, our words and
our silence* (Isaac, *Sermon 25:7*).

The deformity of our spiritual being needs a total reforming before
arriving at conformity to God in Christ. Union with God—it is not
important how this union is expressed: as vision, peace, rest, Sabbath, or contemplation—is the first and final end of our monastic
life. The mystical teaching of our First Fathers is the most precious
part of their, and our, heritage.

Our modern world thirsts for God. It is looking for his face and
seems not to find it. If we have been faithful to the patrimony we
have received, if we have like Moses *persevered* in prayer *as if seeing the
one who is invisible, keeping our eyes fixed on Jesus* (Heb 11:27; 12:2),
then we will indeed have something to offer and to share.

Through him, we both have access in one Spirit to the Father.

The Letter to the Ephesians that has just been proclaimed to us,
announces that Christ has reconciled Jews and Gentiles to each
other and with God. We can ask ourselves if Jesus, the Christ,
does not also want to break down the dividing walls separating the
members of the cistercian family, so as to make us into a single New
Person.

We need to return in trust and confidence to the original inspiration
that gave birth to us as a gift from God to the Church. We need
to embrace without fear the legitimate variety of traditions that
the Spirit has nurtured throughout our nine centuries of following
Jesus. This is the only way we will be able to appreciate and wonder
at the riches that were hidden in that initial gift of the Spirit. But

that is only the appetizer, meant to encourage us to seek an effective communion, which we have to recover and keep establishing.

Let me end by paraphrasing Saint Bernard: Today, dearest brothers and sisters, we have celebrated among ourselves a meeting, a synod, of bodies (*conventum vel synodum corporum*). We should, however, form another, more important synod—the union of our souls. There would be no benefit in having a corporal association together with a spiritual separation. There is no reason to meet in one place—even if that place is Cîteaux itself—if we disagree in the spirit. No matter how holy it may be, the place serves no purpose without the union of spirits (cf. *3 Sent,* 107).

THE SEARCH FOR GOD

Homily on the Occasion of the Celebration of
150th Anniversary of the Foundation of the
Abbey of Gethsemani, December 21, 1998

ONE HUNDRED AND FIFTY YEARS HAVE PASSED since the beginning of monastic life here in Kentucky, U.S.A. If we look beyond these walls and these white cowls, if we look into the hearts and the desires of the men who first came to this place, we find that all began with a group who wanted to search for God and find him, here.

The real history of your monastery is a story of the search for God. This means that the first founders, and all the monks of the last one hundred fifty years, as well as those of today, share a common desire and a common intention. We can apply to every single person who has lived here the principle proclaimed by Saint Benedict in his *Rule*: *The concern must be whether he truly seeks God* (*RB* 58:7). The same is true, of course, for the multitude of monks and nuns who have lived in other cistercian monasteries throughout the nine centuries of the Order's history. It is about us all that it has been said, and is still said: *These are the ones who seek the Lord, who seek the face of the God of Jacob* (Ps 23:6).

The search for God has been the ultimate and deepest motivation of those who have lived here. It still is, for you who live here now. And it will be, for those who live here in the future. *Searching* for God means that we direct our lives to the *mystery* of God, so that we can be *transformed* by God. This is how monks and nuns down through the centuries proclaim the Gospel: we tell the Good News about searching for, and finding, God.

All the spiritual teaching of Bernard of Clairvaux consists in the mutual search of God and the human person for each other. The human person is created to love, so that Saint Bernard's teaching is a love story. This entire adventure of love is condensed into Bernard's last six *Sermons on the Song of Songs* (*SC* 80–85), which are a commentary on the words: *I sought him whom my soul loves* (3:1).

In this mutual search between God and each one of us, there are three elements.

- There is the *theological* foundation: salvation history, especially the grace of the Incarnation and Redemption.

- Then there is the *anthropological* dimension: human freedom accepting divine grace. Grace always precedes freedom and accompanies it from within.

- Finally there is the *phenomenological* aspect of the human person's desire and experience of loving and being loved. At the same time, we know that it is God who first loves, desires, and seeks us.

The end of this story—which is our own story—is the wisdom of love rejoicing in the peace that is the fruit of the communion of wills, or the union of spirits. The whole formation program of the

School of Charity, which is your community, must consist in this mutual, loving search. Its root is the image of God and his likeness, which is lost by us and then recovered through conformity to Christ.

The monk's 'interior' life consists in *tension toward* God and in *attention to* him, since it is God who seeks the monk and loves him. The monastic observances are at the service of this searching, finding, and mutual loving, and are also meant to express it.

The cistercian tradition presents contemplative life in this particular modality of searching for God and finding him in a unity of spirits. This is what the abbot of Clairvaux did in the twelfth century and what your Father Louis did in our own century. Perhaps this is the only real message we have, as contemplative men and women, for the world today. Let me use someone else's words and speak, together with you, to our post-modern world:

> 'The contemplative has nothing to tell you, man and woman of today, except to reassure you and say that if you dare to penetrate your own silence and dare to advance without fear into the solitude of your own heart . . . then you will truly recover the light and the capacity to understand what is beyond words and beyond explanations, because it is too close to be explained: it is the intimate union in the depths of your own, God's spirit and your own secret inmost self, so that you and he are in all truth One Spirit.'

Therefore, as not to trick the world with our words, but rather back up our words with our life, let us pray, with William of Saint-Thierry:

> *Lord, I will seek your face as much as I can and as much as you render me capable of doing. It is your face, Lord, that I seek. Lord, my God, my one hope, hear me, lest I lose the will to seek you through my exhaustion! Let me seek you ardently, and always. Give me the strength to do it, since it is you who have given me the desire. Then when you see that the strength is enough, increase the desire*

you have given. May I remember you, understand you, and love you always! Let me, O triune God, remember you in faith, understand you in wisdom and love you in truth, so that you can reform me into your own image, in which you created me (Enigma, 23). Amen.

PROFESSION OF FAITH IN OUR CONTEMPLATIVE MONASTIC LIFE

For the Solemn Profession of Sister Agnes of Rivet,
October 16, 1999

E XPERIENCE TEACHES THAT WE LIVE BADLY what we do not believe in. The contrary is also true, namely that we live well what we believe in. Anyone not convinced of the value of the monastic life that he or she has embraced will live it in mediocrity.

Being convinced means being conquered by a conviction. The conviction in question is this: if a monastic way exists it is because Christ the monk exists. If I follow his path, I will see his face.

To believe is to have faith and trust: theological faith and human trust. When I say, 'I believe', I either refer to an assent and a certainty coming from the God who lives in me, or to a sureness based on a call and on the testimony of a multitude of monastic witnesses who have gone before me. It is believing like this that I say, 'I believe'.

I believe in the **Father** of the Lord Jesus, Father of each one of us, who handed his only Son over to save those who are lost. His tender mercy transforms us into sons and daughters, brothers and sisters.

I believe in **Jesus Christ**, risen from the dead, the temple of God in whom we meet the intimate life of the most Holy Trinity and the saving plan of the Father.

I believe in the **Spirit**, the Giver of life, who works in Mary and in the Church to make us divine and make us one spirit with God.

I believe in **Mary**, she who is blessed because she believed, and who is the model of theological life according to the Gospel and of intimate union with Jesus.

I believe in the **Church**, the efficacious sign of salvation in which we feel and are sons and daughters of God, brothers and sisters of one another.

I believe in the **community** as a place of prayer, friendship, mercy, service, joy, and forgiveness, which anticipates the promised and longed–for Kingdom of God.

I believe in the **contemplative dimension** of human life, the fact that all persons are called to an eternal dialogue of love with God in Christ through the gift of the Spirit. I believe in contemplative humanity!

I believe in the eternal **Word** of God who speaks in the liturgy, in the dialogue of *lectio*, in authority, community, my brothers or sisters, my own heart, and in many other ways.

I believe in the **Eucharist**, which is banquet, sacrifice, memorial, presence: the source and summit of our christian, monastic, and contemplative life.

I believe in the **Opus Dei** and in the *lectio divina* that prepares for it and prolongs it, as powerful places to hear and answer the Lord who speaks to us.

I believe in special, more lengthy times of silent personal **prayer** to receive the Lord and give myself to him in faith and love.

I believe in **discretion**, mother of all virtue. She alone discovers the 'royal middle road' leading to God through the lurking dangers of excess or defect. She alone establishes the dynamic balance rhythmically uniting liturgy, *lectio*, and work.

I believe in the **asceticism** centered on denying 'self-will', which opens us to charity and the 'common will,' thus receiving as a gift the divine likeness lost by sin.

I believe in **obedience** as a laborious yet joyful listening and assent that makes possible our return to God and our communion with him.

I believe in **humility** as a way of descent to self-truth, and as an ascent to the Truth that is God.

I believe in the **stability** that perseveres with the members of this community in the practice of the spiritual art and never despairs of the mercy of God.

I believe in the **desert** of solitude as a place of trial, temptation, and struggle, but also of discernment, purification, and salvation.

I believe in the **silence** that welcomes and gives, like a womb conceiving and giving birth to the word that is worth listening for and acting on.

I believe in evangelical **poverty** and austerity as signs of the Kingdom and eloquent paths toward the contemplation of a caring

Father in a world that is consumerized, pleasure-seeking, and self-sufficient.

I believe in **work**, especially manual work in imitation of Christ, to earn our daily bread, share it with others, unite with the workers of the world, and show solidarity with those frustrated by social injustice.

I believe in **failure**, **pain,** and **death** as necessary steps toward joy and life, in imitation of Christ crucified and risen.

I believe, above all, in **fraternal charity**, expressed in mercy, service, and unity of hearts, as a condition for receiving and dwelling in the life of God who is Love.

I believe in **contemplation** as knowledge and love, as loving faith, as desire and remembrance, as a presence anticipated in hope, as a vision and a listening with the eyes and ears of the heart of God. *Love itself is understanding!*

I believe in the **contemplative life**, a life of searching and finding, totally oriented toward the prayer and purity of heart that unite us to God the Father and show forth his glory for the salvation of all.

I believe in the **Rule of Saint Benedict** as a monastic interpretation of the Gospel pregnant with discretion, a minimum rule for beginners, leading through humble charity to the perfection of love that casts out all fear.

I believe in **Cîteaux** as a monastic and contemplative way, and as a gift of God to the Church of yesterday, today, and tomorrow.

I believe that in our Order there are more **contemplatives** than is generally thought, especially among the aged and the sick, but less than there should be, because not many persevere in loving faith, which is a crucible that purifies human nature in the light and fire of God.

I believe in the **mystics** and the **prophets**, men and women hidden in God's mystery who shape history by letting God speak through their voices, to reveal his way and his hour.

I believe in each one of **you**, Sisters and Brothers, as pilgrims of the Absolute and mirrors reflecting the face of God.

I believe in **Love**! I believe in Love! I believe in Love! And full of hope I trust that you, too, believe and love.

THE FIRE OF THE KINGDOM AND OUR LUKEWARM PREFERENCE FOR THE 'THINGS BESIDES'

Homily at the Opening of the Chapters General,
October 21, 1999

T HE LORD AND TEACHER IS TALKING WITH HIS DISCI-PLES, those of then and those of now, with them and with us. Though several subjects are touched upon—abandonment to Providence, renouncing one's property to give alms, keeping watch for the Lord's return—everything is focused on one basic concern: *Set your hearts on his Kingdom, and these other things will be given you as well* (Lk 12:31). The conversation concludes with the words we have just heard: *fire, desire, immersion, distress, and division* (Lk 12:49–50).

The fire of the Spirit and of the Kingdom burns with ardent desire in the heart of Jesus. The Kingdom comes at a distressing price: the baptism of the passion on the cross. What is even more distressing, the Kingdom causes family division! Jesus is against any kind of false peace, that is, any peace without demands. Nonetheless, this fire is very different from the one James and John wanted to have fall from the sky and consume the Samaritan city that did not welcome them, a matter that earned them a rebuke from the Teacher (Lk 10:54–55).

And yet, just what is this Kingdom burning in Jesus' heart, that causes division and that must be preferred above all else? In Jesus' day, the Kingdom or the Reign of God was understood in different ways.

- For the Pharisees, the Reign was to have come when Israel had put God's law perfectly into practice.

- For the Zealots, it was a question of the social and political sovereignty of Israel that was to be achieved by force of arms and by the expulsion of the Romans.

- In apocalyptic literature, the Kingdom would coincide with the end of the world.

- According to the tradition of the Old Testament and for most Jews, the Kingdom meant God's sovereignty in terms of helping the needy, the poor, and the weak. It would be established by means of an ideal Messiah King and would be synonymous with justice, hope, salvation, and peace (cf. Ps 72:1–4, 12–13; Lk 4:16–22 quoting Is 61:1–2).

Jesus' understanding of the Kingdom corresponds, then, with that of the Old Testament and apocalyptic literature, but in a way revitalized by the Spirit, giving way to a new and unprecedented understanding of the Kingdom. For Jesus, the Kingdom is filial and fraternal communion with God and with human beings, a communion that begins here but is only completed in the world to come. Transposed into monastic terms, this means for us, mysticism and cenobitism, contemplation and community.

The Teacher did not come to divide but to unite. His plan of filiation and fraternity, however, meets with rejection, both then and now, since it jeopardizes the selfish interests of many. Division is caused, not by God's Reign, but rather by opposition to it.

Perhaps none of us is outright opposed to God's Reign, but it is quite possible that some of us prefer the 'things besides', that come with the Kingdom, to the Kingdom itself. That is to say:

- fine polyphonic singing, a trilingual Bible, an inspiring book, a gothic church and cloister, an ample cowl made of fine cloth, guaranteed solitude . . . to bare, radical and transformative contemplation.

- a warm and efficient group, an intelligent and open abbot or abbess, nice quiet neighbors, rich and influential benefactors, a prestigious place in the Order and in the country . . . to life in common and communion of life.

The 'things besides' that come with the Kingdom are countless, as are those of us who continually gather up more and more of these 'things besides'. The result of all this is:

- a clouded and undefined monastic identity deprived of its Gospel meaning.

- division among persons on account of a fragmented purpose in life.

- a lukewarm flicker that, instead of setting on fire, is sickening to Jesus.

A General Chapter is a good opportunity to evangelize our monastic life by making our commitment more radical, by freeing ourselves from all that divides, obscures, or makes us lukewarm. May the Lord grant that our meeting be, not just another Chapter, but rather something more than a Chapter. Amen.

ON THE WAY TO JERUSALEM: THE PASSOVER TO NEW LIFE

Closing homily for the Chapters General,
10 November, 1999

W E HAVE JUST HEARD IN THE WORD OF GOD: *Jesus went on his way to Jerusalem . . .* (Lk 17:11). We know that in Luke's time, 'the way to Jerusalem' theme served as an initiation to 'the Way' of Jesus (cf. Ac 9:2, etc.). It is in fact a catechesis for Christians of all times. The heart of this teaching is that *life is attained through death*. This statement holds true in various ways, and can be applied to physical as well as spiritual death. To die is always to be reborn. The life of the Christian is a paschal experience. Yet, how does this truth apply to the joint General Chapters we are bringing to a close? Let us attempt an answer.

- In the first week of the Chapter we are primarily the ones at work. During the second week our evil spirits, demons, '*logismoi*' (passionate thoughts or whatever you want to call them) tend to take the upper hand. In the third and last week, the Holy Spirit, whose guiding presence was there all along, begins to come into view.

Being aware of this alternation of spirits, and being attentive to whether or not we are giving heed to their voices, allows us to experience the General Chapter as 'history of salvation', as God's saving action at work in our history. We can therefore affirm that life is a continual rebirth, an ongoing passover.

To put it in a brief yet concrete way, during the first days of the Chapter, it is the program and 'procedures' that point the way. We feel we have an active role to play in our history, we know what we want, and we make an effort to bring it about.

Little by little, however, we get into blustery weather and troubled waters. The evil spirits we discern are not easy to bring to light; we tend to think that our own person is being judged as good or evil. At the same time, who can throw the first stone? One way or the other, we find ourselves trying to impose our own opinions; hidden tensions come to the fore; desire for power causes rivalries; a touch of envy distorts the truth; fear imposes silence; despair darkens the future; impatience wants everything today; suspicion keeps us from looking each other in the eye; the 'flu afflicts our spirits'. A few of us, especially among the sisters, perhaps not altogether aware of this agitation, or else staying on the margins of it, are praying, with praise and thanksgiving, asking the help of the Lord of history.

Their prayer is heard. The sun begins to rise and we begin to get a glimpse of that Jerusalem that is the city of peace. The ever-present Spirit is seen to be at work in many ways, speaking to us from day to day, and, through the liturgy, feeding us with the body and blood of the Risen One. *If we live, we live for the Lord. If we die, we die in the Lord* (Rm 14:8). *The fruits of the Spirit are love, joy, peace, patience, kindness, and generosity* (Ga 5:22). The Spirit inspires us to consecrate ourselves to Mary and to place ourselves in her hands. New ideas and unexpected solutions emerge; prudence finds the golden mean; the Coordinating Commission keeps things in order and gathers together what has been dispersed; we accomplish what we thought was a lost cause; forgiveness heals wounds; hope enlightens hearts; a sense of humor puts problems into perspective; we recognize ourselves as brothers and sisters in the one Father. Indeed, none of this happens of its own accord; the Spirit works and we sweat.

Thus it is that, from one Chapter to the next, we move along the way of history, following Jesus, together, toward God our Father who is in Heaven and in every place. Thus, it is that we experience the christian passover that is a celebration of life. Thus, it is that these Chapters General of 1999 have been, not just another Chapter, but something more than a Chapter.

CISTERCIAN TEXTS

Bernard of Clairvaux

- Apologia to Abbot William
- Five Books on Consideration: Advice to a Pope
- Homilies in Praise of the Blessed Virgin Mary
- In Praise of the New Knighthood
- Letters of Bernard of Clairvaux / by B.S. James
- Life and Death of Saint Malachy the Irishman
- Love without Measure: Extracts from the Writings of St Bernard / by Paul Dimier
- On Grace and Free Choice
- On Loving God / Analysis by Emero Stiegman
- Parables and Sentences
- Sermons for the Summer Season
- Sermons on Conversion
- Sermons on the Song of Songs I–IV
- The Steps of Humility and Pride

William of Saint Thierry

- The Enigma of Faith
- Exposition on the Epistle to the Romans
- Exposition on the Song of Songs
- The Golden Epistle
- The Mirror of Faith
- The Nature and Dignity of Love
- On Contemplating God: Prayer & Meditations

Aelred of Rievaulx

- Dialogue on the Soul
- Liturgical Sermons, I
- The Mirror of Charity
- Spiritual Friendship
- Treatises I: On Jesus at the Age of Twelve, Rule for a Recluse, The Pastoral Prayer
- Walter Daniel: The Life of Aelred of Rievaulx

Gertrud the Great of Helfta

- Spiritual Exercises
- The Herald of God's Loving-Kindness (Books 1, 2)
- The Herald of God's Loving-Kindness (Book 3)

John of Ford

- Sermons on the Final Verses of the Songs of Songs I–VII

Gilbert of Hoyland

- Sermons on the Songs of Songs I–III
- Treatises, Sermons and Epistles

Other Early Cistercian Writers

- Adam of Perseigne, Letters of
- Alan of Lille: The Art of Preaching
- Amadeus of Lausanne: Homilies in Praise of Blessed Mary
- Baldwin of Ford: The Commendation of Faith
- Baldwin of Ford: Spiritual Tractates I–II
- Geoffrey of Auxerre: On the Apocalypse
- Guerric of Igny: Liturgical Sermons Vol. 1 & 2
- Helinand of Froidmont: Verses on Death
- Idung of Prüfening: Cistercians and Cluniacs: The Case for Cîteaux
- In the School of Love. An Anthology of Early Cistercian Texts
- Isaac of Stella: Sermons on the Christian Year, I–[II]
- The Life of Beatrice of Nazareth
- Serlo of Wilton & Serlo of Savigny: Seven Unpublished Works
- Stephen of Lexington: Letters from Ireland
- Stephen of Sawley: Treatises
- Three Treatises on Man: A Cistercian Anthropology

MONASTIC TEXTS

Eastern Monastic Tradition

- Abba Isaiah of Scete: Ascetic Discourses
- Besa: The Life of Shenoute
- Cyril of Scythopolis: Lives of the Monks of Palestine
- Dorotheos of Gaza: Discourses and Sayings
- Evagrius Ponticus: Praktikos and Chapters on Prayer
- Handmaids of the Lord: Lives of Holy Women in Late Antiquity & the Early Middle Ages
- Harlots of the Desert
- John Moschos: The Spiritual Meadow
- Lives of the Desert Fathers
- Lives of Simeon Stylites
- Manjava Skete
- Mena of Nikiou: Isaac of Alexandra & St Macrobius
- The Monastic Rule of Iosif Volotsky (Revised Edition)
- Pachomian Koinonia I–III
- Paphnutius: Histories/Monks of Upper Egypt
- The Sayings of the Desert Fathers
- The Spiritually Beneficial Tales of Paul, Bishop of Monembasia
- Symeon the New Theologian: The Theological and Practical Treatises & The Three Theological Discourses
- Theodoret of Cyrrhus: A History of the

Monks of Syria
- The Syriac Fathers on Prayer and the Spiritual Life

Western Monastic Tradition

- Achard of Saint Victor: Works
- Anselm of Canterbury: Letters I–III / by Walter Fröhlich
- Bede: Commentary…Acts of the Apostles
- Bede: Commentary…Seven Catholic Epistles
- Bede: Homilies on the Gospels I–II
- Bede: Excerpts from the Works of Saint Augustine on the Letters of the Blessed Apostle Paul
- The Celtic Monk
- Gregory the Great: Forty Gospel Homilies
- Life of the Jura Fathers
- The Maxims of Stephen of Muret
- Peter of Celle: Selected Works
- The Letters of Armand Jean-deRancé I–II
- Rule of the Master
- Rule of Saint Augustine

CHRISTIAN SPIRITUALITY

- A Cloud of Witnesses…The Development of Christian Doctrine / by David N. Bell
- The Call of Wild Geese / by Matthew Kelty
- The Cistercian Way / by André Louf
- The Contemplative Path
- Drinking From the Hidden Fountain / by Thomas Spidlík
- Entirely for God / by Elizabeth Isichei
- Eros and Allegory: Medieval Exegesis of the Song of Songs / by Denys Turner
- Fathers Talking / by Aelred Squire
- Friendship and Community / by Brian McGuire
- Grace Can do Moore: Spiritual Accompaniment / by André Louf
- High King of Heaven / by Benedicta Word
- How Far to Follow / by B. Olivera
- The Hermitage Within / by a Monk
- Life of St Mary Magdalene and of Her Sister St Martha / by David Mycoff
- The Luminous Eye / by Sebastian Brock
- Many Mansions / by David N. Bell
- Mercy in Weakness / by André Louf
- The Name of Jesus / by Irénée Hausherr
- No Moment Too Small / by Norvene Vest
- Penthos: The Doctrine of Compunction in the Christian East / by Irénée Hausherr
- Praying the Word / by Enzo Bianchi
- Praying with Benedict / by Korneel Vermeiren
- Russian Mystics / by Sergius Bolshakoff
- Sermons in a Monastery / by Matthew Kelty

- Silent Herald of Unity: The Life of Maria Gabrielle Sagheddu / by Martha Driscoll
- Spiritual Direction in the Early Christian East / by Irénée Hausherr
- The Spirituality of the Christian East / by Thomas Spidlík
- The Spirituality of the Medieval West / by André Vauchez
- The Spiritual World of Isaac the Syrian / by Hilarion Alfeyev
- Tuning In To Grace / by André Louf

MONASTIC STUDIES

- Community and Abbot in the Rule of St Benedict I–II / by Adalbert de Vogüé
- The Hermit Monks of Grandmont / by Carole A. Hutchison
- In the Unity of the Holy Spirit / by Sighard Kleiner
- A Life Pleasing to God: Saint Basil's Monastic Rules / By Augustine Holmes
- Memoirs [of Jean Leclercq]: From Grace to Grace
- Monastic Practices / by Charles Cummings
- The Occupation of Celtic Sites in Ireland / by Geraldine Carville
- Reading St Benedict / by Adalbert de Vogüé
- Rule of St Benedict: A Doctrinal and Spiritual Commentary / by Adalbert de Vogüé
- The Venerable Bede / by Benedicta Ward
- Western Monasticism / by Peter King
- What Nuns Read / by David N. Bell

CISTERCIAN STUDIES

- Aelred of Rievaulx: A Study / by Aelred Squire
- Athirst for God: Spiritual Desire in Bernard of Clairvaux's Sermons on the Song of Songs / by Michael Casey
- Beatrice of Nazareth in Her Context / by Roger De Ganck
- Bernard of Clairvaux: Man, Monk, Mystic / by Michael Casey [tapes and readings]
- Catalogue of Manuscripts in the Obrecht Collection of the Institute of Cistercian Studies / by Anna Kirkwood
- Christ the Way: The Christology of Guerric of Igny / by John Morson
- The Cistercians in Denmark / by Brian McGuire
- The Cistercians in Scandinavia / by James France
- A Difficult Saint / by Brian McGuire
- The Finances of the Cistercian Order in the Fourteenth Century / by Peter King

- Fountains Abbey and Its Benefactors
  / by Joan Wardrop
- A Gathering of Friends: Learning & Spirituality
  in John of Ford / by Costello and Holdsworth
- The Golden Chain...Isaac of Stella /
  byBernard Mc Ginn
- Image and Likeness: Augustinian Spirituality
  of William of St Thierry / by David Bell
- Index of Authors & Works in Cistercian
  Libraries in Great Britain I / by David Bell
- Index of Cistercian Authors and Works in
  Medieval Library Catalogues in Great Britian
  / by David Bell
- The Mystical Theology of St Bernard
  / by Étienne Gilson
- The New Monastery: Texts & Studies on the
  Earliest Cistercians
- Monastic Odyssey / by Marie Kervingant
- Nicolas Cotheret's Annals of Cîteaux
  / by Louis J. Lekai
- Pater Bernhardus: Martin Luther and
  Bernard of Clairvaux / by Franz Posset
- Pathway of Peace / by Charles Dumont
- Rancé and the Trappist Legacy
  / by A. J. Krailsheimer
- A Second Look at Saint Bernard
  / by Jean Leclercq
- The Spiritual Teachings of St Bernard of
  Clairvaux / by John R. Sommerfeldt
- Studies in Medieval Cistercian History
- Three Founders of Cîteaux
  / by Jean-Baptiste Van Damme
- Towards Unification with God (Beatrice of
  Nazareth in Her Context, 2)
- William, Abbot of St Thierry
- Women and St Bernard of Clairvaux
  / by Jean Leclercq

MEDIEVAL RELIGIOUS WOMEN

A Sub-series edited by
Lillian Thomas Shank and John A. Nichols
- Distant Echoes
- Hidden Springs: Cistercian Monastic Women
  (2 volumes)
- Peace Weavers

CARTHUSIAN TRADITION

- The Call of Silent Love / by A Carthusian
- The Freedom of Obedience / by A Carthusian
- From Advent to Pentecost / by A Carthusian
- Guigo II: The Ladder of Monks & Twelve
  Meditations / by E. Colledge & J. Walsh
- Halfway to Heaven / by R.B. Lockhart
- Interior Prayer / by A Carthusian

- Meditations of Guigo I / by A. Gordon Mursall
- The Prayer of Love and Silence / by A Carthusian
- Poor, Therefore Rich / by A Carthusian
- They Speak by Silences / by A Carthusian
- The Way of Silent Love (A Carthusian Miscellany)
- Where Silence is Praise / by A Carthusian
- The Wound of Love (A Carthusian Miscellany)

CISTERCIAN ART,
ARCHITECTURE & MUSIC

- Cistercian Abbeys of Britain
- Cistercian Europe / by Terryl N. Kinder
- Cistercians in Medieval Art / by James France
- Studies in Medieval Art and Architecture
  / edited by Meredith Parsons Lillich
  (Volumes II–V are now available)
- Stones Laid Before the Lord
  / by Anselme Dimier
- Treasures Old and New: Nine Centuries of
  Cistercian Music (compact disc and cassette)

THOMAS MERTON

- The Climate of Monastic Prayer / by T. Merton
- Legacy of Thomas Merton / by P. Hart
- Message of Thomas Merton / by P. Hart
- Monastic Journey of Thomas Merton
  / by Patrick Hart
- Thomas Merton/Monk / by P. Hart
- Thomas Merton on St Bernard
- Toward an Integrated Humanity
  / edited by M. Basil Pennington

CISTERCIAN LITURGICAL
DOCUMENTS SERIES

- Cistercian Liturgical Documents Series
  / edited by Chrysogonus Waddell, ocso
- Hymn Collection from the...Paraclete
- The Paraclete Statutes:: Institutiones nostrae
- Molesme Summer-Season Breviary (4 vol.)
- Old French Ordinary & Breviary of the
  Abbey of the Paraclete (2 volumes)
- Twelfth-century Cistercian Hymnal (2 vol.)
- The Twelfth-century Cistercian Psalter
- Two Early Cistercian Libelli Missarum

FESTSCHRIFTS

- Bernardus Magister...Nonacentenary of the Birth of St Bernard
- The Joy of Learning & the Love of God: Essays in Honor of Jean Leclercq
- Praise no Less Than Charity in honor of C. Waddell
- Studiosorum Speculum in honor of Louis J. Lekai
- Truth As Gift... in honor of J. Sommerfeldt

BUSINESS INFORMATION

Editorial Offices & Customer Service

- Cistercian Publications
  WMU Station, 1903 West Michigan Avenue
  Kalamazoo, Michigan 49008-5415 USA

  Telephone 616 387 8920
  Fax   616 387 8390
  e-mail   cistpub@wmich.edu

Please Note: As of 13 July 2002 the 616 area code becomes 269

Canada

- Novalis
  49 Front Street East, Second Floor
  Toronto, Ontario M5E 1B3 CANADA

  Telephone 1 800 204 4140
  Fax   416 363 9409

U.K.

- Cistercian Publications UK
  Mount Saint Bernard Abbey
  Coalville, Leicestershire LE67 5UL UK

- UK Customer Service & Book Orders
  Cistercian Publications
  97 Loughborough Road
  Thringstone, Coalville
  Leicestershire LE67 8LQ UK

  Telephone 01530 45 27 24
  Fax   01530 45 02 10
  e-mail   MsbcistP@aol.com

Website

- www.spencerabbey.org/cistpub

Trade Accounts & Credit Applications

- Cistercian Publications / Accounting
  6219 West Kistler Road
  Ludington, Michigan 49431 USA

  Fax   231 843 8919

Cistercian Publications is a non-profit corporation. Its publishing program is restricted to monastic texts in translation and books on the monastic tradition.

A complete catalogue of texts in translation and studies on early, medieval, and modern monasticism is available, free of charge, from any of the addresses above.